The Possible Human

The Possible Human

A Course in Extending Your Physical, Mental, and Creative Abilities

Jean Houston

J. P. TARCHER, INC.
Los Angeles
Distributed by Houghton Mifflin Company
Boston

Library of Congress Cataloging in Publication Data

Houston, Jean.
    The possible human.

    Bibliography: p. 222
    Includes index.
    1. Mind and body.   2. Self-actualization
(Psychology)   3. Body image—Therapeutic use.
4. Body, Human (in religion, folklore, etc.)
I. Title.
BF161.H78   1982   158   82-17070
ISBN 0-87477-219-2
ISBN 0-87477-218-4 (pbk.)

The author would like to thank the following publishers for their permission to reprint:

Excerpt from *A Sleep of Prisoners* by Christopher Fry. Copyright © 1951, 1959 by Christopher Fry. Reprinted by permission of Oxford University Press, Inc.

Excerpt from "Burnt Norton" in *Four Quartets* by T. S. Eliot. Copyright © 1943 by T. S. Eliot. Reprinted by permission of Harcourt Brace Jovanovich, Inc.

Excerpt from *The Madwoman of Chaillot* in *Four Plays* (Vol. I) by Jean Giraudoux. Copyright © 1958. Reprinted by permission of Farrar, Straus & Giroux, Inc.

Excerpt from "The Aleph" in *The Aleph and Other Stories* by Jorge Luis Borges, translated by Norman Thomas di Giovanni. English translation copyright © 1968, 1969, 1970 by Emece Editores, S.A., and Norman Thomas de Giovanni. Reprinted by permission of E. P. Dutton, Inc.

    J. P. Tarcher, Inc.
    9110 Sunset Blvd.
    Los Angeles, CA 90069

    Design by Michael Yazzolino
    Art Editor: Jane Prettyman
    Illustrations on pages 10, 15, and 99 by Jeanette Lendino

    MANUFACTURED IN THE UNITED STATES OF AMERICA

    Q   10   9   8   7   6   5   4   3   2   1

First Edition

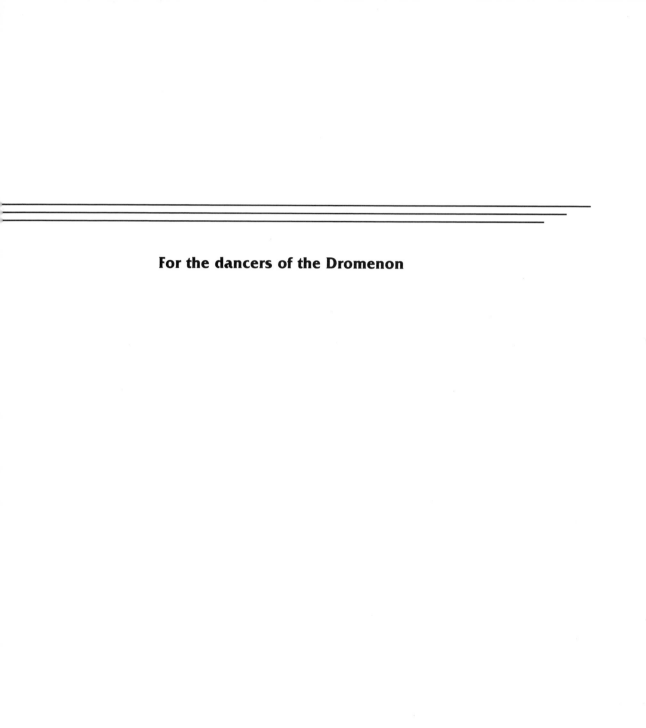

For the dancers of the Dromenon

CONTENTS

ACKNOWLEDGMENTS

I owe an enormous debt of gratitude to my close associate, Robin Van Doren Beebe, whose intensive editorial efforts over many months and in many places did much to bring this book to its final form. Additionally, a good deal of Dr. Beebe's original work and writing is reflected in the essay portion of Chapter 2, "Awakening the Senses."

The always provocative musings, goadings, and lyrical outbursts of my poet friend Rhett Kelly helped inspire the basic form and content of the manuscript.

My publisher, Jeremy Tarcher, provided warm encouragement and lucid, expert advice, as did his editors, Kirstin Grimstad and Millie Loeb. I am particularly grateful to Ms. Loeb for her skillful midwifery in the final months of the book's gestation.

And then there are my students—the dancers of the Dromenon— possible humans all. Their active participation in the exercises and experiences described in these pages, their challenges, questions, and innovations, their willingness to live and explore at their edges, even though they might fall off the map of the known world, ignited and sustained my commitment to the possible human and the possible society. It is to them that this book is dedicated.

INTRODUCTION

The human heart can go to the lengths of God.
Dark and cold we may be, but this
Is no winter now. The frozen misery
Of centuries breaks, cracks, begins to move,
The thunder is the thunder of the floes,
The thaw, the flood, the upstart Spring.
Thank God our time is now when wrong
Comes up to face us everywhere,
Never to leave us till we take
The longest stride of soul men ever took.
Affairs are now soul size
The enterprise
Is exploration into God.
Where are you making for? It takes
So many thousand years to wake,
But will you wake for pity's sake?

CHRISTOPHER FRY
A Sleep of Prisoners

Rhythms
of Awakening

Suppose some genie of space and time were suddenly to put you into the body and mind of your ancestor of a thousand years ago. You would be in for a stupendous reality jolt. If your forebears were anything like mine, your name might be something like *Hugo, Son of Stupid* or *Clothilde the Lame*. Your day would not be much different from your name. In the morning you would wake up on the flea-ridden pallet of your mud-and-wattle hovel because the chicken was walking across your face. After a breakfast of hard bread and gray gruel you would probably go out into the fields of the lord of the domain and push a simple plow all day in the pouring rain (it rained a great deal in the tenth century). Your thoughts were probably not very inspired: "When do I eat?" or "I think I'll kick the ox." And your perceptions would not fare much better: "It's raining . . . I ache . . . I want to eat the ox . . ." At night you and your kin and the animals would gather around the wet wood of a smoking fire to try and catch a little warmth while you scratched your fleas and picked the lice out of each others' hair. On Sunday, after church, you might be lucky enough to find a friend with a hogskin of mead, get drunk, and fall in a ditch until you got dragged home by the bailiff, only to wake up in the morning with a chicken walking across your face.

Certainly, there would be some advantages to your life—you would know your place in the pattern of things, kinship would be close, and the rights and wrongs of things unquestioned. But mostly life would be a narrow, brutish fight for subsistence, and your human energies would be exhausted in the attempt to keep your metabolism going. It is the Dark Ages and its shadow falls across your mind and dulls your spirit.

One hundred years later a rhythm of awakening ripples across the forests, hovels, and castles of the Western world. Invoked by mad monks and greedy nobles, half the population of Europe gets up and goes east—on the Crusades. Slack-jawed and gaping, they pass through gorgeous decadent Byzantium (and no culture is more interesting than a culture in a state of high decadence). Their senses are strummed by the perfumed airs, the silken cloaks, the exquisite foods, the multicolored mosaics, and their ears are ravished by music and speech so sweet it seems the cadence of gods, not of men and women. Everywhere they witness the delectable excesses of a civilization entirely given over to the refinements of its own pleasures, and they begin to awaken to longings they never knew they had. Seeded with desire, they battle on to Jerusalem and see there the enormous complexity of a city of three thousand years of living history. The crossroads of East and West, the womb of world religions, the place that everyone wants and where everyone wants to be, the conquest of Jerusalem gains them the substance of things hoped for, the evidence of things not seen. Thus quickened and awakened, their souls now richer than they had been before, the vast band of Hugo and Clothilde returns to wattle hut and castle and find them . . . impossible. How are you going to keep them down on the farm after they've seen Byzantium and Jerusalem? How are you going to keep them in changeless circumstance after they have known the terrors and the glories of a "holy" Crusade? And so many leave their old life and pour into the burgeoning towns where lie the opportunities for expanding human possibilities. There, new industries flourish, new crafts, and new desires. Leagues of cities and of men, trade networks and guilds for professional excellence crisscross the continent, and lights turn on in an age no longer dark but aspiring. Everywhere there is aspiration. Men and women aspire to God, and the great vaulted cathedrals rise in answer to that longing, stone fingers pointing to the heavens. Minds yearn for meaning, and in Bologna and Paris and Oxford the great universities are founded to provide the intellectual loom upon which the Pattern that Connects can be woven.

The Middle Ages settle in and reality is seen as a comforting tapestry of hierarchies in which everything is interwoven with everything else in a scheme that is absolute for the entire universe. All orders—cosmological, moral, and political—mirror artfully the details of each other in a grand design that at its best gives order, divinity, and meaning to both the parts and the whole. At its worst, however, the medieval tapestry of life smothers and isolates the developing inner world, thus encouraging the spread of superstition. Again, a rhythm of awakening is needed, and it comes in the form of the Renaissance, with its revival of ancient philosophy and myth, literature, and science. Ideas and images are excavated from their Greek, Roman, and Hebraic origins, forgotten texts are translated, esoteric attitudes become available. A veritable archaeology of the Western world's past thoughts and dreams is unearthed, and the horizon of what it means to be human is extended.

Under this stimulus the psyche grows. The imaginal realms of inner space proliferate and spill over into the external world in a phenomenal growth of new science, art, music, literature, politics, and above all in a new vision of mankind and world that is the glory of humanism.

With regard to the effects of the extended psyche on the external world, consider what happens in painting and music. Prior to the general era of the Renaissance, painting was largely flat and two-dimensional with little or no perspective, reflecting perhaps the complacent givens of the medieval universe. With the coming of a more complex consciousness, however, more angles are seen, more shadows and more dimensions. Perspective is the necessary aesthetic response of the Renaissance psyche.

The simple texture of medieval music, which never exceeded three voices, was transformed as the growing polyphony of the psyche demanded a richer and more textured polyphony in music. Whereas before the separate melodic lines were heard together, now music moved toward a complexity of sound that reflected the tensions and multiple levels of the Renaissance soul.

The growth of consciousness spawned in the Renaissance saw us through several centuries of quests within and without, gave us the momentum to extend the "empire of man over things" and to raise the art of exploration into a vehicle for planetary transformation.

Unfortunately, by the nineteenth century, art and artful skill (*techne*) yielded to technique and, more recently, to technology. And skills that were once grounded in the insight that comes from the rhythm of awakening pulsing through the total body-mind-being became the mechanical artifacts of a humanity increasingly fragmented and cut off from its own depths in psyche. This dangerous dissociation did not occur in other cultures to the same degree, but was generally limited to the post-Renaissance European experience. Not that this made much difference, as subsequent events have shown. The "success" of rationalist-materialist philosophy of power joined to the ruthless European policies of colonization served not only to subjugate large areas of the planet but also to inhibit even larger areas of human experience and ways of knowing. All over the planet a Western psychological imperialism has prevailed, one that makes all other imperialisms pale by contrast. The "single vision and Newton's sleep" dominating Western consciousness since the eighteenth century has brought with it the ideal of mind modeled on mechanism, resulting in turn in the materialization of values, the standardization of society through industrialization, and the inability to consider anything other than cause-and-effect relationships as underlying events. In the interests of an extraordinarily narrow notion of "progress," culture is disintegrating, computers are replacing consciousness, and the erosion of human reality is being enacted and mirrored on the stage of nature in the erosion of the planetary ecosystem.

Today the post-industrial global village sleeps. It sleeps beneath a blanket of cross-cultural ties and intraplanetary webbing so thick that all problems and all answers are interdependent. We have seen in our time the death of exclusivity, although in our present sleep we act as if we

knew it not. The weave of persons and nations, of polities and econo-
mies, of exploding populace and diminishing soil, of silent hope and
heady triumph, of air, water, bread, love, death—this is a weave so
thick that it has become a single fabric with few loose threads, so strong
that perhaps not even human beings can destroy it. And formidable
indeed are the social, economic, and psychological forces that confront
us, the atmosphere of chaotic ecclecticism within which it becomes
almost impossible to distinguish narrow and selfish interests from sustained commitment, superficiality from bold experiment, and excessive
claim from genuine accomplishment. This is the case on all levels, be
they social, economic, interpersonal, or governmental. Paranoia has
become a way of life, but we have neither the time nor the resources to
sustain it.

As a professional in human development, I frequently have occasion to attend conferences made up of social planners and heads of
corporations, the forgers and managers of the modern world. Too often,
to listen to their judgments and evaluations is to wrestle with darkness.
It is to engage in seminars filled largely with futile visions, negative
scenarios, the death of hope, with a few technocrats promising a magic
act from some technological panacea. With all the bravado of statistics
and graphs, one still senses strongly the retreat of consciousness of those
who govern before the planetary pathos for which they are partly
responsible.

Underneath the blanket giants tremble, other cultures begin to
sing, the genius of woman emerges, the depths start to rise, and the
other side of the moon of ourselves haunts our becoming and demands
its tribute. It is the first stirrings of the Rhythm of Awakening. Many
have felt it coming. Some have experienced it with joy and hopefulness;
others have felt it as a gut-gripping terror, knowing that its music, when
it comes, demands that they live at their edges. For the first sweepings
of the Rhythm bring chords of dissonance which warn us that our
present problems are not primarily political or economic but are rooted
in the inadequate use of our humanity or, rather, in our persistence in
using those capacities in ourselves that are no longer appropriate to
present times. When so little of the physical and mental as well as the
innate spiritual vitality of person and culture is being tapped, when too
great a reliance is being placed on the rational, the immediate, and the
functional, then consciousness is caught in tunnel vision, inadequate to
deal with the complexities and challenges of the time. Thus we recognize the tragic consequences of this inadequacy and our present seeming inability to use the range of what we are.

We see this especially in the great number of technically "complex" short-term solutions we bring to many-layered social and economic problems, followed by the inevitable long-term failure of these

solutions because of their psychologically simplistic base. When thinking and doing are largely linear, analytic, and hierarchical, and when the self that does that thinking and doing is insular, fearful, and manipulative, is it any wonder that our best intentions and problem-solvings become a crazy-quilt patchwork of Band-Aids.

Impotent before the complexity of things and using too little of ourselves to be capable of finding meaning in the melange of a time of too-muchness, many are retreating into fundamentalist havens, ideological fortresses of "truth," back-to-basics formulas and panaceas that promise to make things real and reliable again while sanctifying our stupidity. This and the mandating of mediocrity is potentially one of the greatest dangers we face, for the world is too interrelated and interdependent to sustain the spread of further reductionism and narrowings.

The Search for the Possible Human

The Rhythm that is coming brings the search for the possible human in ways that it has never been sought before. Previously the ideal of a possible human was one limited by cultural and climatic constraints and gave only limited excellence. If you had been an Arunta in the Australian desert, your notion of the possible human would have been of someone who had the most acute and extended sensory system in order to detect food or water in the parched and barren landscape in which you lived. Similarly, if you grew up in a hunting society, a refinement of sensory and muscular coordination would also be part of the ideal, along with qualities of courage and endurance. Among the educated of Athens in the fifth century B.C., the possible human would have been expected to express the virtues of physical beauty, mental grace, and high skills in speech and rhetoric. For the Romans, a strong mind in a strong body was the *sine qua non*, while for the ancient Hebrews it was a morally upright and righteous ethic guiding every aspect of life. Among the ancient Chinese the noble one was seen to exist in perfect harmony with both society and nature, having the most exquisite sensitivity to the nuances of social and familial relationships. Among certain strata of Northern European society the tough-minded rationalist who is successful in the commercial or professional realm is to be emulated, while among the Balinese a grace in body and mind and a fluidity in states of consciousness mark the possible human, along with the ability, as one Balinese said to me, "to do everything as well as possible."

Given the enormous variety in the nature of the ideal, it is inevitable that the possible human of one society would be the pariah of the next, while the full flowering of one would outrage and seem ludicrous to the other. Memories of these encounters are the great sore spots of history and legend, as complex but harmonious agrarian societies devoted to the intricacies of seasonal ritual and reconciliation are over-whelmed by the conquest ideals of invading warrior cultures. Similarly, as we have seen in the tragic history of frontier America, a native culture whose human ideal revolves around attunement with nature suffers the direst of consequences when confronted with a culture whose ideal includes the constant extension of the "empire of man over things."

We arrive finally at our own time, when the human race can no longer afford the invidious comparisons and psychological imperialism that some "successful" cultures and nations impose upon others. In this time of planetary culture we need the full complement of human re-sources, wherever they are to be found. We need to bring forth and orchestrate all the Rhythms of Human Awakening that have ever been in humanity's search for what it can be.

As we have seen, previous cultures have tended to deny some areas of development while acknowledging and encouraging others. With the present convergence of the findings of anthropology, cross-cultural studies, psychophysical research, and studies into the nature and function of brain, we are beginning to have in hand a perspective on human possibility as profound as it is provocative. This perspective allows us to turn the corner on our humanity, exploring and experienc-ing the astonishing complexity and variety of the world of the possible human. It is virtually a new introduction to the human race.

Some may initially retreat before the magnitude of the vistas that this perspective presents. Our lensing of reality is so conditioned by culture and circumstance that we tend to allow in only familiar, limited notions of what is both proper and possible. In this, our situation is not unlike what might happen should a praying mantis—an insect—suddenly find itself up at the marble podium addressing the United Nations. The mantis would rub its wings together, peer out at its surroundings, and think, "Hmmm, not much food out there," having no idea of the immensity of the human drama that is happening before it. So too with ourselves in our limited lensing of reality.

How do we open those lenses to permit entry to both the vision and the inspiration needed to launch the journey of the possible human? For without inspiration we will have neither the courage nor the momentum to enter upon the tremendous task of responding to the present Rhythm of Awakening, a task and a response in which we quite literally partner evolution in the transformation of our selves.

Let me tell you why I am convinced of the extraordinary opportu-nity that is ours. In 1965 my husband, Robert Masters, and I formed The Foundation for Mind Research in New York City, determined to recover and uncover as many methods as we could to help us explore the nature and range of human capacities. We began our series of experiments by reviewing culture and history and the many varieties of the ideal of the possible human, considering those types of experience that have traditionally been most enriching in ways that are positive and do not present grave dangers to the person or otherwise include certain aspects that might be detrimental. We then inquired further as to which capacities have been highly valued in different cultures throughout history while, at the same time, the ordinary person of our time has been blocked in his or her use of those capacities.

These considerations led us to experimental explorations with over a thousand research subjects during the next seventeen years. We were interested in the immediate experiential and other values of altered and extended states of consciousness, alternative cognitive modes, and new styles of learning. We studied the impact of thinking in images, thinking kinesthetically, time distortion, the acceleration of mental process, sensory enhancement, the modulation of pleasure and pain, and the nature and evocation of the creative process. This work was fertilized by a variety of techniques both very old and very new: the orchestration of dreams and dreaming, the voluntary conscious control of involuntary physiological states (heartbeat, brain waves, skin temperature) assisted by biofeedback and autogenic training, and even the induction of religious and other peak experiences, as well as many other varieties of innate mental and physical capacities, all available to, but rarely used by, most human beings. Because these were all experiences and capacities valued highly by those who have had access to them, we supposed that they would also be found to be of value by the volunteers participating in our research programs.

Our initial procedures had to do with finding ways to open the lenses and unshackle the minds of our research subjects. Visiting different societies throughout the world, searching through time and history, probing both orthodox and esoteric traditions and ways of working with human possibilities of other cultures, we found many procedures commonly used by people across the millennia to alter attention on the spectrum of consciousness so that sensitivity might be heightened, solutions found, inner journeys taken, visions sought and gained. Whether it be through dancing, drumming, chanting, fasting, or employing the many varieties of psychophysical and psychospiritual exercises, human beings have learned to travel to their edges, there to fall off the known world and bring back news from the unknown.

And so we joined ancient processes to modern research methods, even occasionally creating mechanical and electronic devices to help elicit various phenomena of consciousness. As we broadened the base of our investigations, we began to explore ways of extending and refining the sensory and perceptual capacities and the self-modulation of pleasure and pain. This led us more and more deeply into what became the major research emphasis of our Foundation—the investigation of the body-mind continuum. We discovered what many others had discovered before us—that you cannot have a successful and permanent extension of mental, psychological, and spiritual capacity without working toward an enhancement of physiological capacity. One of the reasons that talking therapies do not work as well as they might is that, since they do not knowledgeably involve the body in the therapeutic process, they engage too little of the client's being. A "cure" of psyche is at best a temporary adjustment and undergoes reversals when the uncured body asserts its memories and distortions.

The deterioration of the body that typically occurs before individuals reach adulthood leads to deterioration across the entire spectrum of the brain-body system. We become progressively less able to learn, perceive, conceptualize, relate, and create. It is a path of physical erosion and real loss of human intelligence, this Western division of body from mind, and its consequences are being felt all over the planet. This rationalizing, objectifying mind-set is a direct outgrowth of the loss of awareness of sensorimotor functions, as is the inability to use a larger range of body-mind perceptions for more subtle understanding and complex problem-solving. Quite simply, the holocaust of body-mind has led to the ecological holocaust and to the awful inadequacy of present political and economic solutions.

Consideration of this tragedy led us first to a search for already existing systems, not of physical but rather of psychophysical education—that is, systems that do not divide the body from the mind or ignore the importance of consciousness, but instead seek to work with the unity of body and mind that constitutes the human person.

As our psychophysical work continued to develop, we were able to integrate our imagery and our creativity studies into exercises aimed at improving and developing body movement and awareness. Thus, some psychophysical work was done with imaging in altered states of consciousness and with accelerated mental process. Then, for example, a minute or two of clock-measured time, which may be subjectively experienced as an hour, can give results equivalent to what might be obtained by an hour of actual physical work. Also, it soon became clear that subjects and students who were engaged in the psychophysical work learned more completely and with greater ease to release and apply such more inwardly tuned potentials as the improvement of memory, the capacity to think on multiple tracks at once, and even the ability to tap, at will, into the symbolic and mythic dimensions of the self. It is significant that modern researchers are rediscovering what the early Sanskrit psychophysical philosophers had always known— that the key to transpersonal realities lay in the expansion of physical awareness.

It was becoming apparent that because of the diffusion effect in the brain, the activity of the motor cortex (through psychophysical education) works to disinhibit and activate neighboring neural structures, even those that have to do with complex intellectual processes and intuition. As an exciting extension of this kind of research, we found that people can be taught to "speak" to their own brains directly, thereby entering into the conscious orchestration of mood, attitude, learning, and creativity. In these complex and evocative procedures (some of which are described in subsequent chapters), movement, imagery, intense concentration, and creative intentionality are integrated in exercises that apparently have the most profound consequences upon the conscious repatterning of both our physical and mental lives. These exercises, among the most advanced and sophisticated of our discoveries, apparently involve the bridging and integration of right and left hemispheres, older and newer neural structures, brain and consciousness. Thus we call them "evolutionary exercises," implying that the latency of the human condition is more deeply evoked and made available for conscious use in the course of these procedures.

As news of our research spread, we were invited to make practical applications of our work in many areas of social and institutional change. Among these were school programs in which children learned *how* to learn by using a much larger spectrum of their own sensory and cognitive possibilities. In our programs, the child is taught to think in images as well as in words, to learn spelling or even arithmetic in rhythmic patterns, to think with his or her whole body, and to actively use both hemispheres of the brain. As a rich arts program is always essential to multimodal education, we helped develop and even restore arts-related learning in schools throughout the United States and Canada.

We also initiated programs concerned with helping the elderly restore failing capacities and acquire new ones, knowing full well that when the elders are empowered again, wisdom is restored to the wise and society can regain its most valuable constituency.

People have often asked how we were able to fund this work, since it is very difficult to find financial support for innovative research, and even more so for the social applications growing out of it. We were fortunate in having several generous grants from various enlightened family foundations,* but for the most part found the funding process an enervating and futile task.

By 1973 I had become friends with Margaret Mead, who subsequently became the president of our board of directors, and she advised me to do as she had done in supporting almost all the work of an

* The Foundation for Mind Research received funding from the Babcock Foundation, the Erickson Education Foundation, the Kleiner Foundation, and the Doris Duke Foundation.

anthropological foundation. "Go out and make the money yourself, Jean," she said to me. "Then the job you want to do gets done and you are beholden to no one."

And so I began to earn the funds to support both the research and the projects by lecturing, consulting, and, at our Dromenon training center, teaching intensive seminars in our work to professionals in related fields. This allowed the results of our research to become much more widespread and permitted applications in areas as far flung as finding new paradigms for community growth; helping retarded, autistic, and brain-damaged people; establishing human-development programs in prisons; and applying the premises of the new physics to understanding brain functioning. I continue to teach professional training seminars, but since 1977 the program has been expanded to reach larger numbers of people through Dromenon workshops and New Ways of Being Institutes, which have been held all over the world.

Our programs, begun as rather formal attempts to bring our scientific findings to the general public, soon acquired other dimensions, and included dancing, pulsing, and often wildly funny Rhythms of Awakening in which participants were carried to the edge of their existence, there to find new lenses and polish old ones, to awaken to a vision of what they finally could be.

This book offers the material—the ideas and the exercises— presented in these introductory workshops. It is designed to give you the chance to similarly extend and refine your own lenses of body, mind, and spirit. Its goal is to help you to tap and orchestrate your hidden creative resources. The result is that you will become a partner in the co-evolutionary task, able to perceive the Pattern that Connects, able to take those actions and acquire those skills that help build the earth and nurture the possible human.

How to Use
This Book

Sometimes it seems as if we live out our lives in the attic of the house of our being, rarely visiting the first and second floors and never the basement, which is locked. This book is organized by chapter to indicate some of the other rooms to be explored. Different readers will find different rooms more interesting than others, more familiar, or more alien. Remember that strange dream you once had about wandering through a huge, mysterious house? Well, in some sense, this book is that dream.

I have always thought that we humans are close cousins of the snowflake in that we too are infinite variations upon a starred pattern. I urge you to discover your own variations, your own insights as you go along; you will find the process more rewarding if you keep a journal, recording your experiences in drawings, musings, quotes, questions, and whatever else asks to be written down. This kind of expression will engage you in the most fascinating kind of conversation there is—the conversation with the inhabitants of your own inner crew. (In addition to being snowflakes, we are all polyphrenic as well.)

The book you hold in your hands is intended to serve as a guide in the exploration of the possible human, and as such it attempts to follow a developmental and sequential logic. But life exceeds logic every time, so find the chapter that most appeals to you and begin there if the given order is not yours. My methods are based on the premise that we grow more quickly and effectively if we first acknowledge and celebrate our strengths rather than "working on the problem."

The essay at the beginning of each chapter provides my version of a rationale for the particular capacity being considered, locating its status both in the personal and the cultural domain. The exercises following each essay are designed to help you evoke that capacity. The value of these experiences lies in developing a conscious awareness and use of possibilities that hitherto had been unconscious and dormant. A discussion and some extensions follow the presentation of each exercise. After you are familiar with the exercises, *cheat*! Make up your own variations, play with them, pitch them toward situations and applications that reflect your needs and experience. These exercises are not "writ in stone." If they were, I'd call myself Moses and be leading you in circles . . . which I am. Circles within circles within circles—there are infinite turnings and tunings that can be yours if you would but co-create the material in this book with me. A Promised Land I can't promise you, but I do hope to offer plenty of surprises along the way.

If you are working alone, you may want to put the exercises on tape for more convenient use. (Please don't use an overly dramatic or lugubrious voice, or you'll end up not trusting that person on the tape.) Tapes of some of these exercises and related work are available from the Human Capacities Corporation (see reference in the bibliography). But it's cheaper and easier to make your own.

Quite frankly, the material in this book generally works better when you are exploring it with others. (This is not true for everyone, however. If you are a natural hermit, skip the next few paragraphs.) People working in groups tend to stimulate each other. In their diverse reactions, they prime a diversity of response among themselves. You will allow yourself to have richer and more varied experiences if you are in the midst of a living smorgasbord of experience and reaction.

Working in groups with this kind of material also helps eradicate one of the worst tyrannies that afflicts *homo sapiens*: the tyranny of the dominant perception. This is reflected by such foolish philosophies as "If it was good enough for me, it is good enough for him" and "What's sauce for the goose is sauce for the gander" and "Outside of the Church there is no truth." This is not to deny the importance of consensus and commonalities but to suggest instead that our differences are enriching; I need not be limited, thank God, to my own experience but may share in yours. As you recognize the variety of human responses and capacities, you will become less judgmental, because you will have access to multiple lenses and many ways of being.

A second reason for working in a group is that we need social support to sustain ongoing change. One of the most successful of human potentials is the capacity for sloth. Self-discipline and good intentions have a way of evaporating when the issues are internal ones. The old entropy principle is a formidable foe, and the only way I know to really beat it is through regular participation in a loving, mutually empowering, teaching-learning community. Several hundred of these have sprung up all over the world as a result of our workshops and books, and, to date, they have generally proved rather effective in sustaining continuous growth and development in their participants. Most important, they have had the effect of giving people the courage to grow and then to go out into their communities and with their enhanced sense of the possible, work for social betterment in their chosen field. Many of these celebrational teaching-learning communities have taken the name *Dromenon*, which is an ancient Greek term for a therapeutic rhythm, a dance of renewal that brings the participant into contact with a larger universe and a deeper humanity. If you should decide to start a teaching-learning group, call it whatever you like and use whatever books or resources you deem suitable, but try to involve people who, in their faith in the future of humanity and the planet, are willing to work together with constancy and caring to develop the possible human in themselves and others. Narcissists and psychic exhibitionists are not helpful to the complexion of the group.

To return to the use of this book: When it is used as a basis for group experience, one person will serve as guide, having already done the exercise individually several times and having practiced reading it aloud. The responsibility for being the guide should be shared so that everyone gets a chance to have this role. On no account should you have one person take charge of the guiding. Also, the group should function *very democratically.* If anyone has tendencies to guruship, just remind him or her that *guru* is spelled *Gee, You Are You.*

After the experience is over, participants may take some time for private reflection and recording their experience. Then the experience may be shared with one or two others or, if the group is not large, with the group as a whole. Of course, the inevitable problem of sharing in a whole group is that some feel reluctant to do so. However, the process of verbal sharing in itself deepens the experience for participants, and thus a situation that allows for maximum expression and participation should be encouraged.

In working with groups it is important not to take the role of therapist, and to caution all of those involved against doing so. (If you have professional therapists in your group, they may find this very difficult, but insist that they practice their profession only during regular working hours.) Such comments, which have been heard despite repeated injunctions to refrain from making them, as "You really are blocked!" or "I can see some enormous anger stored up there" do not belong here, and probably they don't belong anywhere. Acceptance of people for who and what they are is as critical here as it is in any other learning experience. Each person is perfectly capable of interpreting his or her own experience and can ask for the comments of others if desired.

In leading workshops and seminars in the United States, Canada, Europe, Egypt, and India, I have worked with diverse groups, groups in which the youngest may be fifteen and the oldest ninety-four, in which some have only a few years of grade school and others are college professors. This variety has always added to the experience for everyone, as culturally determined labels and expectations fall away. I say this in order to suggest to you the value of having a good sample of different kinds and ages of people in your group.

This book is representative of the work used in an introductory workshop and has been used with groups as small as five and as large as three thousand. While many of these experiences are usually incorporated in a three- or four-day workshop, they have been used in school and college classrooms and during religious retreats, by families exploring together, by church groups, by government agencies, in therapeutic settings, and even in prisons—in short, wherever people gather together on an ongoing basis.

While this book stands alone as an introduction to the exploration of human capacities, it may be used in conjunction with two books by Robert Masters and me—*Mind Games* and *Listening to the Body*—to deepen and extend particular areas, specifically the exploration and development of internal imagery and altered states of consciousness, and the development of psychophysical capacities. My book entitled *Life Force: The Psycho-Historical Recovery of the Self* suggests a program of group exploration wherein individuals integrate stages of human historical development with stages of personal development. New and supporting research material originating from the Foundation for Mind Research and from others investigating personal and social transformation is published biannually in *Dromenon* magazine.

While we can give an informed speculation about what seems to be happening neurologically and physiologically, as well as psychologically, in these exercises, there is great need for much more significant research in this area. The impediments to this research are obvious. The human being is extraordinarily complex: cause and effect are very hard to isolate or differentiate. Indeed, where the human being is concerned, there may be no such thing as simple cause and effect. Rather, each phenomenon and experience derives from a rich causal weave of explanation. What we do know, however, is that these experiences and perspectives have allowed many thousands of people to regain or enhance their understanding of themselves and their capacity for growth. You can consider yourself as the object of your own research, thus avoiding invidious comparisons with the experience of others. Over time, you will perceive changes and, generally, improvements in awareness and capacity.

CHAPTER 1

The unity of the perceptual field . . . must be a unity of bodily experience. Your perception takes place where you are and is entirely dependent on how your body is functioning.

ALFRED NORTH WHITEHEAD
Modes of Thought

Eleanor Swett

1

Awakening the Body

Through our bodies we experience the external world and come to know it. Incarnated, we are spirit become matter, interactive with our external environment through our skin, our muscles, our bones—a miracle of highly differentiated and flexible organism, uniquely designed for processing and acting upon information. As the body receives and interprets thousands of bits of information every second, infinitesimal adjustments are made in our chemistry and subtle muscular and neuronal shifts take place remote from our awareness. The well-documented feats of yogis and research from the biofeedback laboratories demonstrate that consciousness can indeed be extended through our bodies and that, as this is done, improved health and increased orchestration of perception result.

This work underscores the possibility that each of us can bring *awareness* to body functions and to movements that we had, in the mainstream of Western thought, only recently assumed to be totally autonomous. Indeed, it has been shown that it is possible, through conscious directed thought, to control the firing of a single motor neuron. With subtly developed body awareness, it is possible for the individual to become the conscious orchestrator of health. We can no longer escape the understanding that *psyche* and *soma* are inextricably woven together.

Over the last eighteen years, our research into the role of imagery in changing body awareness and patterns of body use, combined with my husband's work in psychophysical re-education, has led us to create a series of exercises that allow the individual to develop and extend the natural capacity for body awareness. The aim of this work is to cooperate with the body rather than regard it as a misshapen alien or a rather unreliable but omnipresent companion. The exercises at the end of this chapter will allow you to experience some of this and provide guidelines and models for developing particular exercises that can be used in special situations.

First, however, we need to explore our cultural attitudes toward the body, for it is these attitudes that have shaped our body use and deepened the rift between knowing the body and constructs of consciousness.

Ironically, we are all too often educated *out of* rather than *in to* an awareness of the body. The active, indeed the wriggling, child's body is urged to "sit still," to restrain its natural impetus toward movement and exploration as it is confined to chair and school desk that always seem to be designed for someone else. Under these circumstances the discomforts of the body are best relegated to the unconscious, and the forgetting, the sleeping, begins.

Even when we would direct attention to training the body, we often provide models for doing so that result in a dangerously distorted body image. Thus we are often guilty of regarding the body as something to be "brought into line" as firmly as possible. The resulting rigidity of posture is often mirrored in a similar rigidity of perception, of feeling, and of cognition. My second-grade drill sessions demonstrated this effect in a never-to-be-forgotten way.

When our teacher barked, "Chest out! Belly in! Now march!" the members of grade 2-B sucked in their baby fat, threw out their bony little chests, held their breaths, turned red in the face, and glared, pop-eyed, straight ahead as they high-stepped it around the classroom. I remember feeling especially virtuous as my face purpled and my shoulders began to ache. Virtue, however, was about all I felt, for as my

Gregg S. Cobarr

contracted neck muscles began to cut off the blood supply to my brain, the world became vague and only tunnel vision remained. There was no right, no left, no up, no down, only right in front where I could, from a constrained distance, view a world of objects and "its."

"Now children, this is what we call good posture. You remember that."

I did. Probably you do too. Even now if someone tells me to stand up straight I immediately suck in my stomach and throw out my chest . . . before I realize that posture has other possibilities. This particular one, time-honored in cadre and classroom, prepares the body for war—stiffening joints and muscles into armor, shunting the brain, and equipping the unwary for an unholy crusade against nature, against feeling, against others, against knowing, against self.

If, instead, I stand and put my consciousness into the center of my body, about an inch or so below the navel (what the Japanese call the *hara* and the Chinese call the *t'an chien*), and breathe deeply into this center, letting my shoulders drop and my body feel itself into a place where it is more and more mindful of this center, I notice a significant shift in my perceptions. I have greater peripheral vision, a greater sense of potential freedom of movement, and a greater receptivity to others in my environment. With this simple shift in body posture, not only is the musculoskeletal structure substantially changed, but so, inevitably, are the perceptual and nervous systems. There is a natural grace and fluidity that extends beyond the movement into one's total relation to worlds both internal and external.

You may find it helpful to notice your own posture in different situations. How rigidly are you holding your neck? And what happens to your perceptions and sense of well-being if you relax it? Notice the fluidity and balance of your posture when you are with people you really enjoy. Allow your body to assume this posture in less ideal conditions and see how the external conditions seem to change.

A certain rigidity of posture is characteristic of the Western body. My second-grade experience is by no means unique, and it is altogether likely that you too, at some point in your training, learned to equate "good" posture with a ramrod stiffness that is more suited to the goose step than to the dance.

How did we come to this particular armoring of the body? Quite simply, it results in large part from cultural conditioning. Indeed, it is one of our most human characteristics to shape and be shaped by a larger historical cultural process. This shaping influences our thoughts, our values, our patterns of perception, and, less obviously but more insidiously, our body image. Consciously or unconsciously, we integrate these cultural patterns into our personal patterns. Who we are today is the product of our cultural and genetic experience.

To understand the alienation of the body that is the shadow side of our cultural heritage, it is necessary to look at the deep wounding of the body that has occurred in the West. The doctrine of the body as expressed by the second founder of Christianity laid an institutional base for a hatred and distrust of the flesh that is as fierce as it has been influential. St. Paul speaks to us of "our vile body" and tells us to "bring it into subjection." After Paul, the deluge. The body is seen as the site of temptation and sin, to be hidden from sight and awareness. In all fairness to Paul, it must be said that his profound distrust of the body reflects a much earlier philosophical tradition, which exalted logos and abstraction. These attitudes, however, are still reflected in the art of the Middle Ages, which, more than a millennium later, testifies to the continuing denial of the divinity of the body and a basic distrust of human physicality.

It is not until the new humanism of the Renaissance that we find the classical ideal returning with the remarriage of body and spirit so powerfully portrayed in Michelangelo's ceiling for the Sistine Chapel. The union of body and spirit are exalted in Leonardo da Vinci's drawing in which the outstretched arms and legs of a perfect man form a square and a circle, the square symbolizing the physical world embedded in time and the circle the spiritual one, at home in eternity. Here the body serves simultaneously as bridge and repository of two worlds.

Unfortunately, these Renaissance attitudes were transient and, with the coming of the double-edged sword of industrialization and the body-hating theologies of certain powerful Protestant sects, our physical instrument was dealt a blow from which it has only just begun to recover. The leaders of the Reformation and the Counter-Reformation were, for the most part, no friends of the body, seeing it as the living embodiment of the guilt and sin that keep us in a state of creatureliness far from our home in Spirit. The images of the body that haunt these theologies—"worm bag," "fodder for hell," "tomb of the spirit"—testify to the dread and disgust in which the physical being was held. Nothing would do, therefore, but to turn it into a kind of slave to be prodded and coerced, like some unfortunate beast of burden, into carrying out the will and commands of the master *mind*.

These attitudes prevailed during the age of exploration with the opening up of new continents for settlement and trade. In the dominant psychology of the pioneer, the subjugation and coercion of the body was reflected and reinforced in the exploitation of the natural environment and native peoples. Even such nature-celebrating visionaries as Emerson echo the same denigrating refrain: "Our bodies do not fit us, but caricature and satirize us. Man is physically as well as metaphysically a thing of shreds and patches."[1]

The nineteenth century celebrated the wonders of industrialization and evoked the machine as the metaphor of the possible. Given the "success" of mechanization, this metaphor was taken literally by many, so that today there is an insidious tendency to think of ourselves as the poor relations of complex machines, and to model education, social planning, and therapies on mechanistic and technological processes.

In the twentieth century we have embalmed the body in buildings designed for machines—windowless, humming, electronic urban nests, oxygen-scarce, stewing in sixty-cycle fluorescent pollution. The ensuing ecological holocaust, rooted in the body apocalypse, has evolved until today we have the dying of the earth going hand in hand with the epidemic spread of diseases of stress and dissociation—cancer, arthritis, heart disease, and schizophrenia. The pollution of air and water, the erosion of soil and earth, are only the dark resonance of what is happening in our hearts, our joints, our cells, our arteries. In failing to care for the ecology of our own bodies we have committed mayhem on the rest of the world. It is for this reason that our most acerbic critics have referred to mankind as the cancer of the planet.

Was there ever, then, a paradise of the body, a time when the wedding of body and spirit was known and celebrated? Certainly the fluidity and free-ranging movement of the child recall to us an Eden of physical delight. The young body, still unstressed and unconstrained by desk and chair, highly sensitized by nurture and touch, lives in a state in which the music of muscle and joint and the sensory splendor of each unlensed percept are open to a living paradise, with few intimations of the purgatory to come.

Culturally, the paradise of the body can be seen in some of the living examples of our "primitive" forebears in whom sensory-motor development and faculties of sensing reach levels of the highest refinement. With these people, body awareness is highly developed in order to be better able to hunt, to fish, to sense the cadences of nature, to survive. No switch or machine is available in such an environment to buffer awareness. The feet know the ground they walk on, and the nose recognizes the scents carried in the wind. The divine is present in the cellular structure of matter.

This valuing of the body is not restricted to primitive societies. In ancient Egypt, for example, the body was thought to be governed by the very principles that were seen to organize the universe. The human was the model for that universe, the body the temple designed to permit understanding of the intimate links between microcosm and macrocosm. As the esoteric Egyptologist Schwaller de Lubicz has shown, the ancient Egyptian perceived the body as the cosmic connection linking and expressing the forms inherent in astronomy, geography, rhythm, proportion, mathematics, architecture, magic, healing, and art.[2] Honored as the Temple of Knowledge, the different parts of the body were consecrated to one of the Neters, or divine principles, different organs bearing different gods. A high level of health was seen as a supreme spiritual event. Thus the Egyptian sculptures and paintings show us bodies that are at once supple and lightly held, with a proper relationship to gravity and high muscular definition. The emphasis is on grace, fluidity, and ease of functioning. The current revival of interest in ancient Egyptian magic and art testifies to our desire to recapture these basic connections.

The body as the Greeks represented it from the fifth to the third centuries B.C. was obviously intended to give pleasure to the person and is aesthetically indicative of the unification of *soma* and *psyche*, body and soul. In the Hellenic ideal, the body can be the perfect expression of the philosophic values of the good and the beautiful (*kalokagathia*).

For Christ, the body was apparently a delightful place to incorporate his divinity, for most of the Gospel references to his life in the body seem to involve hiking, fishing, boating, eating, drinking, and generally enjoying a natural use of his physical instrument. His parables are rich in sensuous imagery, full of interesting tastes and colors and showing a fine appreciation and delight in sensory experience. Clearly, the body and nature were for Jesus a living allegory for the action of God in the world. As we saw earlier, however, this perception was to be lost in the institutionalization of Christian practice, although it was kept alive in the esoteric Gnostic traditions, the documentation of which is now, perhaps not so coincidentally, emerging.

Honoring the body as an instrument of intellectual and spiritual knowing, Eastern cultures have developed systems of breathing and yogic postures that tuned and developed this instrument. The temple sculptures of India emphasize rounded, curving bodies with a degree of suppleness almost unknown in the West. In Buddhist art and practice, the emphasis is on centeredness, the shifting of gravity to the belly. It is thought that by being centered in this way a person is able to be receptive to the forces of Being and is consequently shaped, protected, supported, and transformed by these forces. As we have already noted, if you are "belly-centered" you become almost incapable of sustaining the usual tensions and rigidities and are better able to perform all aspects of daily life in an enhanced and enlightened way. For the practitioner of the Buddhist, Hindu, and Tantric disciplines, the body is, as it was for the Egyptians, the supreme temple of transmutation, the place where all the forces of the universe gather to be channeled and transformed into a higher integral order of nature and spirit.

Thus it is apparent that in other cultures and eras the body was indeed viewed with reverence, that practices were developed for its training, and that even the classical world of our Western tradition honored the body. And there is now a profound awakening to the teachings of these various traditions. The emerging new myths of the body reflect this awakening and are not unlike the Christian nostalgia for the Body of Resurrection in their descriptions of the re-creation of the human form so that it may house and express a fuller consciousness and capacity. Previously, many of the Western myths of the physical body partook of the great divide between spirit and flesh, mind and body. The dualisms of Jewish, Greek, Christian, and Gnostic beliefs, best typified in Plato's perception of the body as a dark cave imprisoning the luminous soul, were all myths having to do with the release from the corporeal dungeon to the ethereal light.

I have always thought of a myth as something that never was but is always happening. As with all great myths, the one that tells the saga of the body and its transformations is already happening. The last decade has seen an exotic and varied unfolding of the mythos as countless thousands take up jogging, biking, holistic health care, Eastern disciplines, and martial arts. So we have a veritable potpourri of possibilities—tai chi, aikido, kundalini yoga, methods of ancient Tibetan energy harvesting, acupuncture as orthodoxy, shamanic exercise, Sufi dancing, polarity balancing, rebirthing, biofeedback, the varieties of Reichian experience. It is as if every discipline of healing, health, and becoming whole that ever was has suddenly been called back into practice all over the earth in order that we might have the richest possible inventory of psychophysical opportunities with which to reinvent ourselves. The planetary memory banks of body-mind transformings are available in ways that they could never be before. And we are beginning to use them in ways that previous ages would have considered more mythic than real.

While we have certainly explored many of these alternatives in our research at the Foundation, we have been particularly attracted to the pioneering work of F. Matthias Alexander, Moshe Feldenkrais, and Elsa Gindler and her student Charlotte Selver, all of whom have developed methods to re-educate the body for greater awareness and radically improved use. The key to their work lies in gaining *awareness* of patterns of muscular abuse and then inhibiting these negative reflexes and replacing them with appropriate ones. Once awareness is achieved, conscious control is possible, and you will no longer be constrained by unconsciously held bad habits that inhibit optimal functioning.[3]

These significant discoveries were made in the same way many discoveries seem to be made—by necessity born out of accident. Alexander, a Shakespearean actor, suddenly lost his voice. This tragedy led him to painstakingly search for a remedy. During the process of closely observing the movements of his head and neck, he discovered it was his improper posture that had caused the loss of his voice. This discovery led him from a career on the stage to the development of the Alexander Technique, a method based on the assumption that "bad posture" is really a profound misuse of the self that often results in a malfunctioning of the whole person.

Similarly, Elsa Gindler cured herself of tuberculosis by minutely observing both the movement of her diaphragm and her patterns of breathing and then subtly altering them until they achieved optimal functioning. In this awareness a "primary control" is achieved that, in turn, allows for the creative conscious control of the entire psychophysical organism.

Feldenkrais' Functional Integration focuses on developing "freedom through awareness" by increasing the movement potential of the body and simultaneously freeing the inhibited cells of the motor cortex. This is done either through verbal direction or direct manipulation that guides subtle and gentle movements to re-educate the nervous system. When motor neurons are disinhibited and "re-educated," there is a greater fluidity of movement and a corresponding disinhibition of thinking, feeling, and sensing.

As we studied the work of these pioneers and worked directly with Feldenkrais, we began to focus on developing the "kinesthetic body," or *body image*, directly and on using the active imagination to orchestrate body use. The kinesthetic body is the body of the muscular imagination. Each of us registers directly in the cells of the brain a representation of our body. This representation was charted by the neurosurgeon Wilder Penfield, and it illustrates quite graphically that the neurological awareness of different parts of the body is not proportional to the actual sizes of the parts but is instead related to their use in manipulating and interpreting our external environment.

Our premise has been that this neurological representation of the body can be extended and refined through the conscious bringing of awareness to the subtle patterns of body use and that, as this occurs, there will be an improvement in body functioning. For example, try right now to imagine, as vividly as you can, how you would go about standing up. Now actually stand up. Did you do it in the way you thought you would? Many people find that the actual movements are quite different from the movements they imagined. While this may seem surprising, it is perfectly normal, since we tend to be quite unconscious of our most common patterns of body movements. Repeat this process until your image of how you stand up coincides with what you are actually doing. Additionally, kinesthetic sensing is being developed, and your mind and body are being integrated in a way that will give you a greater freedom of choice of movement. Our work with thousands of research subjects and seminar participants certainly supports the premise that awareness of body use can be developed kinesthetically and that this awareness results in greatly improved body functioning.

As you acquire the habit of inhibiting bad muscular use and

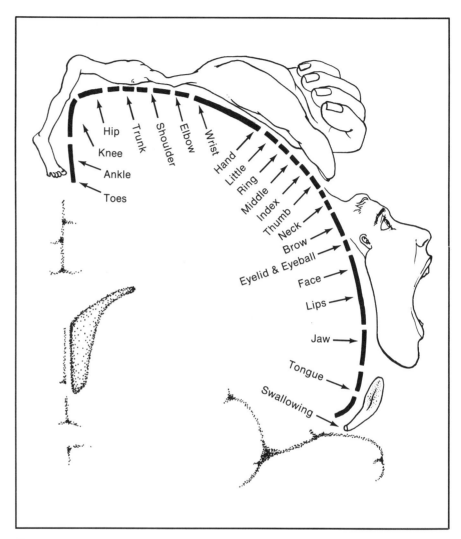

Hip

Knee

Trunk

Shoulder

Elbow

Ankle

Wrist

Toes

Hand

Little

Ring

Middle

Index

Thumb

Neck

Brow

Eyelid & Eyeball

Face

Lips

Jaw

Tongue

Swallowing

The "motor homunculus" as described by Wilder Penfield depicts the areas of the brain that control the motor activity of particular regions of the body.

replacing this with good use, you acquire the art of inhibiting the entire negative spectrum of physical and emotional dis-ease and dis-abilities. As you increase this awareness of the body, a keen and accurate kinesthetic sense is developed that, when married to imagery and verbal suggestion, not only allows you to effect the usual needed healings but also, by extending awareness to organs, cells, and fundamental body systems, allows for the very work of transformation.

In relearning the use of the body, you are living in a state of almost constant revelation. You are likely to find that almost everything you do can be done more efficiently, more pleasurably, and with greater ease than was possible before. You will have much greater stamina and strength, and many of the debilitating "symptoms of aging" will be reversed. In the state of good posture, which is indeed a state of being, your body will feel very light, almost weightless, and will seem less dense—as if your head were a kite and the rest of the body the tail dangling lightly from it!

While we were exploring these possibilities of physical re-education to enhance body use, our basic research into imagery was opening other pathways of tapping into the body's basic wisdom, which in turn can guide the natural healing process. We found that the body has its wisdom that wisdom does not know, to paraphrase poor sickly Pascal. Ordinary waking states tend to inhibit our awareness of this extraordinarily complex body knowing. It is too much for ordinary consciousness to contain and so tends to be revealed in such altered states of consciousness as images, dreams, myths, metaphors, and reveries.

These altered states are well known to physicians who listen to the hallucinations of their feverish patients, and are equally familiar to the shaman and the partakers of hallucinogens. The wisdom available in these states has, however, been blocked from entering the mainstream of modern consciousness.

How does one tap into this body wisdom without inducing a fever or swallowing a visionary vegetable? The ways are many—from the incubation dreams evoked at the temple of Asklepios, the healing daimon in ancient Epidauros, to the monitoring of body signals learned in biofeedback laboratories. For the body knows what it is about but we in the Western world have very largely lost our living connections with these knowings.

To contact this wisdom of the body, we have used visualization and imagery, those techniques that have proven useful for self-healing for thousands of years. Numerous studies have confirmed the fact that vividly experienced imagery, imagery that is both seen and felt, can substantially affect brain waves, blood flow, heart rate, skin temperature, gastric secretions, and immune response—in fact, the total physiology.[4]

There is actually a kind of yogi graduation exercise practiced in the Himalayas in which the adept sits on a cold stone in subfreezing temperatures wearing only a loincloth. Wet sheets are placed on his back and, by visualizing an increase of body heat and practicing certain breathing exercises, he succeeds in drying off these wet sheets. (I like to think it is how many sheets he can dry off that determines how he graduates—that is, five sheets—*cum laude*; ten sheets—*summa cum laude . . .*)

To change the modality we must change the metaphor. In our research we have found that metaphors which provide for the personalizing of body parts and states can often give us the charged imagery that then creates those channels of communication for dialogue with our innate body wisdom.

As an example of this, suppose that you have a stiff hand and wish to free those muscles. Visualize as clearly as you can that hand moving freely. Sense vividly, both in your imagination and your kinesthetic body, what the hand will feel like, the easy vibrant life of the freely moving hand. Through the use of imagery you are beginning to replace one brain program (your stiff hand) with another (your freely moving hand). The body then responds with the appropriate and intricate reorganization that the brain commands, and your hand loses its stiffness more rapidly than would otherwise be expected.

With more serious ailments, the principle is the same. In a relaxed and receptive state, an organ or part of the body is imaged in terms of its optimal functioning. If, for example, there has been an infection, imagine the optimal condition of the infected area as clearly as possible; then imagine white blood cells—seen as either cells or little soldiers—moving in on the infection (seen as some comic-dreadful creature), breaking it up, and carrying it off to be flushed out of the system. Hold images of healthy functioning again, and then speak directly to the brain, advising it to continue orchestrating a situation of healing and health. A child with a broken bone might imagine little people or animals putting bone cement into the crack to help it heal faster.

Exercise 3 in this chapter provides a model for contacting your own body wisdom. Using similar techniques, many physicians in the holistic-health movement have achieved remarkable results with seriously ill patients. Carl and Stephanie Simonton's work with cancer patients, in which they use guided imagery in conjunction with more orthodox therapies to actively and consciously engage patients in their own healing process, is a case in point.

Unfortunately, just as we have the capacity for positive resonance with larger realities, so we also have conditionings for negative resonance with the stalemates of our existence. Nothing is taught the body that does not also teach and inform the minds and eventually the culture. To tell a group of seven-year-olds, "Chest out, belly in . . . now march!" is to give a command that echoes through the rest of their lives. One way or another, the same command is heard again and again, and its cumulative effect is to create walled people and walled nations whose chief feature is their attitude of opposition and denial. It is time to change the command, to allow seven-year-olds and seventy-year-olds to reclaim the glory of their bodies.

The exercises that follow are illustrative of the kinds of practices that will allow this integration of psyche and soma to take place. They can easily be used in conjunction with other physical disciplines and healing practices, and suggestions for doing so follow some of the exercises. As you do the exercises, other extensions and applications will occur to you.

The emphasis in the first two is upon close awareness. The more of your mind that you can bring to bear on each movement, the more highly articulated your body image will become. Thus there are suggestions to note this or note that. What I am urging is that you pay attention to what is going on rather than judge it.

Like most exercises, these won't work if you don't do them, nor do they have much value if they are seen as we ordinarily see much learning curriculum—as something to be "gone through" in some linear fashion. It has been the experience of many of my students that the more they do these exercises and integrate them into their lives and improvise upon them, the more they continue to find in them.

Exercise 1

The Kinesthetic Body

TIME: 45 minutes

There is an extensive tradition both East and West which holds that each individual possesses a secondary, nonphysical, or "subtle" body. Be it the *ka* of the ancient Egyptians, the *pranic* body of yoga, the etheric body of the esoteric schools, or Plato's "the form of things," each tradition shares the belief that this "body" is composed of more subtle matter than the corporeal body and that its development leads to higher faculties of perception and knowing. These traditions may indeed speak directly to the same phenomenon we have been working with—the kinesthetic body, or body image encoded in the motor homunculus of the brain. In any case, all suggest that it is indeed possible to actively engage those processes of physical functioning that are usually unavailable to consciousness.

You might ask "Why bother?" We can indeed be glad that we don't have to consciously regulate all our body functions, that we can trust the body to get on with it, thus freeing our minds for more important matters. If, however, you wish to cooperate with your body's capacity for healing and for knowing, you must be able to bring awareness to your body image.

As a child I was brought to a puzzled awareness that body image and the physical body might be quite different well before I had ever heard anything about Wilder Penfield or the *ka*. I was six years old and spending the summer with my Uncle Paul, an ex-army officer who had lost his leg during World War II. One day he pointed to the empty space in front of him and said, "Jean, would you please scratch my toe?" "Uncle Paul," I protested, "you don't have any toe." "I know that," he said, "but it still itches, so scratch it anyway." Bewildered, and feeling more than a little perverse, I scratched the air in the area where I supposed the toe would have been. "*Ahhh*," exclaimed my relieved uncle, and beamed his thanks at me.

Years later I understood this macabre little comedy as an instance of the phantom-body effect, wherein the toe and its itches may have been removed from the gross external body but not from the subtle, neurological body. In our own research and teaching we utilize aspects of this phenomenon to develop a subtler body sensibility, a "kinesthetic body" (from the Greek: *kinema*—motion, and *esthesia*—sensing).

Here it might be said that some people are "natural" kinesthetic imagers. For these people, the capacity for knowing, indeed for thinking, is closely coordinated with their body movement. These people will find it easier than others to consciously develop their kinesthetic body sense. However, *everyone* can do it. Kinesthetic imagers can often be observed gesturing frequently when they talk and moving around as they think. I am one of them, and for me to have to give a lecture and stand absolutely still would result in my being tongue-tied. While I can attribute (or blame, depending on the point of view) this to my half-Sicilian heritage, it does not much matter. Many non-Sicilians share this trait, and while it may not be the dominant mode of thinking for most people, it is nonetheless *a* mode of knowing for us all. Even if it is not your dominant mode, you can learn to use it just as those for whom spelling is not something they can do with the greatest of ease can learn to spell if they start paying attention to the patterns by which letters are formed into words.

PREPARATION

If possible, have someone else read the exercise to you the first time, or put it on tape. While it is possible to read a few of the instructions, do them, and then return to reading, this can be quite distracting initially, and some of the potential effect of the exercise may be lost. It is possible to read the entire exercise yourself a few times, either silently or aloud, getting a sense of it as you do so and then do the exercise without the book.

When you feel your attention wandering, stop. This is an exercise not in movement per se but in *movement and attention*, and when they have parted company we only reinforce old patterns. This is, again, why a group can be very helpful. The commitment of the group can carry the individual when resolve falters and laughter is needed. If you cannot do this with a friend or in a group, you may find it helpful to create an imaginary group of people to do it with you! The sense of being alone, if that aloneness is not freely chosen, can itself inhibit positive change.

THE EXERCISE

Stand comfortably, with your knees relaxed and your eyes closed.

Focus on your breathing for a minute as a way of directing your attention inward.

The real and the kinesthetic body.

The Kinesthetic Body

Check now to see if your weight is evenly balanced on both your feet and sense your feet in contact with the ground.

Scan your body to ensure that you have relaxed any unnecessary tension, particularly in your shoulder and neck area.

Raise your **real** right arm and stretch, sensing the shifting alignment of the muscles all over your body as you do this. Feel the stretch in your fingers, your hand, your arm, your shoulder, your torso. Now, with equal awareness, lower your arm.

Repeat this several times.

Now stretch your **kinesthetic** right arm, allowing yourself to experience this as vividly as possible.

Stretch again with your **real** right arm, then your **kinesthetic** arm.

Alternate several times between stretching with your **real** arm and your **kinesthetic** arm.

Do the same thing with your **real** left arm and your **kinesthetic** left arm, always remembering to experience your **kinesthetic** arm with as much reality as you had when stretching your **real** arm.

Do the same thing *alternately,* stretching **real** and **kinesthetic** arms.

Let your **real** arms and shoulder circle in a round forward movement like the paddlewheels of a steamboat.

Do the same thing with your **kinesthetic** arms and shoulders, continuing to feel the same momentum you felt with your **real** arms and shoulders.

Alternate.

Let your **real** arms and shoulders circle in a backward movement.

Do the same thing kinesthetically.

Alternate.

Now, with your **real** body, make a fencing lunge to the right.

Come back to the center.

Repeat this several times.

Now lunge to the right with your **kinesthetic** body.

Come back to the center.

Alternate several times between your **real** and your **kinesthetic** body.

Do the same thing with a fencing lunge to the left.

Follow this sequence:

Real body lunges to the right.

Back to the center.

Real body lunges to the left.

Back.

Kinesthetic body lunges to the left.

Back.

Real body lunges to the left.

Back.

Kinesthetic body lunges to the right and comes back.

Real body lunges to the right and comes back.

Real body lunges to the left.

Back.

Now, *at the same time*, your **kinesthetic** body lunges to the right and your **real** body lunges to the left.

Come back to the center.

Now lunge with your **real** body to the right and your **kinesthetic** body to the left.

Come back to center.

Rest for a moment.

Raise both **real** arms over your head and hold them there.

At the same time, feel your **kinesthetic** arms hanging at your sides.

Slowly lower your **real** arms while you raise your **kinesthetic** arms, putting as much attention into your **kinesthetic** arms as you direct to your **real** arms.

Now, lower your **kinesthetic** arms while you raise your **real** arms.

Lower your **real** arms while you raise your **kinesthetic** arms.

Continue with this until the raising and lowering of your **kinesthetic** arms becomes almost indistinguishable from the movement of your **real** arms.

Rest.

Be aware of the space several feet in front of you. Now, with your **real** body jump as high as you can into that space.

Jump back.

Do it again with your **real** body, jumping as high as you can, forward and back.

Do the same thing with your **kinesthetic** body, forward and back.

Now do it with your **real** body.

Real body again.

Real body again.

Kinesthetic body, jumping as high as you can, forward and back.

Real body.

Kinesthetic body.

Jump forward with your **kinesthetic** body and stay there.

Now, jumping as high as you can, jump with your **real** body *into* your **kinesthetic** body!

Standing still, notice how you feel.

Scan your body again.

Is there greater awareness now in your body?

Begin to walk around and notice your awareness.

Opening your eyes, see if your perception of the external world and others has changed at all.

DISCUSSION

It is possible to use very different movements than the ones described above; however, it is best to start with the dominant side of the body, and for most of us this is the right side, because awareness is greater on this side. For the same reason we start with the arm or hand; again, awareness is greatest in this area.

The important principle to bear in mind is that you do the movement with your real body a few times, paying close attention to how it feels and to how the rest of your body responds. Then, when exercising the kinesthetic body, you "replay" this awareness without any "real movement." (Actually, if anyone were to hook you up with a skin galvanometer, subtle muscle reactions would be registered.) Note if doing these movements quickly or slowly increases or decreases the ease with which you register awareness. This will vary from person to person, but finding your own rhythms of awareness will be very helpful to you in doing this exercise.

Some people ask if they are supposed to "see" their body moving when they are doing this exercise. Some people will, especially those who are good visualizers; however, this is not necessary and may even distract from the subtle awareness of internal processes for which we often lack adequate visual images.

As you work with your kinesthetic body, you may notice that your awareness of one side of your body is greater than your awareness of the other. One way to work on this is simply to practice. Exaggerate the movements of the side where there seems to be less awareness, gradually letting the movements become more and more subtle and natural.

APPLICATIONS AND EXTENSIONS

The applications and extensions of this exercise are seemingly endless. I will mention a few here to get you started, with the hope that you will discover more on your own as the power of the body image, or kinesthetic sense, becomes more apparent.

Centering with Your Kinesthetic Body

You can test your kinesthetic sense by slowly spinning your **real** body in one direction while you spin your **kinesthetic** body at the same speed in the opposite direction. If you find yourself becoming dizzy, stop and start again slowly. As your skill increases, you will find that you can spin for a long time without becoming dizzy. Reverse directions for your real body and your kinesthetic body. Continue to do this until you can spin in either direction without becoming dizzy. Those who have done this exercise report that they feel very centered, even still, as the kinesthetic body spins in one direction and the real body in the other.

The Kinesthetic Body

Kinesthetic Dyads

Stand with your weight balanced, facing a partner.

Close your eyes and sense your partner standing in front of you.

Gently place your **real** hands on your partner's shoulders.

Lower your real hands.

Repeat this sequence.

Now place your **kinesthetic** hands on your partner's shoulders, sensing as fully as possible the shoulders of the other and the slight pressure of your partner's kinesthetic hands on your shoulders.

Repeat this several times, alternating between placing your real and your kinesthetic hands on the other's shoulders until a strong sense of your kinesthetic touch is developed.

Now, while playing some dance music or singing a dance melody (preferably a waltz or a box step), begin to dance together with your **real** bodies, circling in one direction.

Change, and dance together with your **kinesthetic** bodies.

Now dance together with your real bodies, circling in the opposite direction. Change, and dance together with your kinesthetic bodies. Alternate several times, dancing together in your real bodies in one direction, followed by your kinesthetic bodies, then repeating the sequence in the other direction.

Dance now with your real bodies, allowing your kinesthetic bodies to dance in the opposite direction!

Keep dancing, sending your real bodies in one direction and your kinesthetic bodies in the other, until you sense the "four" of you dancing together in perfect balance.

This exercise allows you to develop a subtlety of awareness of touch that is often lost in a "slap-on-the-back" culture. It is possible to sense a gentle touch in the thought of another, bringing mind and body in closer communion and a more finely tuned intimacy.

Skill Rehearsal

Once you have a sense of your kinesthetic body, you can practice any sport or physical discipline in your kinesthetic body in a powerful form of skill rehearsal. To demonstrate this, I might ask someone in one of my workshops who regularly practices hatha yoga to demonstrate a yoga position that they would like to improve. That person then executes the posture several times, giving full awareness to all body sensations in the process. Then that person will rehearse the posture kinesthetically, gracefully and without tension or strain. When the person feels that he or she has a full kinesthetic sense of the posture, the posture is repeated with the real body. Usually a very obvious change in the fluidity and ease of the posture is apparent both to the observers and the individual, a change that might normally take weeks to accomplish. The kinesthetic body seems to "forget" errors and awkward movements, thus allowing us to get in touch with our natural grace and fluidity.

Children use kinesthetic skill rehearsal with great ease. One eight-year-old of my acquaintance is a competitive swimmer. Before a race he rehearses the race kinesthetically for a few seconds, imagining himself moving through the water effortlessly and without fatigue. He regards his brief time with his kinesthetic body as his "magic" time—and has become a formidable opponent.

The use of imagery to improve sports performance is gaining widespread support among professional athletes and coaches here. Thomas Tutko, of San Jose State, suggests that it will be "the single most important factor in the sports world" in the 1980s. So even if you are not headed for the pros, you may want to try it before your next tennis game.

The optimal use of your kinesthetic body for skill rehearsal can be enhanced by imagining that you are the master of the particular skill. For example, if you are rehearsing your tennis serve kinesthetically, you might want to imagine that you *are* Bjorn Borg, Tracy Austin, or whoever you admire. We internalize these images of grace and excellence as we watch skilled performers on television, in movies, or in person. With kinesthetic rehearsal we can make the identification between these ideal images and our own movement, letting go of our sense of local incompetence and allowing the expression of our stored imagery of more optimal performance. We could speculate that what is happening is that one part of the brain is training another. The activation of the kinesthetic imagination serves to enable the part of brain functioning that stores optimal images of performance to re-educate, as it were, the part of the motor cortex that informs the usual performance. The motor cortex is then able to release the inferior performance patterns and incorporate the improved patterns, with resulting substantial improvement in the skill needed to perform the task. That this can all happen in a matter of seconds is testimony to the brain's remarkable abilities to re-educate itself. With this comes not just improvement but, equally important, an attitude of greater confidence and courage about the skill.

Speaking of courage, this is one of the great dividends of the theory and practice of the kinesthetic body, since this subtle agent doesn't seem to know the usual fears and blocks of its grosser counterpart. This state of innocence can be employed to great advantage when you need to rehearse some difficult upcoming encounter or interview, challenge, or test situation. Rehearse it in the kinesthetic body until the event seems real, realistic, and realizable. In so doing, you are already prepatterning body, mind, and emotions to make more optimal responses, and so will tend to perform the actual task with greater facility. I do this whenever I am experiencing a writing block. First, I dance to get the blood going and move out of my general state of withdrawal and recalcitrance, dancing—if I can—about the subject I am to write about. Then, all stirred up, I project myself kinesthetically to the typewriter and feel myself writing, and then, some minutes later, I feel *compelled* to go and join my kinesthetic body at the typewriter!

This technique can also be used for more mundane tasks, such as getting yourself and the children off to school in the morning. If you sometimes find this to be an enervating enterprise, spend a minute imaging yourself and your family moving through your morning routine in harmony and with grace. You may be surprised at what happens!

When rehearsing with your kinesthetic body, it is important to rehearse the *entire* sequence—beginning, middle, and *end*. One student who has a strong empathic and kinesthetic sense went to the top of a ski slope and, armed with television images of great skiers, went down the mountain, for the first time, with great ease and even greater speed. Only when she got to the bottom did she realize that she had no image for stopping, since this had never been shown on the races that she had watched, and she landed in an ignominious heap in the parking lot.

Another student developed an ingenious extension of the identification with the skill master. Try as he might, he could not imagine turning a somersault because he was blocked by memories of repeated failures in tumbling classes. Even his kinesthetic body balked. The somersault was clearly not possible for him. Then it dawned on him that it was possible for a frog—a frog flipped so easily into the pond that it could not possibly get hurt. Armed with the flexible image of the flipping frog, he imagined himself to be a frog doing somersaults kinesthetically. This was easy. Still imagining himself to be a frog, he did somersaults with his real "frog" body. In his exuberance, he did a remarkable series of somersaults across the room, celebrating his newfound capacities.

It is our tunnel vision and singular sense of identity that often limits our sense of our own possibilities—and yet it is the genius of humans to imagine being something we are not, and thus to extend what we indeed are. As we define ourselves by the limitations of our personal existential history, we reinforce these limitations, insisting that "this is me." We fail to use our untrained imaginations, our particularly human capacity to act *as if* we were something else, much as the actor on the stage does, allowing us to become shape shifters, more fluid and flexible in our realities and in our bodies.

Kinesthetic Therapies

The kinesthetic body can be used to keep up muscle tone if you are sick in bed or otherwise confined, even during the confinement of plane travel. Make many small movements on one side of your body. These could include a sequence of about twenty-five movements each of rapping your fingers, moving your leg up and down from the hip joint, wiggling your toes one by one, and so forth. Alternate each series of real movements with kinesthetic movements. In doing this, you signal the motor cortex to relax contracted muscles and allow a freer flow of blood, thus improving circulation. As a result of this subtle toning and elimination of muscular contraction, the entire body lengthens, becoming looser and more integrated with other parts of the body. This will reduce the muscular atrophy and poor circulation usually associated with confinement.

This and similar procedures have been used with stroke victims. They exercise the unaffected parts of the body, alternating between real and kinesthetic movements. Improvement of function is often observed in the contralateral parts of the body where there had previously been little or no apparent movement or awareness. This improvement seems to stem from the tendency of the body/mind to generalize, to balance, thus transferring improved awareness from one side of the body to the other. Further specific therapeutic applications are suggested in *Listening to the Body*.

Exercise 2

The Ideal Body

TIME: 30 minutes

As I suggested earlier in the story about marching around the classroom in the second grade, our image of how our bodies "should" look is determined by our cultural experience, constantly reinforced by advertising and admonitions that may have little connection to the reality of who we are. And, often, the "ideal" body suggested by indefatigable advertisements is totally inappropriate for the great majority of us. I will never have a twenty-two-inch waist or weigh a hundred and twenty-five pounds. Nor am I likely to look like I am twenty-one again—if I ever did. It is critical that we break away from these rigid norms and celebrate the union of mind and body that allows for each of us to be unique and not interchangeable Barbie dolls and Clark Kents. Thus many of us are in a constant state of ambiguity, wishing we were taller or shorter, thinner or fatter, resulting in the abuse of the bodies we have. These obvious influences are further confounded by our less conscious imitations of the body use of our parents and the painful and all too present memories of adolescence, when we all believed that the whole world was looking at us and commenting on our awkward bodies and blotchy skin.

It is critical that we again regard the body as ally, as remarkable in its willingness to carry us through life despite the abuse we often administer to it, long suffering as it attempts to communicate with an all-too-often deaf consciousness.

The following exercise has been very helpful in remedying this uncomfortable situation. It will be effective, however, only if you can put aside your "judge" as you observe your body. Allow yourself, instead, to observe with the eyes of a dear and supportive friend.

PREPARATION

It is important to have established a good sense of the kinesthetic body before beginning.

As in the exercise for the kinesthetic body, stand comfortably with your knees and shoulders relaxed. Establish a pattern of regular breathing.

As you do this exercise, do not shift your position; just be aware of it.

THE EXERCISE

Note whether your weight is evenly balanced on your feet, if your body is turned slightly to the right or left.

We are going to scan the entire body, beginning with the feet. Take your time and try not to be critical of what you find as you go along.

Now notice your feet, in contact with the floor, beginning with the right foot if you are right-handed and the left foot if you are left-handed. How much of the foot is actually on the floor? Is the weight on your heels, the balls of your feet, or the edges? Notice the spaces under your arch and under and between your toes.

Notice the top of your foot.

Go through the same process with the other foot.

Notice your ankles. Are they turned in or out? How are they shaped? Is there strain in the muscles of the ankle?

Continue up your legs, sensing and visualizing as many details as possible.

Sense the connection of the thighs to the hips. Is one side higher than the other? Are they turned out or in? Are both hip sockets evenly turned?

Sense now the genitals, the anus, the buttocks and the pelvis. Notice their configuration. Be aware of those areas that seem to be missing from your body image. If you need to move slightly or make some small muscle contractions in these areas to get awareness, do so.

Sense the spine now, from the coccyx to the place above the neck where the spine joins with the head socket. Note its curvature.

Note now the diaphragm as it expands and contracts with the rhythm of your breathing. Continue to focus on your breathing to help your awareness of your rib cage and your chest.

Shifting your awareness now to your shoulders, notice their breadth and width. Is one shoulder higher than the other? More forward? Notice the alignment between your shoulders, your hips, and your feet.

Now move down your arms, one at a time, noting the space between your arms and your body. Compare the left arm with the right arm. Notice your elbow joints and your wrists. Now notice your hands and fingers.

When you have established a full image of your hands and fingers, move now to your neck, noticing its length and breadth, the degree of tension that you might be holding here.

Now work on your head, noticing its overall configuration, the position of the features, including ears and face, hair and hairline, and all the features of the face. Explore the whole and each feature one by one. Is there a difference between the right and left eye? Are the ears evenly placed? Make your awareness as complete as possible.

When you have finished, rest for a minute.

Having made this detailed tour of your body, return to your feet and, beginning there, do a quick scan of your body from your toes to the top of the head, trying to get as complete and integrated an image as possible. Now scan from the top of your head to your toes. Do this several times, pausing in those areas where the image is not clear and doing a little movement to bring that area into fuller awareness, if possible.

Now rest again for a minute.

Having done this inventory of what your body actually is like, imagine, *as fully as you can*, what you would actually like your body to be. Give the same kind of attention to detail here that you did when you were aware of your real body. Include the length of your spine and the size of your earlobes, the position of your feet on the floor and the length of the tongue in your mouth.

In your mind, *create the ideal body that is you*. Hold this image and breathe into it.

Now imagine this kinesthetic ideal body about a foot in front of you so that you can "see" the back of it and *jump into it*. How does it feel? If it doesn't feel comfortable, *jump out quickly*. Adjust those parts, or even the whole image if necessary, to be more realistic. Again, put it in front of you and jump into it. Continue to do this until the body that you jump into feels comfortable.

Begin to move in this ideal body, allowing the knowing of it to be integrated into your patterns of standing and walking, of sitting and dancing.

DISCUSSION

What is happening in this exercise? Essentially, the body image is clarified. Unconsciously held body images that may not be either appropriate or desirable are brought to awareness and replaced with more appropriate ones. Significant parts of the body, such as your ears or the back of your knees, that had previously been missing from your body image may be added so that the image becomes more complete. Our culture emphasizes certain body parts, particularly the face, the breasts of women, the waist and hips, the thighs and the hands. Often the rest of the body image is extremely dim while these parts are vividly and often painfully clear. When seen in the context of the *whole* body, their importance diminishes and they are seen as an integral part of who you are. The results will vary from person to person, depending on the discrepancy between the previous "ideal" and "real" body and the commitment to getting in touch with the "possible ideal" body.

Many have found this exercise particularly valuable for maintaining body weight at an optimal level. The internal body image does not look at scales or count pounds, but instead senses the body as a whole and can respond to a felt shift in the whole image in a way that it cannot and will not respond to the command to shed pounds. Suddenly *and permanently* the desire for sweets disappears; exercise routines are adopted and maintained. At the same time there is no sense of conscious effort or self-denial, perhaps because the "self" is more fully integrated with the body. Those whose body is considerably larger than the acculturated ideal image often find that, for the moment at least, they would not be truly comfortable forty or fifty pounds thinner and are willing to make gradual changes in their body image, repeating this exercise over a period of months until they have achieved a body in which they truly feel at home.

The use of this exercise also seems to be beneficial in self-healing as you maintain an image of optimal body condition and recognize that the body is indeed "talking" to you when it ceases to function optimally. Then we can let go of the idea of mind *over* matter, with its basic adversarial assumptions, and move into a state of cooperation of mind *with* matter. As we now see the body as ally, as trusted comrade on our journey, the ideal body becomes not an illusive dream but an existential reality to be celebrated and honored.

The Ideal Body

Exercise 3

Contacting Your Body Wisdom

TIME: 30 minutes

While I understood the possibility of body wisdom, it remained basically an abstract intellectual construct until I was forced into a dramatic under-standing of its reality when I was twenty-three and woke up to find myself sickening rapidly.

"Influenza," the doctor murmured, and left a few vitamin pills on my nightstand.

"Such a wonderful physician!" exclaimed my Christian Scientist mother. "He doesn't prescribe any medication. Here, read this." She handed me a tract by the wily Mrs. Eddy.

Reading was out of the question, as was thinking, speaking, or even moving. To attempt to lie on my side was to cross the continent. And to turn over on my stomach was half a world away. Never had I been so tired. My name was Fatigue and I knew no other state.

In the hours before dawn my temperature would soar and the halluci-nations would begin. One 3:00 A.M. vigil found me at 105 degrees and being visited by a group of ladies in flowered hats who introduced them-selves as newly dead Westchester matrons who were presidents of their garden clubs.

"Jean," they admonished me sternly, "wake up your mother and tell her to give you the blood test that's given to alcoholics!"

"Go 'way," I whimpered feebly. "You're just my lousy fever."

"Don't tell *us* what we are. We *know* what we are! Now wake up your mother and tell her to give you that blood test!"

"But I've never had more than a glass of wine a month," I protested, knowing even through my fever that all this was a little silly.

The ladies kept it up and so I finally demurred, calling out to my mother and asked her to get me . . . a hot chocolate. I couldn't bring myself to utter that zany message.

"Now why did you do that?" the ladies scolded me as my mother went trundling down the hall. "You know that we are just going to keep after you all night."

And that they did, offering no explanations, no further information, just growing more and more insistent. After about an hour of this brow-beating, I again called out: "Mother . . . Could you get me maybe the . . . uh . . . the . . . uh . . . the blood test that's given to alcoholics?"

"Why . . . yes, Jean. I'll call the laboratory in the morning."

Even I was amazed. Never had my mother been so compliant where standard-brand medical procedures were involved.

The blood tests revealed a raging case of hepatitis from which I duly recovered.

Who were these ladies in their flowered hats, and where did they come from? They were, I am convinced, my collective body wisdom, whimsically decked out but bearing the vital information that was unavailable to my merely conscious mind. Such a drastic methodology, however, cannot be recommended, and I began to explore less radical avenues for contacting the wisdom within. Thus I began to work with guided imagery to find those archetypal or wisdom structures that would allow this body wisdom to become accessible to consciousness.

The exercise that follows combines metaphor and imagery, allowing you to "speak" and "listen" directly to your own body wisdom. This ancient technique in modern dress calls for you to gently alter attention on the spectrum of consciousness, to enter into a world of images, and to have a conversation with a personification of your own innate body wisdom, whom we have called "The One Who Knows Health." If you are not partial to this particular personification, then substitute an image that suits you—the Wise Old Man, the Wise Old Woman, Mr. Healthy, Asklepios, an Eskimo shaman, or the lady in the flowered hat. This personification makes it possible for that wisdom to assume recognizable form and communicate with your conscious mind directly and as unambiguously as possible, in a language that you can easily interpret and understand. One of the problems we normally encounter in our dialogues with our bodies is that we speak different languages. Through exercises such as this, we can evoke a recognizable language as we listen to our body.

PREPARATION

Before you begin, spend a few minutes of practice with your kinesthetic body so that you begin to consciously evoke the body-mind connection. Then select some question or problem related to your health about which you would really like some advice. Your commitment to acting upon your body wisdom is closely correlated to the quality of the advice you will receive. There is little point in asking how you can stop smoking, for example, if you have absolutely no intention of quitting.

THE EXERCISE

Sitting comfortably or lying down, relax your body a bit at a time, starting with your toes and working up to the top of your head. Then do it again and discover that you can relax still more.

Next, imagine and experience as vividly as you can that you are on a mountaintop looking for a way down. You see a rocky stairwell winding

Contacting Your Body Wisdom

down and around the mountain and you begin to descend it. Sometimes the terrain is rough, with boulders in the path. Still, you keep on moving down and around, careful of the rocks, careful not to slip. Go slowly; don't hurry.

When at last you reach the bottom, you discover a door leading inside the mountain. You open that door, enter, and find yourself in a long and pleasant corridor. You are aware that you are walking deeper into the mountain now, but you can trust your own progress. You feel instinctively that this is a place of renewal and learning about the restorative powers of your body.

Allow yourself to look around at the surroundings; you may be surprised to find pictures on the walls portraying beautiful nature scenes as well as fantastic portraits of cellular structures. Continue your walk down the corridor, moving more deeply into the heart of the mountain.

At the end of the corridor is a door. It bears a sign: The One Who Knows Health. Open the door and walk into a most interesting room to meet this being.

This is someone who understands all about you—the one who is the representative of your own body wisdom and has access to billions of bits of information concerning your state of health and what is necessary for its improvement.

Sit down in the chair across from this being and ask both general and specific questions about yourself. Don't demand answers. Allow yourself to be passively receptive to what comes through. The One Who Knows Health may communicate in words or images or even through muscular sensations or feeling states.

Just allow yourself to be relaxed, receptive, and attentive to the messages that you are receiving.

And when you know that these messages have finished, and not before, ask the wise one before you: "What can I do for you?"

Having received this message, sit in silence with this wise being for a few minutes in deep communion, in deep recognition.

And when you are ready to leave, thank this being for the wisdom offered and the understanding received.

Leaving now and carefully closing the door behind you, retrace your steps up the mountain, feeling your body integrating this new knowledge with each step you take until you reach the top. And when you get to the top, open your eyes.

Sense your body now in this familiar place. Get up and walk about. And dance the discoveries you have made.

DISCUSSION

Some people will be able to contact this wise being right away, while others will have to practice the exercise a number of times before they are able to successfully communicate with their hitherto ignored body wisdom.

Impatience won't help. Nor will it help to "try harder." In this domain of the unconscious, attachment to results often seems to be the very thing that will block them, so do this whimsically, with a gentle air.

And if in the room in the mountain you find a dog or a serpent or a child, as some have, do not reject this being but find out the message they carry for you. You may be surprised.

Once you have established contact with this wise being, he or she can become a powerful ally for you in the development of the optimal use of your body. To ensure this, however, you must act on the advice given. As several of my students can attest, if the wise being suggests that you give up smoking (even if you never asked for this particular advice!) and you don't, the wise being will "disappear" from the room in the mountain, not to reappear until the advice is followed. Such is the stuff of myths and fairy tales. Such is also the stuff of our body wisdom.

One person who was always very willing to listen to the advice of others, and often courted it, went to the room only to find a scowling old man who barked at her: "What the hell do *you* want! You know what to do. Get out of here and *do* it!" He unceremoniously ushered her out of the room and slammed the door behind her. She got the message.

Contacting Your Body Wisdom

CHAPTER 2

There was a time when meadow, grove, and stream,
The earth and every common sight,
    To me did seem
    Apparelled in celestial light,
The glory and the freshness of a dream. . . .
It is not now as it hath been of yore,—
    Turn wheresoe'er I may,
    By night or day,
The things which I have seen I now can see no more.

WILLIAM WORDSWORTH
"Intimations of Immortality
in Early Childhood"

Robert P. Carr

2

Awakening
the Senses

Influenced by the developmental psychologists, we have grown accustomed to assigning the "sensory-motor" stage of development to the early years of childhood, thus too rapidly concluding that sensory knowing and delight are something we "grow beyond." But as Jung and others have suggested well before these developmental theorists, there are many whose primary lifelong processing of reality is through this particular mode. It is not something we should hope to "outgrow," for it continually provides a deep access to primary knowing.

In many hunting and tribal societies it is the adult, not the child, who gives evidence of the most acute and orchestral balance of the senses. Thus we are forced to dismiss the comforting hypothesis that our senses "naturally" deteriorate as we get older, and that the sense of wonder before the fresh perception is the sole prerogative of the child.

Each of us is, to varying degrees, influenced if not, as some have suggested, determined by our external environment. We respond to the humidity in the air, the smell of bread baking, the fire siren, the shortening of the days as December approaches, the rubbing of clothes against skin, and countless other constant sensory messages. While we may, and indeed too often do, choose to block our awareness of perceptions, they nonetheless continue to influence us on subliminal levels. Thus although we may not be able to say why we are uncomfortable in a certain place or attracted to another, we recognize the power of these perceptions to shape our actions.

Conceptualization in its finest forms is grounded in the refinement of perception. In our research we have found that there is a real equation between the ability to entertain and sustain complex thinking processes and the richness of sensory and kinesthetic awareness. In the dozens of cases we have explored of high actualizing intelligence, of people who use their intelligence for creative accomplishment, there is a constantly recurring pattern of delight in sensory experience.

Margaret Mead's remarkable capacity for remembering and integrating her experiences was grounded in a capacity for sensory detail. Her mother deliberately exposed her to different colors and textures, great works of art and masterpieces of music; she was encouraged to use her senses in all kinds of activities, even the more abstract ones. When she learned a poem, for example, she would enhance the process of rote memorization with an awareness of vividly seeing the images described, feeling the situation or event as keenly as if she had been there, experiencing the textures and tone of the poem, and empathically identifying with its feelings.

As you read this book, you feel the texture of the pages, see the relation between print and space, perhaps smell the memory of type against paper, hear an inner voice reading aloud, and conjure up mental images and associations. All these perceptions, inner and outer, influence your understanding of the concepts.

The blunting of perception occurs as we develop the capacity for abstraction, in the labeling of our perceptions and the conceptualizing of the thing perceived, or, as stated in Houston's Law, *Concept louses up percept*. Conceptualization isolates consciousness from its object, thought from experience, and the local consensual reality from the larger Reality about. If I can label you as Man or Woman, Catholic or Jew, German or Chinese, Primitive or Sophisticate, I can put you safely into culturally conditioned categories that separate us. Thus we are conditioned to respond to the abstraction and generalization of the label, with the result that many of our best insights and intuitions, our clearest percepts and glimpses of a wider realm are shut down by the insistent immediacy of the reflex. Worse, this keeps us from experiencing the complexity of things, leaving us in a state of puerile innocence not unlike the dogs and cats that William James speaks of as occupying our living rooms and libraries without any idea of the intricate and absolutely fascinating goings-on around the house or of what's in all those books.

If we close down our senses, it is possible to distance ourselves from the information we receive from these senses, to quantify objects rather than integrate gestalts, to simplify and to abstract. From a distance it is possible to see a number of things simultaneously, to ignore differences of detail, to classify, and to readily shift our attention when we don't like what we see. At a distance we can see, and perhaps hear, but we cannot touch, we cannot taste, we cannot smell, and thus our most primary senses are relieved of conscious involvement.

As I have suggested, the denial of the senses comes in part from the increasing reliance on the word, the concept, the abstraction. We have adopted an essentially dualistic posture before these responsibilities, choosing alternative paths rather than an integrated landscape. The cultural conditionings that reinforce this dualism are essentially the same for the senses as for the body, at least in the West. The pleasures of the flesh have been viewed as obstacles to the perception of the divine, as St. Augustine so vividly testifies. And yet there has been a time in our own cultural development when this was not the case. As Paul Friedlander, the great commentator on Plato, points out, for the Greeks "the sensual element is not merely mask or veil. It is a steppingstone to a higher level, but a necessary steppingstone whose absence would make that higher level inaccessible."[1]

And yet there is a profound ambiguity inherent in our traditions. Catholicism provides a richness of sensory experience in the lighting of candles, the immense splendors of the cathedrals, the resonance of the litanies, the smell of incense, the richness of the bishop's robes and, *at the same time*, advocates the scourging of the flesh, the penance of fasting, and the insistence on celibacy for those who would bring the word of God. The Puritans forbade dancing and bright clothes and rich feasts, forcing their poet, Anne Hutchinson, into the wilderness.

In the East, Krishna tells Arjuna to "first control thy senses and then slay desire, for it is full of sin, and is the destroyer of knowledge and of wisdom." And this is the same Arjuna who then says:

> Know that among horses I am Pegasus, the heaven born;
> among the lordly elephants I am the White one, and I
> am the Ruler among men.
> I am the Thunderbolt among weapons, of cows I am the
> Cow of Plenty, I am Passion in those who procreate, and
> I am the Cobra among serpents.
> I am the Wind among the Purifiers, the King Rama
> among warriors; I am the Crocodile among the fishes,
> and I am the Ganges among disputants.

And what could have a more powerful appeal to the senses![2]

Our senses are indeed our doors and windows on this world, in a very real sense the key to the unlocking of meaning and the wellspring of creativity. What many religions have done is to reserve the richness of the sensory world to the religious institution and deny it to the secular life of its practitioners, making one rich and various and the other impoverished and sterile, thus reinforcing the dualism of matter and spirit.

It is time to change this practice, to awaken and celebrate the senses, to encourage the bridging of "sacred" and "secular" worlds, and to allow perception again to inform conception so that we may conceive of new possibilities.

Conceptualization is, of course, essential to the creation and continuation of culture—it sustains the very fabric of civilization. But, as the patriarch Sigmund Freud has warned us, civilization has its profound discontents. These discontents would seem to arise when the conceptual base is too narrow and confining to contain the knowing of our perceptions. How are we to explain the boat people and the dolphins that come into our living rooms via television, the astonishing feats of yogis that are documented in our laboratories? We see these things and hear them. Increasingly mobile, we get on airplanes and fly to previously distant lands to touch and taste and feel. Our concepts ache to expand in order to encompass our undeniable perceptions. And no longer are these sensory experiences available only to a small minority who can safely be ignored or assimilated as "interesting but insignificant." If we are to reconceptualize, to re-create a reality large enough to incorporate this complexity, we must be willing to integrate and acknowledge as much of this information as possible.

The capacity for awareness of sensory experiences is critical to the development of meaning. And it is just this lack of meaning that is creating an epidemic of crisis proportions today, with its corollary violences against self and society. Meaning derives from a profoundly held relation to the revelatory power of the symbol. Yet the symbol becomes an objectified "other" if it is not grounded in the senses. The tree of life does not carry meaning for the people of the desert, nor the sea for those who are landlocked. Would we have traveled to the moon, coordinated thousands of people working together for this fantastic, this almost absurd, voyage, if this symbol had not been so powerfully and universally grounded in our senses? Many of the traditional symbols derive from an intimate contact with nature, a contact that is not experientially available to those who have lived in modern cities.

Even food, that very primary experience become symbol, sustaining life, is deprived of its sensory values and thus of its symbolic potential as it arrives with little taste or odor, uniform in size, texture, and color. The capacity for refinement of the senses is denied opportunity for discovering itself. How different are our supermarkets, with their frozen and packaged products, from those glorious French markets that in the early morning overflow with abundant aromas of cheeses, sausages, and freshly picked fruits?

We can now see, at least among the urban middle class, a reaction to this basic denial in the return to homemade cookies, to real soups, to breadmaking, to the restoration of "farmers' markets" in some of our cities, to the turning of abandoned lots into communal gardens. We have left the isolation of our farms and mountains and small towns for the variety and excitement and complexity of the metropolis only to find a soul-yearning of the senses for the smells and textures and tastes that remind us of a less ephemeral reality.

I am not suggesting that we be prey to local famines or that we abandon our cities, but rather that we design them in such a way that they do not force us to turn off our senses if we are to survive, for this "survival" will inevitably be short term. As we close down our senses to protect ourselves from pollution in the air and jackhammers in the street, so do we close down our passion for life.

We must remember that life was not always so. In the nineteenth-century schoolhouse, the children who sat at those desks spent proportionately little of their time in this sterile environment. They did not live in today's cities and go home to eat potato chips and watch the world go by in disjointed form on television. They were connected to the rhythms of nature; they grew and harvested and prepared food, saw animals being born, and raced before the storm. Babies did not come from hospitals and old people did not go there to die. The rich sensory base of life experience was there to inform their knowing.

We are living in a very different reality today. As the schools of the nineteenth century provided a place to learn things that could not be learned and experienced elsewhere, so must the schools of today. Our schools, from the first grade through graduate school, are all too often places of extraordinary sterility and depersonalization, reflective of the sterility and depersonalization that marks all too much of public urban life, particularly for the poor. Laboratory experiments have shown that even rats raised in a rich sensory environment they can actively explore and manipulate have heavier brains and better-developed dendritic connections than their brothers and sisters raised in bare cages where they have no opportunity to explore their environment. Surely we can do better for our students than our scientists do for their rats!

I vividly remember a schoolteacher who came up to me during a workshop and announced: "I am so glad that I teach kindergarten." Well, I was too, since she seemed very vibrant and alive, but when I asked her why she was so happy with this prospect I was less than thrilled with her explanation that only in kindergarten were the children allowed to "mess with things," to cook and taste and touch and smell and really get into the thickness of the mystery of their environment. In first grade, then, comes "society's teaching time," when we learn "about" rather than "with."

Ironically, in gaining one perspective we often lose another, as Wordsworth laments. In his classic story of this loss, St. Exupéry explains all of this to his new friend, the Little Prince:

> Grown-ups love figures. When you tell them that you have made a new friend, they never ask you any questions about essential matters. They never say to you, "What does his voice sound like? What games does he love best? Does he collect butterflies?" Instead, they demand: "How old is he? How many brothers has he? How much does he weigh? How much money does his father make?" Only from figures do they think they have learned anything about him.[3]

In the exaggeration, we recognize an uncomfortable truth. We have forgotten how to ask about essences. Distancing ourselves from the multidimensional world of the senses, coming to label and quantify and classify as our primary mode of knowing, we relieve ourselves from the abundance of these realities and say, with a sigh of relief, "This is *only* this, and that is *only* that."

In fact, any single lensing is the enemy, restricting our freedom of choice, distorting both percept and concept. What I am urging here, and what my work is about, is the conscious development of awareness in all our modes of knowing so that we may choose to use them freely and selectively.

The primary reality of the senses is home for both the scientist and the poet, a coupling that we would often oppose. However, to do so closes down the opportunity for the leap into the creative insight. Michael Faraday "smelled the truth." As his biographer comments: "There was given to him . . . a sense of the spatial. He would almost see the moving wire slice through the lines of force and the current stir within. Perhaps, after all, it was the reward of this incapacity for abstraction, this vision of nature in the round, and in depth."[4] The aroma and taste of the madeleine cookie stirred memories in Proust that flowered into expression in *The Remembrance of Things Past.*

Poets and storytellers have long recognized and deliberately used sensory images to evoke the creative imagination of the listener. Their stories survive political upheavals and social change because they call forth the deep and powerful memories of our senses, building patterns of connection that extend beyond existential time and space. The Brothers Grimm were masters of this, telling us that

> Once it was the middle of winter, and the snowflakes fell from the sky like little feathers. At a window with a frame of ebony a queen sat and sewed. As she sewed and looked out at the snow, she pricked her finger with the needle, and three drops of blood fell in the snow. And in the white snow the red looked so beautiful that she thought to herself: "If only we had a child as white as snow, as red as blood, and as black as the wood in the window frame."[5]

When you read these words and feel the needle prick your finger, you gain *direct* access to the story, you are present and involved. The epics of Homer and the dramas of Shakespeare involve us fully through the richly textured weavings of sensory images. Think of those stories you remember and notice the senses they evoke—the images, the sounds, the smells, even the tastes. As I write this I am reminded of a Christmas story I loved as a child called "Granny Glittens' Mittens." Granny Glittens knit Christmas mittens that could be eaten because the wool was dyed with candy, and I can still remember speculating upon the taste of chocolate and strawberry wool.

Wordsworth is wrong. He is wrong when he cries that "nothing can bring back the hour of splendour in the grass, of glory in the flower." It *can* come back, bearing, however, a different splendor and a different glory. The appreciation felt is more poignant, not unlike that of the prodigal son returning home. Having come home, he is given so much, his father withholding nothing.

So it is for those who in their maturity return to the birthright of their senses. As it has been stated in the Upanishads: "Abundance is scooped from abundance, and yet abundance remains." There is more now than there was then. The brightness is heightened because the shadows are seen and felt as they were not in early childhood. When remade, the connections are felt more keenly. The excitement of paradox acts as a constant provocation to transcendence, as it cannot in childhood. Eros and aesthetic joy, passion and contemplative intelligence give to maturity the experience and perspectives to deepen and create from the sensory experience.

In our own society we honor the keen ear of the musician, the olfactory sensitivity of the wine connoisseur, the gustatory subtlety of the great chef, and the visual acuity of the artist. Those who retain the capacity to make use of one or several of these usually atrophied categories of perception and communication belong among the specially gifted. They are the composers, musicians, dancers, and acrobats. The capacities of the adult need not be those deliberately developed in childhood. Grandma Moses came to her painting late in life. Most children do not go around sniffing wine, and adult-education courses attest to the fact that people are discovering latent abilities in themselves every day.[6]

This gift does not seem to be the sole property of those whom we would quickly label and dismiss as exceptional. Participants in workshops and seminars report greater facility and awareness in perceiving their environment and, at the same time, a greater sense of purpose after working on sensory awareness. As you become a keen observer, you will develop a sense of delight and wonder, a freshening of perspective, feeling much as the inhabitants of Los Angeles feel when a storm blows away the smog and the air is cleared and the mountains are visible once again. It is as though an all too familiar shroud, whose weight is so habitual that we no longer feel it, has been lifted, as though fig trees are laughing and shimmering in a Brooklyn backyard. And we are reminded that we are "trailing clouds of glory."

Exercise 1

Cleaning the Rooms of Perception

TIME: 45 minutes

In this exercise we will evoke the power of the metaphor and the active imagination to begin to lift the veils that have grown over our perceptions. Although we know that there are many more than five senses, it is our cultural conditioning to identify them as five—sight, sound, smell, taste, and touch—and so we will accept our given categories and seek to enhance and extend them.

PREPARATION

Before you begin, think about what is involved in each of these senses. For example, when we see, we interpret color and form; our binocular vision allows us to sense perspective and depth; we can focus on particular objects, screening out peripheral vision; and so on. Take a moment to consider what is involved in each sense before you start. In this way perception and concept can be integrated.

THE EXERCISE

Close your eyes and focus on the evenness of your breath, tuning in to this rhythm for a while.

Now imagine that you are traveling through the blood vessels of your body, transported by a little blood platelet.

Beginning in your small toe on your right foot, go through that foot and travel up your leg in a great arterial channel until you reach your pelvis.

Continuing upward through your chest, note things you see on the way: the luminous latticelike bellows of the lungs, the steady expanding and contracting of the pumping heart, the bronchial tubes branching like sea anemones.

Ascending now through the veins and arteries of the neck into the facial muscles, you arrive finally at the folded hills and valleys of the cerebral cortex of the brain.

Move now to the pineal gland, or third eye, a spot midway between the eyes, the seat of inner seeing.

Here you will see a house, the House of the Senses. There is a golden key in the door with your name on it. Turn the key to open the door and put the key in your pocket.

As you enter the house you will turn on the light and notice in the front hall that there are all kinds of cleaning equipment: buckets of water, vacuum cleaners, dustcloths, mops, sponges, hoses, and a host of other objects you do not quite recognize. There are also large empty trash bags and cans. Everything you might need for cleaning is here.

Go now into the room on the right and find yourself in the visual centers of your brain. This is the Room of Vision, of Sight.

Walk around in it, noticing the dusty corners and the darkened windows, the heaps of rubbish and the burned-out lightbulbs. Begin to clean it, going back to the hall for any equipment you might need. Scrub the floor and walls. Polish the windows and fling them open. Remove the dusty drapes. Throw out the accumulated rubbish. Put as much effort into this as you can. You are actually doing real work here, cleaning up your perceptions at their neurological base. Get the dust out of the furniture and out of the air, letting the wind help you.

When you have cleaned the room and cleared away all the debris, walk around in it, begin to dance in the sparkling light, feel the light flood your sight. Look out the window and see for miles, seeing a world bright and shining as after a great rain when the sun comes out.

Notice now that there is a door at the end of this room, a door that is locked. Use your golden key to unlock this door and enter now into the Room of Hearing, leaving the door open behind you.

What a junk heap this is! Look at all the cobwebs on the walls and that thick wax buildup all over the place. Clean it up! Get in there and scrub! If you find that the room is too small, push the walls back, make the ceiling higher. Let the whole room expand until it feels like the right size. Make it bright and shining, knowing that as you do so you are improving the quality of your hearing.

When you have finished cleaning and enlarging the room, walk around and listen to the reverberation of your footsteps on the floor. Open the windows and let the fresh air swoosh in, hearing it swoosh in and letting it blow out any remaining dust. Hear the wind in the trees, the singing of birds, the laughing of children playing, the sneeze of a rabbit beneath the window. Move around the room, humming and singing in this freshly cleaned room of sound. Let the room fill with sunbeams and dance to their music.

As you dance, you notice that there is another locked door at the end of the room. Open the door with your golden key and step into the Room of Smell. This is one of the oldest rooms in the house, filled with trunks piled on trunks, with all kinds of clutter, with old deodorant bottles and air fresheners. Clear it out and throw away the garbage, maybe even paint it a different color. Open the windows and let the fresh scents of the outside flood the room.

Enjoy this room now, breathing in the lovely fragrance blown in by the wind. Feel this fragrance filling your whole body, reminding you of the forgotten delight of smelling.

Go now through the locked door at the other end of the room with your golden key, leaving the door open behind you, into the Room of Taste.

This is the gustatory garbage heap. There is so much deposited here, and it's been here for so long. Clear it out! Get rid of the cigarette butts and ashes, the left-over cold coffee in cups, the wrappers from instant hamburgers. Be aware of all the accumulated plaque: scrape it off and sweep away the encrusted garbage. Use scouring pads or whatever you need to remove the grit and grime. Clean the windows to the garden and open them, letting the winds sharpen your taste buds.

Savor the refinements and subtlety of the cleaned room, the saltiness, the sweetness, the bitter and the sour. Let these sensations be distinct and then let them flow together into one mouth-watering treat.

When you have finished, notice another door at the end of the room. Again you will use your golden key to open this door, leaving it open behind you. Now you are in your tactile center, the Room of Touch.

What a pigsty it probably is, covered with calluses and old rubber gloves, with sludge and refuse that are barriers to clear and sensitive tactile sensations. Clean out this room until it is vibrant with life, glowing with texture, sensitive to heat and cold, a caress and a tap, the slippery and the silky, the rough and the nubby.

Notice the feel of the window frame as you open the windows, the light brush of the air moving past you to help you clean the room. Walk barefoot on the floor and feel the bare wood or the carpet or the tile against your feet. Touch the walls and feel their texture. Enjoy all the feelings that are available to your body, which is now vibrant with sensation.

When you have finished, notice another locked door and go through it, leaving it open, back into the hall, where you will deposit all your rubbish.

Notice now that there is a stairway leading to the floor above, and, with your senses refreshed, go up the stairs. At the top of the stairs, you find yourself in a very large room.

This is the Room of the Sixth Sense, the home of all the senses that we have not encountered below and the place where all these senses come together.

Explore this vast place, becoming aware of its grand perspective and ample proportions. Move around and notice the nooks and crannies. Now

Cleaning the Rooms of Perception

begin to clean it up, opening the windows and making yourself at home in this unfamiliar place.

Let the light and air circulate and fill the room. After cleaning out so much debris accumulated from childhood, you may feel refreshed in all your senses, and may even be aware of new senses.

Notice that this room has a balcony and walk over to that balcony. From the balcony you can look down into all the rooms below, the Room of Sight, the Room of Hearing, the Room of Smell, the Room of Taste, and the Room of Touch. All these clean rooms are connected by the open doors you have left behind you, and you sense the patterns that connect them.

Now, being aware of the gentle, warm breeze blowing through the open windows and doors of your senses, inhale deeply the fresh air of the Room of the Sixth Sense and then, swinging your head down, blow through all five rooms. Bring your head back up to the second-floor room and inhale again. Now, again, circle with your head down and blow like the wind through each room, cleaning and connecting all the rooms and each sense with the other. Keep on doing this, gently and powerfully circling with your head and blowing through the rooms at least a dozen times.

Then fully relax for a minute and sense your whole body flowing with this new awareness, feel it coursing through your nerves and your blood, your muscles and your flesh. Sense a gentle tingling and exhilaration and allow yourself to deeply remember this. Promise these rooms that you will keep them clean and come back often.

Now go down the stairs to the front hall, getting rid of the garbage there in whatever way seems appropriate to you, perhaps in some totally unexpected way you have never thought of before, and go now out the front door, keeping the key in your pocket. Whether or not you close the door or lock it is up to you; just be sure you know how to get back in easily.

Open your eyes now and look around. Notice how much your senses have changed. Does the room seem larger or smaller? How does your skin feel? Notice the scents in the air. Bite into a crisp apple or some wonderful bread and notice the texture and the taste and the aroma.

At this time you may want to play some richly textured familiar music—perhaps the Bach Brandenburg Concertos. Begin to move to this music and see how different it sounds from the last time you heard it.

When you have enjoyed this experience, continue to explore your environment, remaining aware of your sensory perceptions as you do so. Have a conversation with another person and notice the sound of that person's voice, the texture of hair and skin, the shape of the head and the features. Be aware of how these sensations may have become so familiar, so automatic, that they were no longer consciously available for you.

DISCUSSION

This exercise may be repeated every day, with slight variations, as a meditation and a way of enhancing the senses so that you begin to think more creatively and see more freshly into new insights for old problems. You can change the order of the rooms or decide to concentrate on one particular room for a while.

People who work with this exercise notice a freshness of perception that seems to be accompanied by the sense of wonder we often nostalgically attribute to our childhood. Several people who had previously worn glasses found they no longer needed them. One man who lived alone reported that he began to plan his meals more carefully and enjoy them more when he gave up instant dinners and watching TV while he ate. In general, people experience a refinement of perception and an awareness of subtle details and nuances that bring greater richness to many aspects of their lives.

The clarity of the sense of any particular room can be used as an indicator of your primary sensory mode. In working with a sense that is not well developed it is important to *go from strength*. Work on getting an ever-expanded awareness in the dominant sense and then let this spill over into the less vivid senses.

For most of us, the Room of Vision will be most clearly defined, because the visual cortex has grown enormously as we have evolved, and for the human being it is a primary mode of knowing. Based on brain size, however, the Room of Touch should be the largest; however, in a culture that labels things and people with "Don't touch" signs, this is often not the case. Expanding and working on this room can help improve this situation and make us more aware of the sense that is usually forced to work unconsciously.

EXTENSIONS

Children love this exercise, although you might want to change the language for them. For example, the Room of Taste is not likely to be cluttered with cigarette butts and coffee cups but with Big Macs and Twinkies. Younger children enjoy building the rooms from blocks, while older ones enjoy making floorplans and dioramas of the different rooms. Children particularly enjoy comparing the similarities and differences in their rooms and freely build on the perceptions of others, thus often expanding their own experience. Once you start using this exercise with children, you can allow them to lead the others through the different rooms, an experience they enjoy very much.

The same exercise can be applied to the *inner* senses or the imagination. In other words, the imagination can be used directly to work on the imagination. Thus you would imagine going to the Room of Inner Seeing,

Cleaning the Rooms of Perception

cleaning it up so that inner imaging becomes clearer and more defined. Then go to the Room of Inner Hearing and so forth. As you become more proficient in doing this, you can move back and forth from inner to outer, noticing how the rooms differ and which senses are stronger in the different modalities, using one to strengthen the other.

Exercise 2

Fine-Tuning the Senses

TIME: 15 minutes

Most of the time we act as though our senses have an on-off switch. We either hear or don't hear, see or don't see, feel or don't feel, failing to recognize the subtle nuances that are possible. Most of the preceding exercises have been designed to turn the switches on, to break the patterns of conceptualization and labeling that have blocked our awareness and caused us to turn the switches off without even noticing that we have done so. This exercise goes a step further and invites you to begin to tune your senses so that you can regulate the degree of inhibition you want. Sometimes you will want to be totally focused on one thing, oblivious to other experiences and events, which then are labeled *distractions*. A few people suffer intensely from switches that are permanently in the on position. This is similar to the memory expert described by the Soviet psychologist Luria who was unable to forget anything, to sort out field from ground, to make distinctions and order priorities. It is not a blessing to be constantly and consciously bombarded by our senses. The following story is one of many possible illustrations of this point.

Susan, a four-year-old girl, came home from nursery school every day absolutely exhausted and begged not to go back ever again. Every morning there was a scene of tears and turmoil. She seemed to have friends at school, and the teachers reported that she was a very bright little girl and seemed to be happy. When questioning her failed to reveal the source of Susan's exhaustion, her mother decided to visit the school. As she followed Susan through her day in the noisy, bustling classroom, she noticed that Susan was occasionally muttering something under her breath. "What was that?" she asked. "Oh, I was just saying that Tommy was wrong when he said that we were going to the store to buy apples tomorrow. It's the day after tomorrow." The mother was a little puzzled, since Tommy was nowhere around, and she mentioned this to Susan. Susan looked up and said, "Oh yes, he's over there in the other corner; didn't you hear him?" Sure enough, there he was, using the blocks with some other children. Soon the mother became aware that Susan was picking up on every sound in the room and responding to them all in some way, however slight. Nonetheless, Susan still seemed to stay focused on whatever task she was doing. No one would have called her hyperactive or easily distractible.

Armed with this insight, her mother observed Susan on the playground. Susan headed for the farthest corner and sat quietly, and then asked the teacher if she could go back into the room and show her mother around while "it was nice and quiet." The teacher commented that Susan would frequently ask to stay alone in the room when the class went out.

The source of Susan's exhaustion became clear. She simply could not inhibit sound from consciousness and was overwhelmed by the assault. A program was worked out for her so that she could leave the room whenever she wished and go into a quiet office to work, and going to school was no longer such a traumatic experience for her.

It was necessary, however, to help Susan develop a way of learning to inhibit this bombardment, and her mother began to work with her, using a variation of the rheostat exercise given here.

Susan's case is an example of a phenomenon we have seen in the laboratory with psychedelic experiences in which the subject is overwhelmed by sensory stimulation, by the "too muchness" of it all, as he or she consciously tries to respond to everything. In unguided experiences this can lead to the "bad trip."

It is also the curse of the super-sensitive people who seem to operate with one particularly acute sense always all the way open. They are just as "stuck" as those who habitually block everything. The key lies in developing access to a continuum of sensory awareness rather than living with an either/or model.

PREPARATION

Seat yourself comfortably in a quiet place the first time you do this. Allow yourself to relax, letting go of the tension in your muscles as you focus on your breathing. Don't try to control your breathing, just pay attention to it and let it serve as a point of focus.

THE EXERCISE

Imagine a dial like a light dimmer that tunes your sense of hearing. There are numbers on this dial going from one to ten, 1 being the least awareness of sound and 10 being the greatest acuity. Allow 5 to represent your accustomed mode of hearing.

Listen now to some fairly even sound, such as a radio or television playing in another room or the sound of traffic going by. As you turn your attention to this sound you will probably notice that it seems louder. This is because we normally block the awareness of routine noise. Imagine your normal awareness of this sound to be associated with a number on your dial, say 2 or 3. Give a number to the awareness you have now of that sound. Concentrating now on the dial rather than on the sound, turn the dial up to 8 . . . and listen . . . and to 9 . . . and listen . . . and finally to 10. Now turn it quickly back to 3. Starting from 3, turn it slowly down to 2 . . . and then to 1. Now turn it back to 5, sensing this as the middle place between 1 and 10. Slowly, slowly, move it up to 6 and down to 4; up to 7 and down to 3; up to 8 and down to 2, sensing the subtle gradations between these settings. Continue to do this until you can move easily from 1 to 10 and back.

DISCUSSION

All of this is much more easily written and read than done. It takes a lot of practice. As soon as you find yourself becoming frustrated, stop. Just drop it for a while. You will find that having given yourself the suggestion that doing this is possible, it will become progressively easier each time you try it. It is, not so simply, just a question of bringing the rheostat to consciousness all the time.

As one of my students began to do this exercise she found that she was not the "tone-deaf" person her sixth-grade teacher had labeled her, but was instead extremely sensitive to sound. She began to train her ear and tentatively began to explore playing the piano and singing. Finally, she has been able to move from a distrust of music to a recognition of the music within. She had been overwhelmed by the "too-muchness" of what she heard and had no tools for sorting it out, for modulating and discriminating.

You will probably find that this kind of regulation is much easier for some of your senses than for others. Notice this and see what it tells you about yourself. If you find that it is particularly difficult to do with seeing, you may be particularly sensitive to visual information. Here conceptualization can be helpful. Work on fine-tuning not the entire visual field but depth perception as well, noting background and foreground, and then work on light and shadow. You can tune each color one by one. Thus you will begin to orchestrate this sense, identifying its properties and exploring its subtleties. The same principle may be applied to any sense.

Exercise 3

Listening to Music with Your Whole Body and Synesthesias*

TIME: 20 to 60 minutes (depending on music used)

This exercise follows very well after Cleaning the Rooms of Perception, but it also works well independently and can be used to refresh yourself.

First, we are going to listen to music with the whole body. This is not a metaphor for what we are doing but the actual experience. Music, like all sound, comes through the air in waves that flow over the entire body, subtly interacting with the frequencies around our bodies and the hair follicles, which are particularly sensitive. You know this already because you can remember all too well what happens to your *body* (not just your ears!) when chalk scratches on the blackboard. After the music is flowing all over, you will begin to experience synesthesia, or a crossing of the senses, to "see" sound, to "taste" texture. Many children do this spontaneously and naturally, and it is the basic experience that informs much poetry and multimedia art.

PREPARATION

Select some music, preferably music that is not so familiar that it will elicit automatic listening responses. Remove heavy or tight clothing, including shoes and socks, so that your body is free to experience the touch of the music all over your body.

THE EXERCISE

Lie down in a comfortable position on the floor. Allow yourself to relax. As you focus your attention on your breathing, feel your body melting into the floor, letting go of stress and unnecessary tension.

As the music begins, allow it to flow over you . . . through you . . . caressing your entire body . . . moving through and around you . . . entering and leaving . . . playing itself through you.

Do this for a complete piece of music and then change the music.

After this has been fully experienced and the music has become a part of you, allow yourself to feel the colors and textures of the music . . . its smells and tastes . . . heat and chill . . . its light and darkness . . . so that the

*Adapted from *Mind Games 1 and 2.*

music sweeps through the senses . . . blending them together in a full orchestration of the sensorium . . . carrying you into and beyond the hearing of the music.

Do this for a complete piece of music.

When the music has ended, lie still and savor the experience. It may be appropriate to write down the words or images that have risen, to dance the patterns that have emerged, or to sing the song that your senses have played.

DISCUSSION

Once your capacity for synesthesia has been consciously explored, it will be possible to call it forth with ease. Many find this much more relaxing when they come home from work than the habitual cocktail—and much better for their health! I know a writer who uses it as a mini-vacation when he finds himself getting stuck or stale, and then returns to his writing refreshed and invigorated, hackneyed phrases and stale vocabulary having been replaced by the vivid imagery of his senses. A therapist working with a highly imaginative group of people who wish to enhance their creative productivity uses this exercise at the beginning of each meeting, finding that it serves to evoke the power of the sensory base of creativity.

You may have noticed that you spontaneously moved your arms or your whole body as you did this, the music moving you, rather than you moving to the music. This is a common but by no means universal response to this experience; it is more common among musicians and dancers who have, consciously or unconsciously, experienced sound through their whole body and have not inhibited the body response.

EXTENSIONS

Children love to do this exercise. The all too frequent temptation in working with children is to use very simplified or familiar music. Just as children are enriched by listening to great literature that they do not "fully understand," so are they enriched and responsive to the complexities and subtleties of great music. After they listen to the music in this way, they can make vivid and dramatic collages and drawings of their experiences.

Exercise 4

Pleasure and Then Some . . .

TIME: 30 minutes

One day, as an experiment, I asked a group of friends who were in the house to jot down a list of their most pleasurable experiences and associations. After some initial laughter and skepticism, they came up with the following list, their enthusiasm growing noticeably as they continued with this project. The sampling that follows is a regular Noah's ark of pleasure, an adventure into lands forgotten but now found again, a banquet to regale the body and captivate the soul:

Lying on the beach listening to the waves, with my toes wriggling in the hot sand.

Climbing between freshly ironed sheets that have been dried in the sun.

Nursing my baby in the middle of the night, curled up in a big chair.

Roller-skating at breakneck speed down a steep hill.

Picking! My own navel, my own scalp, ears, nose.

Cuddling, singing to, and rocking my children, and scratching their backs—which I did every night until they were at least eleven. It was like the evening blessing for me.

Walking in the quiet of New York City after a heavy snowfall.

Listening to a Beethoven symphony and imagining that I'm the conductor.

The electricity in the air after a thunderstorm has blown away.

The sensation of a purring, enraptured cat as she kneads my body with her paws.

Saturday afternoon at the movies with a giant Mr. Goodbar.

Dancing with my huge dog.

Hearing a choir rehearsing as I walk down the street.

Sitting by a fireplace and watching the images come and go in the crackling flames.

Blowing the paper wrapper off the straw into the fans at Robinson's Drug Store before guzzling my strawberry ice cream soda.

Reading a great novel in a hot bath on a cold night.

Diving naked into a cool lake.

Telling ghost stories while the wind demons howl outside the house.

Cool green grapes in July.

Watching the cork disappear beneath the water and feeling the sudden tug of a big fish on the line.

How often do we make such lists? Most lists are lists of things to be done, reminders of duties unattended and obligations reluctantly remembered. For our doctors we list our symptoms, for our therapists our problems. A catalogue of woes is much more frequent in our society than a catalogue of pleasures.

The reasons for this, I suspect, are due not so much to a cultural pathology as to a pervasive puritanism. There is an ethic of "pain as virtue" insidiously pervading our culture; we admire the fortitude of the stoic and are more than faintly suspicious of the epicure. We associate the refinement of the senses with the effete, the morally lax, the intellectually lazy. This attitude is the inevitable result of the rift between man and nature, body and mind, I and Thou, and it is so pronounced that the world outside of self is seen as fundamentally alien, a world of pain to be exploited, manipulated, and mastered. Parents are suspicious that their children aren't really learning anything in school if they are having a good time there, and then blame the teachers when their children drop out.

Trying to control the world is hard work; sunsets are elusive and dandelions insistent. We are urged to grin and bear it, keeping a stiff upper lip as we grin—a difficult exercise if there ever was one.

These pleasures are the stuff of the rich murals of the temple of Hatshepsut, the medieval tapestries of the Unicorn, the dancing peasants of Breughel, the feisty sensuality of Fielding's *Tom Jones*, the haunting play of line and texture in Vivaldi's *Four Seasons*, the riotous combination of sawdust and animals and blaring trumpets and lights and spangles and magic of the tented circus. It is also the glory of the setting sun and rioting daffodils, the sparkling chill of hillside waterfalls, and . . . and . . . . The list is endless. All there to be celebrated, caught, danced with, cherished, and *shared*.

Perhaps our insistence upon standing alone, on being "individual," has locked the doors of these memories and knowing. They call for celebration, and we have forgotten how to celebrate, or else we turn celebrations into an opportunity to get drunk or high.

What I am suggesting, therefore, is that we have a culture with a tendency to long pains and short pleasures. There is evidence that a few cultures have long pleasures and short pains, indicating the importance of a subjective cultural attitude. An example of such a culture would be that of the Balinese, who have a culture rich in song and dance and storytelling.

What are the outstanding characteristics of these cultures? Inevitably, they are the ones in which the artist and the singer are honored, where the arts are integrated into the daily experience of all people, where furniture and clothing are crafted and honored, where the making of a meal is an occasion for high play. In these cultures there are traditions of celebration in which all members of the community, young and old, are actively involved.

Remnants of these traditions live in isolated pockets of our own culture, in nursery schools where birthdays are celebrated with pomp and dignity, in the ritual gatherings of some families that have cherished traditions, and in those religious communities that honor the whole person.

There is a renaissance going on, albeit a quiet one, attested to by the festivals of Woodstock and the growth of Dromenon communities. Here pleasures can flourish and be affirmed. Food and music and dance are shared. All these speak of the joy and empowering that are inherent in shared pleasures. And the people who commit themselves to this are more "productive" rather than less, finding in the sharing of pleasures a sense of renewal, of coming home, that allows them to carry this sense of commitment into other aspects of their lives.

If a Martian anthropologist were to study our notions of pleasure as reflected in the popular magazines, he would have to conclude that either we are missing many organs or we suffer from a surfeit of banality (witness the *Playboy* philosophy).

THE EXERCISE

Make a list of your own pleasures and delights. If you are anything like my friends, once you start, the remembered pleasures will trigger more memories to relish and you will not want to stop. These memories prime your sensorium, and you may find, after making and recalling this list, that your awareness will have a keener edge, your capacity for pleasure will deepen, and your body will feel lighter. More important, the recovery of more skeins in the tapestry of pleasure will give you a larger room upon which to weave delight.

Having listed your pleasures, choose one that is particularly vivid for you right now and feel it intensely. Visualize the experience as strongly as possible, hear it, taste it, smell it, let it fill your entire body. Experience it down your spine, breathe into it, laugh into it, smile into it. Reach out and hug it. Hold it to you and then let it go. Begin now to move with this knowing flooding your body.

Sing or draw or paint or write or cook or garden with this knowing flooding your being—and note the difference. What has happened? And now remember some "problem" or something that may have been bothering you when you began this exercise. How does it look now?

Pleasure and Then Some . . .

DISCUSSION

After doing this exercise one person commented, "What problems? They're gone!" For others, their problems look smaller and more manageable. Another person in the philosophy department of a large university said later that she had tried this before going to a particularly difficult meeting with her department chairman, who had previously terrified her. She found herself smiling as she went in, barely able to contain her mirth. (She had been remembering the time she won the children's pie-eating contest at the county fair.) Her good will toward the world in general encompassed the chairman as well, and the meeting resulted in a new spirit of cooperation and the beginning of a lasting and productive working relationship.

I have found this to be true over and over again in my work. Those people who are in touch with their pleasures inevitably share this pleasure with those around them. Somehow they seem to be protected from the adversities that afflict others. Waiting in line becomes an opportunity to meet "just the right person," people help them with cumbersome suitcases, New York taxicab drivers embrace them (not often, it is true, but this did happen!), total strangers invite them home.

This is not as farfetched as it sounds. Consider those people you know who are bursting with a sense of fun and delight, with an openness to and availability for what is possible. Invariably they are the ones who are in touch with their senses and pleasures and are remarkably successful in what they do. They are not the people of denial and the quick put-down, frowning behind a fortress of folded arms; they have remembered that we are *homo ludens* (man the player) and invite us to join in the serious delight of high play.

Exercise 5

Sensuous Bouts

TIME: 30 minutes

Listing the varieties of our pleasures is meant to broaden the base for understanding and recognizing pleasure. In this exercise, the aim is to deepen the experience of pleasure and transform the relationship between that which gives pleasure and that which receives pleasure.

PREPARATION

Get a piece of fabric. It may be an article of clothing, a soft blanket, or anything else that appeals to you, and seat yourself comfortably with it.

THE EXERCISE

Put the fabric on your lap and touch it in the ordinary way. Be aware of your sensations.

Now, closing your eyes, change your state of consciousness slightly by making a zzz-zzz-zzz-zzz sound for a few minutes.

Allow your whole body to vibrate slightly with this sound. Feel the sound going down your spine and then down your legs to your feet.

Now block your ears with your hands and continue to make the zzz-zzz-zzz sound, feeling the vibrations ever more intensely, until your whole body is humming with the zzz-zzz-zzz.

Stop this and sit quietly for a moment, breathing into this awakening of your body.

Relaxing your body now, think of the fabric as an intense source of pleasure. Think of the fabric as personal, as "thou," as a dear friend wishing to give you pleasure. Now touch the fabric, regarding it as the giver of pleasure. Allow the fabric to brush against your face, over your closed eyes, your neck, the sides of your arms, and against your bare feet.

Know now that objects have the potential to give you pleasure and extend this awareness now to the chair that you are sitting in . . .

And now to the room . . .

And to the world beyond this room, being aware of this world as a source, an ever-renewed and renewing source of pleasure, allowing yourself to receive this gift fully.

DISCUSSION

After doing this exercise it is common to feel a deep awareness of the sources of pleasure that surround us. The lasting result for many is a much greater mindfulness of the environment and a detrivialization of the commonplace. Once we become aware of the power of the familiar and ordinary to so inform us, we begin to honor it more deeply and escape from banal routines and automated response patterns. Those who have done this exercise report that they no longer want to wear clothes that are too tight and binding or are made of fabrics that irritate rather than delight the skin. Fewer unworn clothes are sitting in the back of their closets and they are less prey to the inducements of advertisements to get the latest fashion. Possessions are honored and cherished rather than discarded and replaced. Less becomes more as this awareness deepens.

In this exercise, the fabric becomes personal, and is no longer an object. To increase sensory acuity, we often have to suspend that mode of consciousness which insists on objectifying the world. Since "I" is more receptive to "thou" than to a distanced "it," there is a natural increase in pleasurable sensation. As many creative and innovative thinkers can attest, the most powerful ideas are often sensuously held. They are tasted and touched, felt and smelled, and rich in images. Thought, at its best, is on a continuum with pleasure. Let us have sensuous bouts with ideas!

EXTENSIONS

This exercise can be done with almost any object and is particularly effective with those who eat mindlessly, stuffing their mouths but barely knowing what they have tasted. Instead of fabric, they could use a piece of fruit or a slice of bread or any other food they might ordinarily eat without paying much attention. First they should sense its texture with their hands, noting the appearance of it and accepting the pleasure of it as they do so. Then they should bite into it, noting the texture again with their tongue, and the taste, receiving all the pleasures the food has to give, slowly and with full attention.

Gluttony becomes almost impossible, and fast foods and instant this-and-that become less desirable, as food is again honored as a source of pleasure. We have chosen to "grab a bite" rather than receive a gift, and so we grab and we bite and we supplement our deficient diet of too many calories and too little nourishment with hosts of capsules from brown bottles reverently placed on the altar of the kitchen shelf or the medicine closet. Honoring food as a source of pleasure, as a gift, informs the traditional grace: "Oh Lord, make us grateful for the food we are about to receive." Yet, for many, the gracing of the food is a ritual forgotten, lost in the desacralization of the events of daily life as we eat our meals in front of the evening news or standing before the counter.

Exercise 6

The Epiphany of the Moment

TIME: 20 to 60 minutes

This exercise, which flows quite naturally from the preceding one, emerged the way many exercises do, from one of my students, Judith Morley; I will let her tell the story herself:

Although I am a writer of plays, I have not been much of a poem-maker since adolescence. And none of the few recent ones pleased me; they were pompous and strained. Then suddenly the most mundane subjects were filled with laserlike delight and I could not write my impressions down fast enough.

What had happened? At a workshop on March 11, 1979 (you may note that I am a journal keeper!), Jean had given us an assignment: "Throughout the day, several times an hour, stop whatever automatic, ordinary thing you're doing and become luminous . . . experience the moment as one in which all of creation is blooming and you are a part of it . . . and do it not in the high moments of ecstasy, but when you are engaged in trivial acts."

Being a journal keeper, I decided to address the trivial moments as I felt them. I caught them wherever I was—stirring the oatmeal, washing the sink, running for the bus, awaking from dreams. And I discovered that in the act of being distilled and recorded, they became no longer trivial but translucent, that every moment became extraordinary when you paused to look at it. And I have a book of poems to prove it.

Here is a sampling of Judith's poems:

March 29, 1979
8:35 A.M.
An invisible
Self-propelled eggbeater
Blathers my blood
Down to the least, tiniest cell
As I race the bus
To the corner
And lose.
Easy there, kid,
Say I to my hysterical heart,
On what cosmic calendar
Is it written that
Only on this bus
May you pursue your destiny?

March 29, 1979
7:30 A.M.
It looks as if I'm stirring the oatmeal,
but the spoon is in my left hand

The Epiphany of the Moment

and the pot handle in my right
instead of the other way around as usual.
And I'm slowly breathing down my legs
so that I'm held up by my feet
and not my thighs.
And I'm humming a sound
that fills my head with images
as my kinesthetic body
takes a short hop
into the stratosphere and looks around.
And I'm wondering how
my next-door neighbor makes oatmeal.
Before I learned this new recipe
stirring the oatmeal
was so boring.

June 10, 1979
The pond stinks
The wind is still
The carcass
of a mallard
lies rotting
on the spillway
The five goslings
are all dead
Goldfish gasp for breath
in the shallowing water
The pond is dying
If I were God
This would not be happening
But I am
and it is.*

You don't have to be a poet or a journal keeper to do this yourself. Try it now, taking a common experience and sensing it fully, the feel of it, the sight of it, and let it emerge. Here are some suggestions to get you started:

Tying your shoes
Brushing your teeth
Opening the mail
Locking the door
Washing the dishes

*Copyright 1979 by Judith Morley.

Making the bed
Paying the bills
Wrapping a gift
Folding the laundry
Answering the phone
Emptying the wastebasket
Starting the car

Just as our individuality is coded in our fingerprints, our signature, our voice, indeed in each cell of our being, so too does each of these actions have something to reveal about our worlds, inner and outer. No two people will experience the same thing, however common the experience may be. Locking the door isn't *simply* locking the door.

The Epiphany of the Moment

CHAPTER 3

So many things fail to interest us, simply because they don't find in us enough surfaces on which to live, and what we have to do is to increase the number of planes in our mind, so that a much larger number of themes can find a plane in it at the same time.

ORTEGA Y GASSET

Deborah Koff

3

Awakening the Brain

We have entered upon one of the greatest explorations of all time as we begin to probe the mystery of the brain. This small organ weighs less than three pounds and, in the mature adult, comprises less than 8.5 percent of our weight, and yet it is complex beyond our wildest imaginings. Here is encoded the wisdom of the millennia and the dreams of tomorrow, the capacity to decode the abstract symbols of this page and the desire for communion and community. Language, memory, and the great achievements of civilization emerge from the complex interaction of billions of neurons. Recent brain research has underlined the extraordinary complexity of the brain and provided a rationale for an extraordinary education. We know now that many of the dualistic ways of thinking historically attributed to the human—spatial and temporal, analogical and digital, intuitive and rational, divergent and convergent, subjective and objective—may be linked to the two very different ways of processing information in the two hemispheres of the neocortex; that by taking thought we may control the firing of a single muscle cell; that different states of consciousness are correlated with different patterns of brain waves; that we respond to subliminal perceptions; and much more.[1]

Here I want to suggest that it is possible to "speak" directly to the brain, to exercise it, if you will, just as you might use calisthenics to exercise your body when you get up in the morning. Such an idea is not new in itself. Over a century ago Oliver Wendell Holmes suggested that we could increase our brain use by thinking ten "impossible thoughts" before breakfast. And I have been known to begin seminars by asking people to tell each other three outrageous lies! The resistance that some people experience to such a suggestion may be indicative of the extremely literal mind-set that results from an acculturation that worships "the fact" and logical proof. This kind of brain exercise is designed to increase the capacity of the brain to consider multiple possibilities, however outrageous, without the premature interference of The Judge in each of us who is well trained to slam down the gavel and declare "Impossible! Won't work! Case dismissed!" before the trial has even begun.

Cross-cultural studies hint at the dormant possibilities, as do the studies of the "exceptional" person. Feats of prodigious memory are now well documented, as is the deliberate use of dreams to elicit healing and great conceptual insights.

For our purposes here, the primary findings to be underlined are that this process we have called "thinking" is much more complicated than any purely rational model would suggest. Further, relying on such a model limits and inhibits our understanding of much that is actually going on, and what we think deeply influences who we are and how we behave.

As a Westerner, I have grown in a culture that rewards the rational logical thinker. Such a tradition has its roots beyond the Age of Enlightenment, before Descartes declared that being and thinking are synonymous, predating the sublime ordering of the *Summa Theologica* of Thomas Aquinas. The tradition of a hierarchy of the mind in which reason is given dominion over the untrustworthy and potentially rebellious vassals of instinct, emotion, intuition, and revelation finds its roots in our Hebraic and Greek heritage.

The marriage of Athens and Jerusalem was not an altogether harmonious occasion for the brain. The child of this union, distinctly male, found himself a wanderer in this universe, separated from nature and at a distance from his gods. Alone in a potentially alien universe, he is part of neither the natural nor the divine order and must instead create his own. He looks for a ruler who will restore a structure that gives meaning.

Plato enthroned reason to rule over and combat the shamanic world, which had fallen into decadence, threatening the glory of Athens with superstition and soothsayers. The light of reason was to come into the cave to relieve the darkness. Like many contemporary commentators, Plato was to remark on the similarities between mediumship, poetic creation, and certain pathological manifestations of the religious consciousness. Each of these, Plato claimed, involved a degree of possession or mania that must be subjected to the active and unifying force of reason. The role of the prophet and korybant as channeler of divine or demonic grace was indeed acknowledged and honored, but it was an honor that masked a basic distrust, much as we honor or give lip service to the functions of the right, or "minor," hemisphere of the brain. Athens saw the development of Plato's Academy, which was to serve as a significant model for our formal education, as the home for the spirit of reason and the dialogue of analysis.

Similarly, the emphasis in Judaism, and subsequently in Christianity and Islam, upon linear rather than cyclical time with a concurrent development of written law and a reliance upon the word served to reinforce our insistence on the temporal, or left-hemisphere, way of knowing and thinking.

However, both the Greek insistence on logos and the Hebraic emphasis on temporality and legalisms were leavened by a much larger cultural context in which there was still room for mystery and ritual, for the great story and music and dance. Two thousand years ago there existed a supporting sea of aesthetic expression and spiritual depth to carry the craft of logos and law and order.

So we see how some of what we have come to call left-hemisphere learning, with its insistence on time and order, are rooted to some extent in aspects of our cultural dawnings. We have labeled the empathic knowing of shamanic cultures as primitive and naively anthropomorphic, insisting on the long-distance telescopic lens, with its illusion of objectivity, as the only valid perspective of reality. We have gone further, to the deification of efficiency and quantification and the acceptance of a profound materialistic dualism of right and wrong, and we have found our basic metaphors in the machine and the computer.

The result is distance, the worshiping of facts and products that can be evaluated and held constant at a time of radical change, rather than risking the challenge of process and the evocation of the full potential of the brain. Our education reflects these unfortunate biases, with the result that we are inhibited in the consciousness of much of our knowing. If we had deliberately planned to fetter our brains, we couldn't have done better.

Accepting this basically reductionist and single-lensed notion of the brain—as a thinking instrument that is essentially rational and logical—we have developed a whole series of programs to train this brain and have embalmed these programs in our educational institutions. Thus we "analyze" Shakespeare, reduce our traditions to a historical time line, learn arithmetic through rote memorization, outline uncountable pages of information, copy life off the blackboard into our notebooks to be reproduced as accurately as possible on examinations, and reward those who survive this ordeal by putting them on the Honor Roll of the Well-Trained Brains. This disaster has been compounded recently by standardized testing, with its reliance on a multiple-choice format that asks the test-taker to select *the* correct answer from a limited number of alternatives. The more complex but academically less efficient challenge to come up with an original response is not possible in the present Reign of Quantity, and our model of the brain seems to have become that of a primitive and rather inadequate computer. Holmes' suggestion of the "impossible thoughts" has no room to percolate in the confines of such an environment.

Just as there has been a renaissance of the body, there is a less perceptible renaissance of the brain, reinforced by an outpouring of research from the biological sciences. At the same time there is a renewed interest in the work of Gurdjieff, who dedicated his life to developing processes that would allow the brain to "wake up." Gurdjieff stated that we have three "brains," or centers, that direct action. Each of these brains can be trained, and this training can be generalized so that students will be able to develop their mental faculties to such an extent that a great deal of learning can be accomplished with great ease. As Gurdjieff's student A. R. Orage suggests, "It need not be claimed that . . . Einstein becomes easy. The special language of every province of science must be independently acquired even by the most perfectly developed mind. But it can be claimed that when the language is familiar, the ideas themselves, no matter by whom expressed, offer less and less difficulty to a mind trained in these exercises."[2]

While I do not envisage a division into three distinct centers with different loci that are respectively the seat of the emotions, the body, and the intellect, I have certainly witnessed the profound potential of the exercises given here for increasing the fluidity of conceptualization and expression, a fluidity that releases the motivation to learn the language of Einstein—and of Bach and Escher and the Upanishads. The myriad worlds of conception and perception become richer and more accessible as we gain access to more of ourselves.

In the exercises in this chapter we will explore ways to "talk" to the brain, actively recruiting it as an ally, and to develop the capacity of being conscious of multiple patterns. It is not yet possible to generalize about the physiological responses to these exercises. Nonetheless, reports of research subjects and seminar participants convincingly suggest that they do have an effect, and that it becomes easier to entertain multiple possibilities, do serious intellectual work, focus on ideas without becoming fatigued and distracted, and, in the acceptance of brain as ally, enter into a dialogue with it.

Exercise 1

Left Brain/Right Brain

TIME: 60 minutes

We begin within an adaptation of an exercise created by my husband, Robert Masters, and called "Left Brain/Right Brain." Although a version of this exercise appears in *Listening to the Body,* its inclusion here is critical because it serves as a prototype that can be adapted in various educational and therapeutic settings. Moreover, of all the exercises we have developed of this type, it seems to have the most profound effect. Although we have called this exercise "Left Brain/Right Brain" and work with the metaphor of right and left sides of the brain, we cannot claim that this exercises the function of two distinctly separated hemispheres of the cerebral cortex. Instead, this exercise would seem to integrate many functions of the brain, bringing together words and images, senses and emotions, the abstraction of numerical symbols, and the unity of the mind field.

To do this exercise the first time, you will need to put it on tape or have someone read it to you. As you put it on tape or have it read aloud, be sure to allow enough time for the images to develop.

PREPARATION

Seat yourself comfortably with your spine straight and your body in a supported and relaxed position that you can maintain comfortably for about forty-five minutes.

Consider now what you would say to your brain if you could speak to it directly. Apart from "Hello there," "Wake up, stupid!" or "Where have you been all my life?" what would you really say if you had the opportunity to begin a friendship and ongoing communication with your own brain? Remember what this is, because toward the end of this exercise you will have the opportunity to say these things directly to your own brain.

THE EXERCISE

Close your eyes and direct your attention to your breathing. Allow the rhythm of your breath to become regular. As you do this, allow your consciousness to rest in your solar plexus and gradually move up through your body, passing through your lungs and then your heart, moving up the left carotid artery to the left side of your brain. Move your awareness forward now to your left eye.

Keeping your eyes closed, look down with your left eye. Now up. Look to the left . . . and to the right. Keeping your awareness in your left eye, allow that eye to circle clockwise . . . and counterclockwise. Which direction is easier? You may find it easier if you imagine you are looking at a clock and follow the numbers of the clock as you move your eye.

Now shift your attention to your right eye. Keeping your eyes closed, look down and then up. Repeat this several times. Now move your eye from right to left. Allow your right eye to circle to the right and then to the left, clockwise and counterclockwise. Is this easier with the right eye than the left?

Relax your eyes, feeling them get soft and releasing the muscles around the socket. Rest for a minute.

Keeping your eyes closed, direct your attention to the right side of the brain . . . and now to the left. Shift back and forth easily a few times, noting any differences between the two sides of your brain. Does one seem more accessible than the other?

Keeping your eyes closed and relaxed, imagine the images that will be suggested as vividly as possible. Don't strain as you do this.

On the left side of your brain, imagine the number 1 . . .

And on the right side the letter A . . .

On the left side the number 2 . . .

And on the right side the letter B . . .

On the left the number 3 . . .

And on the right the letter C . . .

On the left the number 4 . . .

And on the right the letter D . . .

On the left the number 5 . . .

And on the right the letter E.

Continue with the numbers on the left and the letters on the right, going toward the number 26 and the letter Z. You don't have to actually reach 26 and Z. Just continue for a minute or so. If you get confused or lost, go back to the place where the letters and numbers were clearly together and begin again.

Rest for a minute, relaxing your attention as you do so.

Now reverse the process you have just done, putting the letters on the left and the numbers on the right.

On the left image the letter A . . .

And on the right the number 1 . . .

On the left the letter B . . .

And on the right the number 2 . . .

Keep going toward the letter Z and the number 26.

Stop and rest for a minute. Note whether it was easier on one side than the other, whether numbers or letters were more clearly imagined.

Continuing with your eyes closed, on the left side of your brain imagine a festive outdoor scene with a big picnic and fireworks.

On the right image a couple getting married.

Let that image go and, on the left, imagine a procession of nuns walking two by two through a lovely medieval cloister.

On the right there is a hurricane sweeping through a coastal town.

On the left is an atom.

On the right is a galaxy.

On the left are fruit trees bearing new blossoms.

On the right the trees are weighted down with frost and snow.

On the left is the sunrise.

On the right is the sunset.

On the left is a green jungle forest.

On the right is a snow-covered mountain in the Alps.

On the left is a three-ring circus.

On the right is a thick fog.

Left Brain/Right Brain

On the left is the sensation of climbing rocks. Try to capture the feeling and sensation of the rocks and breathe easily as you experience it.

On the right, imagine how your hand feels caressing a baby's skin.

On the left, the feeling of plunging your hands into warm soppy mud.

On the right, that of making snowballs with your bare hands.

On the left you are pulling taffy.

On the right you are punching a punching bag.

Now, on the left hear the sound of a fire engine.

On the right the sound of crickets chirping.

On the left the sound of a car starting up.

On the right somebody is singing in a very high voice.

On the left the sound of ocean waves on a beach.

On the right the sound of your stomach growling.

Now on the left the smell of a pine forest.

On the right imagine smelling freshly brewed coffee.

On the left the smell of gasoline.

On the right the smell of bread baking.

Now on the left brain, the taste of a crisp, juicy apple.

On the right the taste of hot buttered toast.

On the left the taste of a lemon. On the right the taste of nuts.

Now on the left side of the brain, experience as fully as you can the following scene: you are riding a horse through the snow and sleet carrying three little kittens under your coat, and you are sucking on a peppermint.

On the right side of the brain you are standing under a waterfall singing "You Are My Sunshine" and watching a nearby volcano erupt.

Now, eyes still closed, with your left eye look up toward your left brain. Move the eye so that it circles and explores this space. Roam around for a while.

Now do the same thing for a while with your closed right eye on the right side of the brain.

Now with the left eye trace some triangles on the left side of the brain. Now make some rectangles. Now make some stars.

With the right eye trace some triangles on the right side of the brain. Now make some rectangles. Now draw some stars.

Now make many overlapping circles on the left side, leaving spirals of light streaming from these circles into the left side of the brain. Imagine the brain as charged with energy by this light.

Make many overlapping circles on the right side with the right eye, leaving energizing light streaming from these circles.

Now, with both eyes, circle vertically just in the middle of the head. You should circle along the corpus callosum, the ridge where the hemispheres of the brain come together. With both eyes together, circle as widely as you can inside your head.

With both eyes, create spiraling galaxies throughout your brain. Fill the whole of your brain space and the inside of your head with them.

Stop and let your eyes come completely to rest.

Try to make horizontal circles with both eyes just at the level of your eyes, and circling as widely as possible inside your head. Now try making smaller circles horizontally at the level of your eyes. Make them smaller . . . and smaller . . . and smaller . . . until you get down to a space that is too small for circling and then you will want to fix on that point and try to hold it. Continue to breathe freely with your muscles relaxed as you do this. If you lost the point, make more large circles, letting them become smaller and smaller until you get back down to a point, staying fixed on that point for as long as you can easily.

(Circling inward and holding on the point in the center is an excellent meditation exercise when done by itself.)

Rest for a moment. Then, in the middle of your forehead, imagine a huge sunflower. Then erase the sunflower.

Simultaneously, imagine a sunflower on the left and some green damp moss on the right. Let them go.

Imagine that there is a big tree growing right in the middle of your forehead.

Let go of that, and imagine that there is a golden harp on the left, and just a little to the right of the harp is a drum. Try to hear them as they play together.

Let them go and imagine on the left an eagle, and on the right a canary, both of them there together at once. Let them go now, and imagine the canary now on the left and the eagle on the right.

Let them go, and imagine two eagles on the left and two canaries on the right. Let them fade away.

Breathe easily, and if you need to adjust your position to be more comfortable, do so.

Now, in the middle of your forehead, imagine a small sun. Then imagine the sun just inside the top of your head. Try to roll it down the inside of your skull to the inside of the back of your head, so that if your eyes could turn completely around in your head, they would be looking at it.

Now raise the sun along the back of your head to the top and then down to the forehead. Now raise it along the inside of the head from the forehead back to the top and then to the back of the head, and then to the top of the head and back to the forehead. The sun should be making vertical semicircles on the inside of your skull.

Now let that sun move out in front of you and see it setting over the sea. From somewhere in the direction of the sunset comes a sailboat. From what direction is the sailboat coming? From the left, from the right, or from some other direction?

Left Brain/Right Brain

Tom McHugh/National Audubon Society   Jeanne White/National Audubon Society

Imagine on the left an eagle, and on the right a canary.

Let that image fade away and imagine an elephant walking. Try to become more and more aware of him as he walks. He stops and eats something, pushing his long trunk into his mouth, then he walks some more, then he sees you and breaks into a run. He slows down and then he stops and eats some more.

Let the elephant go, and imagine seeing Santa Claus in a sleigh pulled by reindeer. Observe the sleigh and watch it accelerate, then slow down and stop, then start up again, going faster and faster as it circles around and down a spiral track that is inside of your head.

Starting from your chin, the sleigh spirals up and around and around and around until it reaches to the top of your head. Then it spirals down and around and around and around to your chin. Then it rushes up and around and around and around to the top of your head. Then it circles down and around and around to your chin. Circling now up and around and around and around to the top of your head. Let it stop there poised on the edge of the front of the top of your head.

Now yawn and let Santa and his sleigh and reindeer drive down over your nose and into your mouth, swallow the sleigh, and forget all about it!

Now focus attention on the left side of your brain for a while. Concentrate on it and try to see or imagine what your brain looks like on the left side. Be aware of the gray matter and the convolutions of the brain. Concentrate in the same way on the right side of the brain. Pay attention to the thick bands of fibers that connect the two hemispheres of the brain.

Now try to sense both sides at once, the whole brain. Sense its infinite complexity, its billions of cells intercommunicating at the speed of light. Meditate on it as a universe in itself, whose dimensions and capacities you have only begun to dream of.

Now, breathing very deeply, imagine that by inhaling and exhaling you can expand and contract your brain. And do this for a while, expanding your brain when you inhale slowly and deeply, and contracting your brain when you exhale slowly and completely.

Let your brain rest now and, holding its image, speak directly to your own brain, suggesting, if you wish, that its functioning will get better and better.

Suggest that you will have more brain cells accessible to you and that the interaction of the cells and all the processes of the brain will continuously improve as time goes by.

Tell it that the right and left hemispheres will be better integrated, as will older and newer parts of the brain.

Advise your brain that many of its latent potentials can now become manifest and that you will try to work together with the brain in partnership to allow these potentials to develop in your life.

Listen now and see if your brain has any messages for you. These messages may come as words or images or feelings. Give the brain time to respond, withholding judgment. Does your brain want something from you? What does your brain want to give you?

Again being aware of the whole of the brain, begin to feel a real sense of both communication and communion with your brain.

Think of it as a new friend and of this friendship as a profound and beautiful new fact in your life. In the weeks to come, spend time nurturing and deepening this friendship so that the two of you (your brain and your consciousness) can work together in useful ways. But now, spend some minutes communing with your brain. Images may come to you, or feelings, or words, as together you move into a more complete partnership and friendship.

If you wish, while you do this place your hands about half an inch above your head and have the sense that you are caressing the "field" around your brain, in the same way that you might pat or stroke the hand of a dear friend. (Allow about three or four minutes for this to happen.)

If you have some special intention for your brain, offer it now.

Continuing to feel a communion with your brain, open your eyes and look around. Observe whether there are any changes in your sensory perceptions. How do you feel in your body? What is your mood and your sense of reality? Do you feel that your possibilities have changed? Observe these things.

Left Brain/Right Brain

As you do this, stretch and move around the room. When you wish to, suggest to yourself that you are becoming more and more wide awake.

DISCUSSION

What seems to be happening here? Certainly, many things on many levels. Teachers who have used this exercise with their classes report that their students enjoy the experience and then are more relaxed and alert as they address the other areas of their schoolwork. They begin to regard their brains as allies rather than poorly programmed robots, and they are delighted to find that their brains have a sense of whimsy and play. Some who have felt sluggish and sleepy experience renewed energy. One Texas rancher found his brain saying to *him,* "Where have *you* been all my life?" Many experience an unexpected sense of reverence for their brain; the brain has truly become Thou, an active partner in the process of co-creation.

As attention of this kind and duration is directed toward the brain, more blood goes to the brain, bringing nourishing oxygen. As this attention is directed toward different areas of the brain in different ways, more of the brain seems to be nourished and available. The principle is the same as that used in autogenic training for the relief of migraine headaches. As you image the hand becoming warm and heavy and the forehead cool, the congested blood in the head is relieved and more blood is directed toward the hand. Patterns of blood circulation are thus directed by conscious imaging. For this same reason, some people experience a temporary feeling of constriction in the skull after doing this exercise. This is often followed by increased mental acuity and cognitive clarity.

If you feel fatigued after this exercise, you may have been trying too hard. As in all psychological exercises, it is important to work without strain, letting images happen rather than making them happen. Your brain will cooperate with you if you let it, but if you bully it, the level of cooperation drops drastically. Scolding yourself or feeling inadequate if Z and 26 do not come out together at the end won't help Z or 26. With practice, you will find this exercise increasingly easy, indeed child's play. Then you may want to vary it in your own way or follow any of the suggestions in the Extensions section below.

You can also use this exercise diagnostically for yourself and with any individual or group you may be working with. If someone experiences considerably more difficulty with one side than the other, you can strengthen the image on the dominant side until it becomes as vivid as possible and then allow this image to gradually slip over to the nondominant side.

Letters or numbers that are reversed can be "corrected" by a magical wand that turns them around. This is particularly effective for those who have reversal problems in writing. Have the children draw the images they see. If they are reversed, tell them that there is a special magic wand in their brains and have them touch the reversed letter with this magic wand so that it turns around. Then they write it again as it is now. One eleven-year-old boy found the magic wand a rather inadequate instrument to deal with so complicated and old a problem, so he imagined a heavy crane with steep grippers that turned the recalcitrant letter and held it firmly in its correct position! The possibilities are endless.

This exercise also has been very helpful to those who are natural lefties but were switched to right-handedness by parents or teachers. Stroke victims, too, have found it useful. In such a case it is often better to start with sensory images rather than letters and numbers, since smell and taste are our oldest senses and are located in the older central portion of the brain. Beginning with these senses, it is possible to reactivate connections that seem to have been damaged in the initial trauma of the stroke.

The most remarkable aspect of this exercise is the variety of different responses that people report—everything from the obvious falling asleep to imaging in color for the first time to mystical experience. Even the same person doing the exercise at different times, without changing the instructions in any way, usually reports a very different experience each time. The brain seems to be a veritable kaleidoscope, revealing new patterns and insights with the slightest shift of the lens.

EXTENSIONS

1. Change the particular images, or, working with a friend or small group, take turns suggesting the images to one another. In the sharing comes a new level of mindfulness.

2. Set up a deliberate rhythmic or singsong pattern and change images with the beat. You can use a heartbeat or a metronome or even "Mares eat oats, and does eat oats, and little lambs eat ivy . . ." Keep the beat constant throughout the exercise and see if this makes it easier. Notice what tempo is most comfortable for you. Try it faster and slower. Try varying the beat within the exercise.

3. Vary the direction from which you are doing the images. If you find yourself always going left—right—left—right, interject a few left—right—*right*—lefts and notice how you respond emotionally to this variation. Often surprise combines with irritation when a pattern that was going so nicely is suddenly interrupted. Yet, at the same time, you are developing the flexibility to shift patterns with ease, and after a while the resentment dissolves as a subtlety of awareness develops.

Left Brain/Right Brain

Exercise 2

Multitracking

TIME: 45 to 60 minutes

Have you ever wondered why we have such difficulty in thinking of several things at the same time? Our brains seem to be locked into a single idea, unable to sustain a play of thought in which a variety of ideas, perceptions, and emotions can be consciously entertained at the same time. We seem to be unnecessarily shackled to a serial view of reality, moving doggedly in a single track until we painfully shift gears and continue our journey on another single track. In so doing we belie our nature, our brain, and reality itself. For the world within and without is multiple, various, and simultaneous.

We know that we can hear and see, smell, taste, and touch simultaneously. Yet we have great difficulty in being *aware* of all these sensations at the same instant. I can see, at once, earth, sky, snow, fence, mother, car, dog, trees, postman. This is "automatic" and does not seem to involve separate frames of conscious attention; it involves a gestalt of knowing and requires little mental effort, little conscious attention, to appreciate the whole in its many parts. You will recognize this quickly if I ask you to recall the details of the whole picture you saw. Was there moss on the side of the tree? Did the postman carry a letter in his left or right hand?

We know on the subliminal level but have a difficult time in getting this knowing across the threshold of our consciousness.

And yet, go up the scale of human performance a bit and you begin to see how readily we can begin to self-orchestrate our several realities and be able to exist on multiple tracks and with multiple knowings. Consider the young man at the piano playing the "Moonlight Sonata" to his beloved, his right and left hands fingering different musical patterns while his eyes gaze soulfully at the one standing there, his lips promising eternal love and a part of his mind occupied with the cost of dinner at her favorite restaurant.

Is this a case of fragmented consciousness? Not at all. Our hypothetical young man is operating quite well on all those tracks at the same time. He is "multitracking," as all of us do in our personal, professional, and unconscious lives. This is enough to remind us that we are capable of much, much more, and indeed that we can learn to *consciously* put these capacities for multiple tracking into the service of a more richly textured mental and emotional life. We all have the capacity to recognize and work with complex patterns and varying perspectives, yielding creative insight at any moment. We also have the faculty to pull together the parts of any process, be it personal, artistic, or scientific, so that the ensuing weave becomes a new design on the fabric of reality. Such is the stuff of which world-making is woven.

The autonomous functions of the brain's neural networks could allow us to discriminate in full consciousness dozens and perhaps even hundreds of separate functions and ideas. Certain states of consciousness, especially those related to moments of high creativity or mystic perception, seem to give a person access to the knowledge of the one and the many, in which everything is seen as separate but unified, uniquely what it is and an essential member of the pattern that connects. Thousands of studies of the phenomenology of these "higher" states of consciousness confirm this thesis: to create, commune, advance, evolve, we must multitrack and open our lenses to simultaneous knowing and doing.

How can we begin to do this? We could start, perhaps, with the whimsical recalling of the childhood game in which we rubbed our stomachs while patting our heads and then reversed the process, rubbing our heads while patting our stomachs. Try it now! It is a game we should never have stopped, for in its simple formula lies the key to an articulation of separate motor functions that in turn gave us an increased capacity to function in thought and feeling on several levels at the same time. Sufi masters have known this, as did Gurdjieff and a thousand other evocateurs of the extended use of our capacities. Teach a person to articulate a variety of distinctively different motor functions, add thoughts, sounds, rhythms, and paradox, and you are laying the neural and conceptual basis for a flexible multifunctioning person.

PREPARATION

Think of this exercise as a childhood game raised to an adult level, knowing that as you perform these steps, however unlikely they may seem, you will be doing real neurophysiological work, activating latent functions of the brain and reorganizing others. Gradually you will become aware of a functional improvement and experience relative ease in performing many different tasks at the same time. Follow the directions playfully without striving for literal accuracy, as that will only yield frustration and make the natural impossible.

The last part of this exercise depends upon your being familiar with the practice of the kinesthetic body, which is Exercise 1 in Chapter 1. You can omit this part of the exercise if you have not already worked with the kinesthetic body.

THE EXERCISE

To begin. Stand up and make sure that you have enough room to move freely. Get centered and balanced.

Let your head and shoulders move from left to right together in an even swinging movement.

Now let your head and shoulders swing apart—that is, your head and shoulders are moving in opposite directions from each other, your head going left while your shoudlers go right, and your shoulders going right while your head goes to the left.

Now your head and shoulders swing together . . .

And apart . . .

Together . . .

And apart . . .

Now, with your head moving in the opposite direction from your shoulders, let your eyes follow the shoulders. It's rather like flirting!

Don't get cross with yourself if you can't do this. Remember that we are just playing a game as well as asking you to awaken circuits in your brain that may never have been used before.

Now return just to the head and shoulders moving in opposite directions, your eyes doing anything they like. At the same time, tap dance.

At the same time sing a song like "Tea for Two."

Stop at the end of the song and rest for a minute.

Now let your head go right and your face go left.

Now reverse and let your head go left and your face go right.

Keep on doing this, reversing the order each time.

Add a little jog and snap your fingers. At the same time move your hands in circles.

And hum "Yankee Doodle Dandy"!

And, simultaneously, think about a hive of bees, a spiral staircase, and a bowl of Jell-O!

Stop and rest for a minute.

Now let your hips and arms swing back and forth together.

Now let your hips and arms swing in opposite directions.

Now together again.

And now in opposite directions.

At the same time, jump up and down.

Add a boxing movement with your hands.

And whistle "Dixie."

And think about Marie Antoinette, a ski slope in the Alps, and a giraffe.

Add a giant traffic jam and buttered popcorn.

Stop and rest for a minute.

Lie down on your back on the floor with your knees bent, the soles of your feet on the ground, and your hands on your chest.

Begin to raise and lower your elbows in a flapping motion.

At the same time bicycle with your legs.

Now put your feet on the ground and open your knees wide and bring them back together in a flapping motion while you bicycle with your arms.

Now flap with your arms and bicycle with your legs.

Change.

Change once again.

And sing "A Bicycle Built for Two" or "Row, Row, Row Your Boat," changing the movement of your arms and legs at the end of each line.

Stop and rest for a minute after you have done this for a while.

Still lying down with your knees bent and your arms at your sides, begin beating very slowly on the floor with your right hand.

Now add a fast beat with your left hand while your right hand continues to beat slowly.

Keeping these two motions going, let your right foot begin to tap a slow beat.

Keeping all these motions going, let your left foot begin to tap a fast beat.

Stop.

Let your left hand beat a slow beat.

Now add your right foot tapping a slow beat.

Now add your right hand beating a fast beat.

Now add your left foot tapping a fast beat.

Keep all of this going for a few minutes.

Stop and rest.

Stand up now, and again let your head go right and your face go left.

Now reverse and let your head go left and your face go right.

Keep on doing this, reversing the order each time.

Add a little jog and snap your fingers.

At the same time move your hands in circles.

And hum "Yankee Doodle Dandy."

And, simultaneously, think about a hive of bees, a spiral staircase, and a bowl of Jell-O!

Stop and rest for a minute. Be aware of any improvements you have noticed.

Now for the most interesting and subtle of the sequences:

Standing in a comfortable and relaxed position, close your eyes and become totally centered and balanced.

Take four steps forward and imagine, kinesthetically and actively, that you are taking four steps backward.

Now take four steps backward while thinking four steps forward.

Keep repeating this for a few minutes until it seems natural.

Now, as you move forward, allow your arms and hands to move in clockwise circles.

As you move backward, reverse the direction of your arms and hands. Continue to do this for a while.

Now, keeping all of the motions and thoughts going, think counterclockwise while you are making a clockwise motion with your hands, and think clockwise when you are making a counterclockwise motion.

At this point you are taking four steps forward and making a clockwise circle with your hands while you are thinking four steps backward and thinking a counterclockwise circle for your hands. Then you are taking four steps backward and making a counterclockwise circle with your hands while thinking four steps forward and clockwise with your hands.

Continue to do this for five to fifteen minutes, until it becomes a simultaneous dance of movement and thinking. Should you lose one or more of these tracks, stop and begin again, adding movement and thinking sequences gradually until you are comfortable with all of them.

DISCUSSION

In this exercise, thinking, moving, expressing, and, often, laughter at the absurdity of it all are consciously combined. What may have seemed initially impossible begins to seem natural and easy. The purpose of this exercise is not, however, to learn to lie on your back and sing while you bicycle in the air with your feet, but rather to regain a natural flexibility and fluidity of thought and intention. The rigid tracks and expectations that shape much of our thinking are playfully stretched and extended, reaching out for new connections and unexpected patterns.

After completing the last sequence in this exercise, many people are aware of a deep sense of centering and serenity. Some feel that as a result of the paradoxical nature of the exercise they are now able to see and resolve paradox in ways they could not have done before. Whether this is because of a conceptual change or a physiological reprogramming with a greater integration of the two hemispheres we do not yet know, but it is a very common response. Suffice it to say that the exercise is, in itself, a wonderful moving meditation and seems to prepare the individual for a day of balanced perspectives and the capacity to entertain at least ten impossible thoughts before breakfast. Of itself it is a sophisticated and subtle spiritual practice that may also be done beneficially at any time of stress or decision making.

EXTENSIONS

Multitracking with Partners

Working with a partner, you can create multitracking exercises for one another. One of you will suggest and demonstrate a motion and the other will execute it.

The suggester does only one motion at a time, but the partner will attempt to execute them all simultaneously. Thus you might stamp your foot. Your partner will copy you. You stop and your partner continues. Now you pull your left ear while your partner is stamping his or her foot *and* pulling his or her left ear. Keep adding movements, sounds, thoughts, and so forth until your partner has five or more tracks going. And then give your partner an opportunity for revenge by shifting roles!

Multitracking

CHAPTER 4

Time present and time past
Are both perhaps present in time future
And time future contained in time past.

T. S. ELIOT
Four Quartets: "Burnt Norton"

Jane Prettyman

4

Awakening Memory

One of the profound miracles of the human brain, and one whose ultimate explanation still defies the efforts of the best researchers, is our capacity for memory.

As we grow older, we store more and more memories—literally nothing is lost. While we may have suspected this for a long time, Wilder Penfield's reports of patients undergoing brain surgery confirm this suspicion by demonstrating that the stimulation of a particular neuron in the brain will result in the patient's reporting vivid sensations and experiences that he or she had experienced as a child. Our problem is not that we do not have these memories but that we have failed to harvest them.

The rooms of our memories are locked, bolted, and in some cases protected by large armed guards who say simply, "Thou shall not enter." Caught in the modern tumult of enormous sensory stimulation of the moment, we save our reminiscences for our rocking-chair days, thus dividing present from past. This phenomenon transcends the personal, to be reflected in the diminishing status of history departments in universities.

Increasingly, teachers report that their students, of whatever ages, have poor memories and bemoan those days when students memorized twenty lines of Shakespeare a night or ten verses from the Bible (forgetting, of course, that Tom Sawyer, among others, did not memorize quite so much as he claimed). At the same time, we have lost the tradition of *telling* the stories of our past, listening instead to the stories of NBC and CBS. So we, like those before us, take courses and read books on how to improve our memories. Such a practice is not new, nor are many of the techniques.

Come with me now on a journey. It is the year 10 B.C. You are wandering through a temple in the Roman Forum. You stop to admire the burly, muscled marble statue of Jupiter but are soon distracted by an undertone of muttering coming from a young man standing nearby who is eyeing the statue intently. A religious devotee, you think, and pass on down the hall, careful not to disrupt his meditations.

Thirty feet away you halt to study a graceful Minerva. Again, the young man is close beside you, his mouth moving, and occasionally he even gesticulates in what appears to be a style too theatrical for prayers. "An ancient Roman bliss ninny," you may comment as you walk away.

Your eye catches the glint of a marble pool, and you go to sit by its sculptured edge. As you observe the movements of a fish you are once more distracted by the same muttering fellow, who is regarding the fish with a zeal more properly directed to the gods than to a carp. Every so often he looks at a wax tablet he is carrying. You move closer to try to catch his words and discover, to your surprise, that he is speaking of tax reform and is asking his fellow Romans to recall the agrarian simplicity practiced centuries ago by the great leader Cincinnatus, whose righteous actions contrast sharply with the present crop of sybaritic senators. The young man, still rapturously engaged with the fish pool, waves his arms dramatically, and you move on.

Throughout the temple and in the forecourts, atriums, and impluviums of other temples and public buildings, you come across similar meandering, murmuring fellows who seem to be neither priests nor parishioners, nor to belong to the staff and company of the buildings. Who are they and what are they doing?

They are students and practitioners of rhetoric, and they are using the different loci of public buildings to fix the stages of their speeches in their minds, for one of the chief amusements of the ancient world was listening to very long speeches. The giver of the speech, devoid of printing and without paper for taking notes, had to become a master of *mnemotechnics*, the art and skill of memory. In the century before Christ, the masters of rhetoric—Cicero, Quintilian, the unknown author of *Ad Herennium*—devised remarkable texts and essays that taught the earnest pupil to develop powerful visual and verbal memories using techniques similar to the ones you just saw employed by our muttering friend. He had probably just been reading Cicero, who told him that "one must employ a large number of places which must be well lighted, clearly set out in order, at moderate intervals apart, and images which are active, sharply defined, unusual, and which have the power of speedily encountering and penetrating the psyche."[1]

The would-be rhetorician deposits the sequence of his speech in the sequence of the rooms, statues, and ornaments of a familiar building. "This done, as soon as the memory of the facts requires to be revived, all these places are visited in turn and the various deposits demanded of their custodians." The ancient orator travels in this way in his imagination through these buildings in the very process of giving speech, drawing from the memorized places the images he has placed on them. A long speech might go on for miles of buildings, while a short one might be limited to a small temple or even to the contents of one room. We still retain vestiges of this ancient practice when we say, "In the first place . . . in the second place . . ."

As expertise grew, so did prodigious and bizarre feats of memory. The elder Seneca could repeat two thousand names in the order they were given. Upon listening to a class of over two hundred students, each in turn speaking a line of poetry, he could recite all the lines in reverse order, beginning with the last and going right back to the first. St. Augustine tells of a friend, Simplicius, who could recite Virgil backward.[2]

Such formidable if feckless feats give proof to the teachings of the ancient texts which tell us that if we keep up a good visual recall of our architectural memory places, we can travel along them at will, forward and backward, upward and downward, recovering our memories through a technique that may be more artifice than art but that has changed little in method or madness over the last twenty-five hundred years. A paperback, *How to Build a Phenomenal Memory in 10 Easy Lessons*, shows us that those lessons are more often than not a poor, if hyped-up, rewrite of Cicero. Consider the modern memory expert who asks us to memorize the Portuguese word for *clam* (*ameijoas*) by imagining a grotesque and gooey six-foot version of said clam rising out of the waters and lurching down the beach, to which you respond, "Oh what a mess you is!"

Our expert is indebted for this technique to the author of *Ad Herennium*, who suggested, circa 85 B.C., that, for memory's sake, we must astonish ourselves with striking and active images: "If we assign to them exceptional beauty or singular ugliness; if we ornament some of them, as with crowns or purple cloaks so that the similitude may be more distinct to us; or if we somehow disfigure them, as by introducing one stained with blood or soiled with mud or smeared with red paint, so that its form is more striking, or by assigning certain comic effects to our images, for that, to well ensure our remembering them more readily."[3]

That huge and messy clam belongs to an ancient and honorable tradition, the tradition of artificial memory. Useful and entertaining as it is, it remains a brain trick that allows us to remember a particular bit of information. It does not really encourage and deepen real memory, which remains a much more subtle, elusive, and valuable thing. With real memory, we harvest our seeds and recover our lives. We engage in time travel to the eras and arenas of our personal histories, meeting the selves that we were along the way, giving new life to things past, making present and available that which should never have been lost and, finally, weaving together the threads of our lives into a living tapestry that is both current and eternal. For in real memory the categories of time are strained by the tensions of eternity.

How faulty is our sense of history of the planet, our species, and ourselves. Like the fatuous inhabitants of Flatland who could not conceive of a three-dimensional world, we assume that time is singular, linear, and irreversible. Yet in the realm of the psyche and of higher physics (which may well be close neighborhoods, if not the same realm), time is dynamic, relativistic, whimsical, and incorrigible. It warps, it weaves, it quakes with synchronicities and chronological hot spots. It primes its cousin memory with the power of its flow, but it also confuses with its acrobatics and legerdemain.

When we acknowledge the comedy of time, we recover the power of memory. Like time, memory can be recovered at any point and brought into the eternal now. Like time, too, all its strands and forces can be gathered for the edification of the present. If you have lost or blocked your memories, chances are you have also blocked or lost the times of your life.

A little test: If you were here in the room with me now, along with about a hundred randomly chosen people, and I asked those with good memories to raise their right hand, about 10 percent of the group would do so. I would then ask those in the entire group who often review their childhood memories to raise their left hand. If we now looked around the room, we would discover that almost everyone who had raised their right hand would have raised their left hand as well. I have made this test many times with many different individuals and groups, and the results have almost always been the same.

People with good memories for all sorts of things—recent and distant, general and specific, abstract and sensually vivid—are often engaged in stoking their memories at their roots in the active recollection of their childhoods. It would appear that we can prime our general memory bank by reliving earlier memories. This activation of early sensory memory seems to have the effect of improving memory in general.

Margaret Mead, who had perhaps the best general memory I have ever observed, kept her childhood memories as fresh and vivid as if they had happened the previous day. She had the remarkable capacity to remain on current and familiar terms with all the different eras of her long life. In her mind's eye (and ear and nose and mouth and skin) she could walk around a memory of 1937 or 1977. This was probably due not only to the liveliness of her childhood memories but also to the fact that much in her memory was tied to sensory images and bodily feelings, which seem to provide for deeper chemical encodings than do abstract memories.

If you asked her how the people of Manus expressed sympathy, for example, she first summoned a specific memory: a child fell down in 1928 while she and a group of people were watching an old woman from Mbuko make a pot. Margaret then seemed to move back in time to a certain veranda in the New Guinean village of Peri. She felt the same physical and postural sensations as she did then. Sitting in *that* group, looking at *that* scene, she observes the child falling down, sees it being picked up, and watches closely to see what happens next. She described the proceedings in detail, cautioning, however, that these descriptions are not valid, scientific data.[4]

They may not be scientific, but they are revealing of a person who was *present* to so much of her life. Too many of us fail to exercise this particularly human capacity. Years accumulate like a gathering of shadows, and we cannot tell you what we did or were or even what we felt during that time. We were chimeras in a dream play, sleepwalkers in the corridors of time.

We know that a great deepening of the recovery of personal memory and the harvesting of its potential is possible. In the early 1950s, Dr. Milton Erickson, one of the world's foremost authorities on hypnotherapy, worked with Aldous Huxley to explore the earlier stages of Huxley's life. Erickson led Huxley, in trance, to experience a divided consciousness in which he was fully himself, aged fifty-two, and at the same time conscious of being himself at other ages extending from infancy to his current age. Erickson describes the procedure as it unfolded:

> As he [Huxley] watched, he became annoyed with me since I was apparently trying to talk to him, and he experienced a wave of impatience and requested that I be silent. He turned back and noted that the infant was growing before his eyes, was creeping, sitting, standing, toddling, walking, playing, talking. In utter fascination he watched this growing child, sensed its subjective experiences of learning, of wanting, of feeling. He followed it in distorted time through a multitude of experiences as it passed from infancy to childhood to school days to early youth to teenage. He watched the child's physical development, sensed its physical and subjective mental experiences, sympathized with it, empathized with it, rejoiced with it, thought and wondered and learned with it. He felt as one with it, as if it were he himself, and he continued to watch it until finally he realized that he had watched that infant grow to the maturity of 23 years. He stepped closer to see what the young man was looking at, and suddenly realized that the young man was Aldous Huxley himself, and that this Aldous Huxley was looking at another Huxley, obviously in his early fifties, just across the vestibule in which they both were standing; and that he, aged 52, was looking at himself, Aldous, aged 23.[5]

The possibility of such regression, of the active and vivid recovery of our past, has been documented in many cases of age regression under hypnosis. Those who have known "out-of-body" experiences in a life-threatening situation often report that their entire life passes before them with vivid clarity of detail during this "no-time" experience.

Wilder Penfield's work, mentioned earlier, suggests a neurological basis for this phenomenon. During surgery on epileptics, he would stimulate one small area of the patient's cortex and suddenly the patient would hear the sounds and see the sights of some very early event in his life—perhaps his third birthday party. Stimulation of another discrete area would evoke other distant memories, experienced as living realities. Parallel neurological experiments have confirmed this phenomenon. Apparently all that we have ever been is totally present now, coded within us. Thus there is an abundance of evidence to suggest some remarkable possibilities for "time travel" within the reaches of our own historicity.

One of the possibilities is suggested by Erickson's further account of Huxley's experience. Erickson writes:

> Then Aldous, aged 23, and Aldous, aged 52, apparently realized simultaneously that they were looking at each other and the curious questions at once arose in the mind of each of them. For one the question was, "Is that my idea of what I'll be like when I am 52?" and, "Is that really the way I appeared when I was 23?" Each was aware of the question in the other's mind. Each found the question of "extraordinarily fascinating interest" and each tried to determine which was the "actual reality" and which was the "mere subjective experience outwardly projected in hallucinatory forms."[6]

This suggested to me that we can enter into an interactive relationship with our earlier selves. In 1968 I began a series of experiments along these lines while working with a gifted but tortured young woman whose childhood and adolescence had been full of deep trauma and chronic insecurity. Abandoned by her mother almost at birth, she had spent the next sixteen years of her life in and out of foster homes, always to be taken back by her mother. By the time she was nine years old she was the prey of the endless succession of her mother's boyfriends. At twenty-six, Meredith was a beautiful woman of high intelligence and a compassionate and caring nature, but she was often in the throes of insecurities and anxieties so pervasive that she would frequently shake with uncontrollable and unspecified terror.

In our initial interview, I put her into a light hypnotic trance and asked her to find within herself an image with which she felt an affinity that would be for her a source of security and delight. A few moments later she reported, "I seem to find myself to be a white mare running in a green field." She further described a freedom and strength in being this image, the white mare giving her an exuberance and natural surety she had rarely felt before. I asked her to stay with that image for the next few days until she felt some of its strength and security extending into her everyday life. This she did, and several days later we met for our next session.

Remembering the Erickson-Huxley experiments, I put her into a much deeper trance and asked her to be present at her own birth. I explained that she—Meredith, twenty-six years old—would attend the birth of Meredith, the infant, as she emerged from the womb. I further suggested that there would be a divided consciousness and that she, Meredith, aged twenty-six, would hold the newborn Meredith in her arms, and when the infant felt loved then the twenty-six-year-old would know it and say, "Yes, she is loved." (Meredith was actually a wonderful mother to her two children and had remarked to me that if only she had been her own mother she would never have suffered as she did.)

For the next fourteen hours, I had Meredith meet herself at various stages of her life, progressing hour by hour, then day by day, then week by week, then allowing months to pass. At each of these stages she became a great friend of herself as an infant, a child, an adolescent, and an adult, giving herself the guidance, love, and nurturing that she felt she had never had in her childhood and early adolescence. As we proceeded from stage to stage, the Meredith of twenty-six stayed with the young Meredith, and when she felt that the other knew she was loved, she would say, "Yes, she is loved." In this way many hours went by, and when finally the twenty-six-year-old Meredith embraced the twenty-six-year-old Meredith the process had completed itself and the trauma of years had apparently ended. As follow-up studies showed, at that time she was released from the denigrations of years past. She felt that these torments were still recorded in her, but it was as if her own ministrations to herself had resulted in an alternative and enriched time track in her mind/brain system. This alternative time track in which she had become the great friend of all the stages of her life apparently detoxified her traumas and, by giving sustenance and support to her earlier years, resulted in a healing of her present life. The insecurities left, the shaking terror departed.

Subsequent work has convinced me that it is possible to enter, from the present time, into an earlier time frame, enriching the reality of the earlier self with an alternate track and often, as a consequence, healing the present self. You do not, in this way, ever abolish or erase the pathos or tragedy that may have occurred as you might erase a tape recording. The brain/mind system is too complex and interrelated to be treated successfully as a mechanism from which you can simply remove and replace a faulty or trouble-producing part. But neither are we merely a succession of historically frozen selves. Nearly a century of psychoanalysis has proven our capacity to be healed of the effects of childhood lacks and traumas. The psychoanalytic process, however, tends to stress the abreaction, or discharge of earlier painful memories in your present development, and to fortify the distance between who you are and who you were. I think it wiser to integrate these "past" selves and explore the resonance and cross-fertilization created among the generations of your selves. In this resonance lies the enrichment and expansion of the reality tracks of the times of your life.

What would you be like if you started today to attend the rest of your life, if you turned a corner and awoke? Suddenly, you are right there, an intense observer and participant in all the inner wit and wisdom, in knowings, growings, havings, being more present and alive in several moments than you had been in the previous drowse of years. Many of the so-called larger-than-life people differ from the rest of us chiefly in this one respect: not that they are actually larger or greater or more brilliant, but rather that they are profoundly present to the continuum of their lives. Of course there is more to them. The ages one to ten are present and accounted for, as are ages twenty to thirty, thirty to forty, and so on. There occurs an exponential gain and growth in the creative living use of all one's experience. Thus some die at seventy with an experiential age of seventeen while others are closer to a hundred and seventy, so intimate are they with the happenings of their lives.

To gain access to our past—both distant and recent—and learn from the patterns of our lives is to move into a life of incalculable richness and meaning. The tiniest incident has a grandeur that ties it to the moral flow of the universe, while giant events are taken in stride, denouements in the great drama of which one is both engaged participant and co-author.

Exercise 1

Priming the Memory Bank

TIME: 45 to 60 minutes

My observations of the penchant of people with good memories to actively recall images and incidents from their childhoods led me to develop the following exercise. In this process we discover that by activating childhood memories we apparently prime the memory banks generally, so that regular practice brings with it a substantial improvement in all aspects of memory and recall. It may be that the freshness of perception and uncensored receiving of experience that one has in early years is stored in brain and body in such a way that eliciting it exerts a tonic quality upon our more recent perceptions and experiences. Thus one time stream is invigorated with the vitality of the earlier one. In biological terms, we might hypothesize that the neurochemistry of childhood is still available to our present organism, and that childhood memories awaken the untrammeled neurological excitement that was ours before maturity took its toll and a cerebral reducing valve shrank our experiences to the mindscape of the cultural trance.

As you do this exercise it is important to focus clearly and not get caught up in long, lugubrious recollections. The memories are to be short, quick recalls, not unlike the flashings of a stroboscope. So if your partner says, "Tell me from your childhood memories about the family dog," you might say something like, "Oh that was Spot. I remember the time that Spot stole the fudge icicle away from the Good Humor Man. Now I see Spot running after the fire engine. Ah, I remember the time Spot chased Grandpa up the tree. . . . And there was the time Spot had puppies on my bed and we discovered that Spot was a lady. And now I see Spot wolfing down the liver I gave her under the table at dinner so that I wouldn't have to eat it . . ." These flash recollections seem to stimulate the brain and memory in ways that long narratives ("Spot and I took a walk down Mulberry Street and crossed Jefferson Avenue to Hopkins Store and turned right . . .") do not.

PREPARATION

The first part of this exercise must be done with a partner, for reasons that will soon become apparent. One person lies on the floor with eyes closed. This person will be the Rememberer. The other person will be the Guide and read the suggestions to the Rememberer. At a certain point the roles will be reversed.

To do the second part, you can either put the instructions on tape so that you can follow them together, since no speaking is involved, or you can take turns reading them aloud.

THE EXERCISE

Part 1

One of you will lie down and your partner will sit by your head and say the following, allowing about two minutes or so for each response.

Tell me from your childhood about a very young boy.
Tell me from your childhood about an old lady.
Tell me from your childhood about your favorite foods.

Tell me from your childhood about a much loved or hated teacher.
Tell me from your childhood about eating an ice cream cone.
Tell me from your childhood about your bedroom as a child.
Tell me from your childhood about climbing a tree.
Tell me from your childhood what you ate for breakfast.
Tell me from your childhood about a pair of shoes you wore.
Tell me from your childhood about a family trip.

Now reverse roles so that the person who was lying down will ask the questions and the one who was sitting will lie down and respond to these suggestions.

Tell me from your childhood about a balloon.
Tell me from your childhood about going to the store.
Tell me from your childhood about going to the beach or playing in water.
Tell me from your childhood about songs you sang or heard. Sing one of these songs now.
Tell me from your childhood about a birthday party.
Tell me from your childhood about blowing bubble gum.
Tell me from your childhood about a very young girl.
Tell me from your childhood about an old man.
Tell me from your childhood about interesting smells that you remember.
Tell me from your childhood about a character from radio, TV, or the movies.

Now stand up and see how you feel. How does your body feel? Your head?

Part 2

Now sit down and close your eyes. Without speaking, but as vividly as you can, for one minute do the following:

Remember getting up this morning.
Remember what you were doing at this time yesterday.
Remember your high school graduation or its equivalent.
Remember, if you are old enough, hearing about John F. Kennedy's assassination.
Remember some event from last summer.
Remember the first time you fell in love.
Remember your first day at school.
Remember the last time you went to the grocery store.
Remember your earliest memory.
Remember ten years *from now*.
Remember the signing of the Declaration of Independence.

Remember Abraham Lincoln delivering the Gettysburg Address.

Remember William Shakespeare watching a performance of *Hamlet* at the Globe Theatre.

Remember Leonardo da Vinci painting the *Mona Lisa*.

Remember Joan of Arc leading the armies of France.

Remember King Arthur and the Knights of the Round Table.

Remember Cleopatra floating down the Nile in her perfumed golden barge.

Remember the crucifixion of Jesus of Nazareth.

Remember the building of the Great Wall of China.

Remember the building of the great pyramids in Egypt.

Remember early man hunting the wooly mastodon.

Remember the giant dinosaurs dragging their huge bodies across the swampy marshes millions of years ago.

Remember the creation of the earth.

Remember the creation of the universe.

Remember a million years from now.

Remember yourself totally at this present moment.

Open your eyes and share your experiences.

DISCUSSION

For many people, the first part of this exercise evokes a sense of light-headedness, buzzing, an "expanded" head, a sense of many lights going on in the brain. These are physically felt metaphors which correspond to the stimulation that has just occurred.

For most, the relating of childhood memories causes these memories to become clearer and more abundant. As you begin to recall them with all your senses, they in turn trigger the further remembering of related memories. For some, immediately following the exercise and for some hours thereafter, sensory perceptions will have a greater clarity and fresh-ness not unlike the sensory acuity you knew as a child. This is because the exercise serves to prime childhood sensations and perceptions as well as memories. We seem to gain access to some of the uncensored neural strategies of childhood. The lid's off, as it were.

In the next part of the exercise, which dealt with a broader range of personal memory, the previous priming of childhood memories seems to have the effect of improving memories of things past even though more recent memories may still be vague. With practice, however, even yester-day's grocery list offers itself for review, present and accounted for, if often uninspired.

The eliciting of imaginative historical memories is often experienced with as much liveliness and realism as the recall of personal memories. This does not mean that "you are there" with Cleopatra on her royal barge or that you have hooked into some memory trace of Joan of Arc recorded in the collective unconscious of the human species, but rather that all the things you have learned, seen, or imagined have also been imaginally primed by the activation of stored imagery that occurs in the priming of the memory banks.

As for the remembering of the future, why not? If nothing else, it is the stuff out of which novels, music, art, statecraft, and religion are created.

Exercise 2

Recalling the Child

TIME: 45 to 60 minutes

What would it be like if you, like Aldous Huxley or Meredith, at your present age and knowing what you now know, could go back and become the great friend and guide of yourself as a child? Many who have explored this possibility with me report that the child in them seems to respond to this friendship in such a way that makes them feel their past life is enriched, although not necessarily changed. In their present adult state they feel the effects that come from experiencing an enriched earlier life, often feeling stronger, more secure and resilient, more creative, and even beginning to lose some disabling and neurotic behavior that may have started in childhood.

Remember, as you go back in your life to meet the child living within you, to choose to encounter that child at some time when he or she would have been receptive to the arrival of a sympathetic stranger. Very few children are capable of welcoming someone new in the midst of great emotional trauma. Once you and your child have become acquainted and accepting of one another, you can repeat the exercise on other occasions and approach more sensitive areas. You might want to meet your child as he or she goes to school for the first time, or when a tooth is lost, or when your child needs a push on a swing or someone to talk to in the dark.

In the second stage of this exercise you will contact the person you will become in the future, allowing the three of you—yourself now, yourself past, and yourself future—to experience the renewal that is inherent in this meeting. As you saw in the previous exercise of applying active imagination to memory, it may be possible to go forward in time as well as backward. If we hold this perspective, future selves may be both willing and able to nurture and redeem our present existence. Certainly modern physics has suggested that time is not linear but rather is an omnipresent dimension of reality, and that it is only our experiential limitations which keep us locked into a serial view of this dimension.

PREPARATION

This exercise is best done with one person serving as a guide and reading the instructions. The guide will need a drum or gong to mark the passage across time. If this is not possible, the instructions and the drumming can be put on a tape.

THE EXERCISE

Stage One: Befriending Yourself as a Child

Sitting with your eyes closed, breathe deeply, following your breath in and out. For this exercise act *as if* the following were true: that there still exists in your being yourself as a child, a child who does not know that in some other time frame of its existence it has grown up.

As the drum (or gong) sounds, call upon this child to come forward from wherever it exists. You might even want to open your right hand so that it can be reached by your child. The child, who was yourself, may appear during the sounding of the drum or gong or it may appear at the ending of the sounds. In either case, as soon as you feel your child to be present, be attentive to the child. Some will want to do this with the active imagination, others will actually rock the child or walk around with it, and be very active during this exercise. Find the way that seems appropriate for you.

You may find that you actually feel in your right hand a little hand holding yours. Feel the needs and personality of this child. Hold your child in your arms if the child is willing. Talk with your child. Walk with it. Take it, if you like, to some place like the circus or the beach or the zoo, or let it take you somewhere. Play with this child who was you. Give it love, friendship, nurturing, and allow yourself to receive from the child, who may actually have as much if not more to offer you than you have to offer it. You have fifteen minutes to begin the friendship with yourself as a child.

If you go outside, you will be called back by the ringing of a bell.

The guide will then beat a drum or gong slowly thirty to sixty times.

At this point, depending on whether or not you want to go on to the next sequence in this exercise, you can do one of several things. If the exercise has been done in a group, you can meet with one or two others in a small circle, each of you with your child so that adults and "children" share their experiences. Allow your child to talk and act through you as well as sharing from your own mature consciousness. In this kind of group sharing, the reality of the child is honored and so becomes clearer.

If you are doing this alone, make something with your child—a drawing or clay figure or poem—that will serve to remind you of this meeting and what you have learned. Work with your child as partner in this process.

When this process has been completed, you can tell your child goodbye, assuring it that you will come back and visit often if you plan to do so. If you choose to go on to the next sequence, in which you are befriended by your extended self, tell the child you will call it back in a few minutes.

Stage Two: Becoming Befriended by Your Extended Being

In this next sequence you become as a child to the extended version of yourself. This extended self is the *entelechy* of you—who you would be and could be if your potentials and capacities were fully realized. This High Self is the oak tree of which you at present are still the acorn. We are assuming that in some realm of the psyche this being already exists, just as the child that you were still persists.

Closing your eyes and following the path of your breathing in and out, become aware of the following: Your extended being is about to enter your present reality and be for you as you were for your child. This is the high being of yourself, full of wisdom and grace, free of meanness and pettiness, filled with empowering love, who has multiple ways of knowing, learning, sharing. This is you as Sage, you if you had a hundred more years to consciously work on yourself.

Now, as you hear the sound of the gong or drum, this potential being is becoming real, for it truly is real. This richly extended self is coming to meet you from a dimension beyond space and time.

Sound the gong or drum slowly ten to twenty times.

As this being comes and cares for you, allow yourself to be nourished, empowered and awakened. Let yourself receive and be refined by the gifts that your High Self has for you.

Allow five to ten minutes for this experience.

Guided and cared for, loved, acknowledged, and evoked, call forward the child that was you. Hold the child in your arms, as you are being held by your own extended being. The three of you are now together, a trinity that is a perfect oneness. Let a continuum of love, encouragement, and empowerment flow among the three of you so that the child gives its freshness of vision to the extended one, while he or she quickens the child, and you give to both.

Allow about five minutes for this experience.

Release now the child and the extended self so that they may return to their own place of being, knowing that they can be called into your reality frame whenever needed. Know also that each of these parts of yourself has access to the other, and that this communion and communication is a high practice that must be nourished in order to be known.

Recalling the Child

And coming back now to regular reality, be still for a few minutes as you open your eyes. Reflect upon what has been given to you and what you have given. Sense the extension of yourself flowing through your body as you begin to move around. Share this, if you wish, with another person or by writing in your journal.

DISCUSSION

As I suggested earlier, an extended sense of being is evoked in this exercise. Knowing the living presence of the child within and the promise of the person you are becoming, you are free to draw on these beings, to see the current reality through their eyes and so gain multiple perspectives that still have the integrity of your own experience and your own nature.

While this seems to be true for most people, there is still the possibility of a wide range of individual responses, ranging from poignancy to pathos to falling-out-of-the-chair laughter. One woman who had no memory at all of her father, who had died when she was three, found herself with her two-year-old child being sung to by her father. Others have been surprised to find the great resiliency and strength of their child.

You can extend the power and possibilities of this exercise by allowing your child and your High Self each to have a bit of your day that is theirs, a time in which you might play or listen to music—or pay your bills!—guided by the particular knowing of this being. Some parents and teachers have found that their child within has been most perceptive about the children without, offering helpful advice and insights about the headstrong nine-year-old or tearful adolescent. The High Self provides a different sense of time, putting the drama and trauma, and even the tedium, of the moment into a longer and larger perspective. As these beings become your allies, you extend the horizons of the timebound self.

CHAPTER 5

Nature attains perfection, but man never does. There is a perfect ant, a perfect bee, but man is perpetually unfinished. He is both an unfinished animal and an unfinished man. It is this incurable unfinishedness which sets man apart from other living things for, in the attempt to finish himself, man becomes a creator. Moreover, the incurable unfinishedness keeps man perpetually immature, perpetually capable of learning and growth.

ERIC HOFFER
Reflections on the Human Condition

"There's a quality of frogness that I find lacking in our world today."

5

Awakening Your Evolutionary History

Beyond and within the realms of personal memory are locked the archaic memories of evolution, guiding us with the wisdom of the millennia toward the calling future. Often unintegrated into our conscious verbal awareness, these memories war with conscious intention, baffling and betraying us until we welcome them into conscious partnership. Scripture abounds with quotations reflecting this warfare: "The spirit is willing but the flesh is weak," "The things that I would do, I do not, and that which I do, I would not." The poet's query as to whether we are apes who have learned to talk or angels who have not yet learned to dispense with words is a classical reflection on this state of affairs.

We are all witnesses to the awful daily spectacle of our own bewildering behavior. Why, we wonder, do we overreact to trivia and routinely commit mayhem on the anthills of our life with elephantine trompings and leonine roars? Why, after years of education and the active cultivation of the most urbane and civilized attitudes, do we

Left: Tribal display ritual in New Guinea—two warriors about to fight. *Right:* Two men in cars about to fight.

regress to fanged-lip screechings and fetal crouches upon middling provocation? Surely this is no common garden-variety neurosis but a deep-seated, marrow-born anomaly that comes with the condition of being human.

Clearly, this reminds us that we need a corrective to our own archaic equipment, that physiological equipment we developed tens and even hundreds of thousands of years ago that once was helpful and necessary to our survival but that now, in its atavistic phase, is very harmful and could indeed destroy life on this planet.

Ethnologists have demonstrated extensively that our glandular system as well as our entire autonomic nervous system and the emotion-controlling centers in the midbrain reflect their development at a time when conditions were very much harder than they are now, and when the appropriate responses to the very real dangers in the environment were those of jump, bristle, fight, or run for your life.

Although these conditions have changed, the emergency mechanisms of the sympatho-adrenal system remain, causing our emotional and physiological responses to be grossly overstated, as though nature were indeed hostile and threatening. How often have you been driven to outrage by the smallest provocations, to fierce and unholy fury by simple misunderstandings? For the most part, our deepest expectations have changed very little from those of the distant past: life is hard, stubborn, intractable, to be conquered, manipulated, and, if we are triumphant, to be bent to our will. Reinforced generation after generation with the views of a far-removed age, many of us still feel ourselves as helpless against an impervious fate, our atavistic instincts keeping us robots trained to shoot on sight and to question, if necessary, later.

The pity is we act in such a way that our belief turns our reality into a sophisticated version of life as it was lived fifty thousand years ago. Listen to the nightly news, read the newspapers, watch the catalogues of violence and destruction that are the regular fare of television viewing, and you witness a point of view about the nature of things that was cooked in ancient caves. The possibilities of altruism, of social concern, of humor, of delight, of love are more often than not reflected in the occasional human-interest column or a story in the "women's section," or in the vapid vapors of the sitcoms. Religious traditions have fed this evolutionary estrangement, building elaborate theological edifices upon these great divides. The doctrine of original sin can be seen as early apologia for the split between our modern selves and our original nature, while the story of Adam and Eve and their fall from the unitary consciousness of the Garden is in some sense the tale of leaving the stability and certainty of the older areas of the brain for the proliferating ambiguities and differentiations of the new.

Nor is this doctrine of primordial ineptitude limited to Old and

New Testament writers. In more recent years, a similar ideology has grown in embellishment. From John Calvin to Karl Marx to B. F. Skinner we find the same beleaguered tale of righteous threats, admonitions, inquisitions, and operant conditionings offered as a modus vivendi to lead fallen humanity away from the twin illusions of freedom and dignity. Salvation in every case seems to involve inclusion within the band of the enlightened who have "succeeded" in denying the dark nature of their ancient yearnings.

It is time to become modern, to stop nursing our fossilized thought patterns, which demand as their birthright that life be hard. As life always obliges our expectations, and in the present technological environment could apocalyptically exceed our worst imaginings, we had better grow up very fast. It behooves us to discover a subtler dialectic between ourselves and the world, one that, in Arthur Koestler's words, "rings the bell of man's departure from the rails of instinct . . . signals his rebellion against the single-mindedness of his biological urges, his refusal to remain a creature of habit governed by a single set of 'rules of the game.'"[1]

In the scientific world ethnologists and others have excavated the neurological base of this continuing psychological catastrophe. In drawing attention to the "naked ape" syndrome that reputedly affects so much of our behavior, they have speculated that some of this behavior derives from the fact that much of our brain and nervous system is still deeply committed to the physiological and behavioral matrices of more primitive life forms.

Paul MacLean, chief of the Laboratory of Brain Evolution and Behavior at the National Institute of Mental Health, has, over the last thirty years, developed a model of the brain based on its evolution, which he calls the "triune brain."[2]

As MacLean has shown in his research, the human forebrain has expanded to its present large size and dominance while still keeping the essential neurological and chemical patterns of our reptilian, paleomammalian, and neomammalian ancestry. We bear the tragicomic burden of being the three-brained ones, and our triunity is not unity at all but an uneasy and easily violated truce. Indeed, a form of madness that goes beyond schizophrenia is the natural neurological given of our species. One might call it a kind of evolutionary polyphrenia stemming from the fact that we look at reality through the receptors of three quite different mentalities of different ages and functions, with the two older "brains" lacking the possibility of verbal communication. The striving and territorial protectiveness of the reptile, the nurturing and family orientation of the early mammal, the symbolic and linguistic capacities of the neocortex may multiply our damnation or grace our salvation.

We find, for instance, that the routine and ritually driven behavior

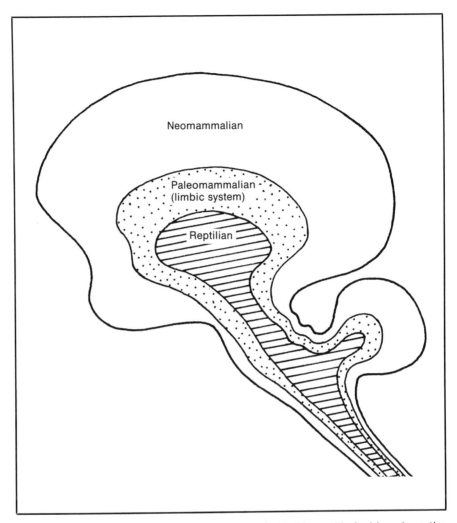

The human forebrain has evolved and expanded in hierarchic fashion along the lines of three basic patterns, which may be characterized as reptilian, paleomammalian (limbic system), and neomammalian (neocortex).

of reptiles and amphibians translates in our human expression into obsessive-compulsive acts and a tiresome devotion to sundry habituations. When you find yourself stuck in the rut of an intractable pattern, blame your reptile. But thank this same reptile if you want to maintain some stability in an ever-changing world.

In our midbrain the battlings and nurturings of mammals as well as their elaborate preparations for partnership and procreation provide the emotional momentum for the development of family, clan, and the early basis of civilization. Yet this same early mammal within each of us is a Trojan horse gifting us with the neurochemical patterns that make for war, aggression, dominance, and alienation.

Finally, there is our neomammalian brain, a Pandora's box of ideas, inventions, and idiosyncrasies—not the least of which is its often tentative and ambiguous relationship to the two earlier brains from which it has sprung. Part a cold, calculating computer, part the home for paradox and a vehicle for transcendence, it is that aspect of ourselves that apportions our fate and determines whether as a species we will grow or die.

Unlike our paleolithic ancestors, we are now, as MacLean has pointed out, the highbrowed ones because of the late evolutionary development of the prefrontal cortex. In the crucial link between the prefrontal lobes of the neomammalian brain and the limbic system of the paleomammalian brain, we are able to look inward, gain insight into the feelings of others, have compassion, reflect upon where we have been, and orchestrate all of these to become what we might be. The development of the prefrontal lobes, with their capacity for empathic understanding, for dreaming of the possible, and their deep connections to our earlier knowings, allows redemption to move beyond its theological metaphor and become the critical fact of our continuing existence.

How can we do this? Several years ago Moshe Feldenkrais and I held a week-long conversation during which we speculated together on the nature of the ontogenetic development of the first thirty-six months of a child's life in the light of the phylogenetic development of mankind from the fish stages to our present condition. Our conversation reinforced and added pragmatic and practical dimensions to MacLean's model of the triune brain.

Feldenkrais has had years of experience observing and analyzing the developmental stages of movement in infants. From this he has proposed that the development and integration of older with newer parts of the brain might be dependent upon the child's being able to recapitulate, within the first three years of life, the critical movements of phylogenetic development. Such a kinesthetic experience would constitute the second time that the developing human had gone through the stages of evolutionary development, since, within the first six months of fetal development, it structurally recapitulates these stages.

We speculated that if the developing human failed to go through any of these evolutionary sequences of movement this would inevitably result in real damage to both body and behavior. It seemed likely that the inhibition of any of these stages would in turn inhibit the making of appropriate connections between one evolutionary level of the brain and another.

The phenomenological evidence suggests that at birth the fish brain is dominant and may account for the infant's early rolling movements. These movements in turn activate growth of the area of the brain that deals with the amphibian and reptile part of development—what MacLean calls the R-complex. At this stage, the child crawls on its belly and gradually coordinates bilateral movements of arms and legs. These movements in turn activate the paleomammalian parts of the brain, and the child begins to crawl on all fours and to demonstrate the emergence of the limbic functions and emotional structures of behavior. The crawling movements in turn activate the neomammalian brain, and the child proceeds to make movements similar to those of the monkey, swinging from side to side and moving limbs crosslaterally. At this time there is also a rapid increase in eye-to-hand coordination as well as an enormous growth in learning and imitative and adaptive behavior. Anyone who has been a close observer of growing children will certainly recognize the emergence of the monkey stage complete with great curiosity, interminable "whys?" and a seemingly unlimited potential for hugging.

Normal development appears to be linked to the full expression of these developmental stages. For example, during the reptilian stage there is an integration of arms and legs as well as of the upper and lower axes of the body. If this is inhibited, there may be damage to sexual development and many other kinds of basic survival behavior. If the child is kept, quite literally, in a harness during the primate phases of development, not only would this interfere with postural growth but there would also be a consequent diminution of curiosity, exploration, skill building, and imitation. MacLean has noted that the autistic child exemplifies "the devastating effects of an inability to imitate." This leads me to wonder whether some autistic behavior could be the result of inhibition of primate behavior and movements in early childhood, an inhibition that could have resulted from social restrictions or neurological immaturity. If so, some autistic behavior might be alleviated by enabling the child to re-experience primal patterns of movement, thus activating the necessary neural mechanisms that would allow for therapeutic development.[3]

As I have suggested throughout this book, we clearly need to go beyond our limited conception of "normal" development if we are to meet the challenges of our time. We must all become conscious co-partners of all that we have been so that we are no longer prey to the inchoate dictates of evolutionary history, able to recognize and embrace our past so that we move into the future with grace and mindfulness.

Exercises in Evolutionary Memory

TIME: 2½ to 3 hours for entire sequence

Feldenkrais has worked directly on the body, using evolutionary movements to facilitate therapeutic functional reintegration. In my own work I have developed the following series of exercises to allow individuals and groups to recapitulate the evolutionary sequence of brain and behavior as well as the corresponding developmental movements of the first three years of life. This can be used both as a therapeutic procedure and as an enhancement of growth and integration.

In doing this series of exercises, you will be incorporating the work of the previous four chapters, integrating body, senses, brain, and memory as you recapitulate these stages. Certainly evolution occurred to the entire organism, and just so did it occur in entire groups of organisms. While these exercises have been done by individuals working alone, they are enormously enhanced by being done with a group; it can be your family, a few friends, a class, or any other kind of group. Evolution was a social and collective event. The more varied the group doing these exercises together, the richer and more complex the experience will be for each participant. The discovery of one person within the group frequently becomes the understanding of the entire culture of the group, and the dynamics played by individual and group in the evolutionary process quickly become apparent.

Several years ago, those who witnessed the spectacle on the lawn of the University of California at Santa Barbara, where a wriggling sea of bodies—three hundred and fifty teachers, professors, physicians, psychiatrists, ministers, nuns, social workers, and other members of the professional establishment—crawled over and under each other in a state of active reptilian regression, stared at one another and me with total disbelief. And yet this scene and similar ones have by now been repeated hundreds of times.

Only the observer seems to experience the disbelief; the participant soon experiences some knowing even deeper than belief as the brain and body begin to respond to these ancient ways of being in the world.

PREPARATION

Ideally, this exercise will be led by a guide who has already done it several times. The guide will read the instructions for each stage to the entire group and adjust the timing to fit the experience of the particular group. The exercise can be put on tape, but this is less satisfactory since the timing is important and varies considerably each time the exercise is done.

This series of exercises is most effective if it is done sequentially with no break, at least initially; the momentum is continuous and the contrast between the beginning and the end more striking.

If you can do this exercise outside on a lawn or beach, so much the better, but it can be done in any fairly large open space where no one and nothing will be hurt by people crawling around. Clear everything out of the way so that there are as few interferences as possible.

Before you begin this exercise, remove your shoes, belt, watch, glasses, jewelry, and anything else that will inhibit or interfere with your old fish and reptilian self.

If you find yourself too exhausted to continue at any particular time, stop the actual movement but continue the same state of consciousness and do the movements kinesthetically. Resume the actual physical movements as soon as possible. Many people have found that although they may become fatigued at one particular stage, they experience renewed energy in the next stage; they report that they feel they are actually tapping into different levels of themselves.

As you do this exercise, note those stages that are particularly comfortable and familiar to you, those where you have the least awareness of knowing what is going on, those where you find the greatest resistance to continuing, and those where you have the greatest energy. When do you begin to feel self-conscious? To be aware of your sexuality? To experience fear? And joy? We will be coming back to this, and the more awareness you can bring to this whole process the richer it will be for you.

The exercise occurs in three stages and altogether takes at least two hours. You are going to be rather uncomfortable trying it with either a full stomach or a full bladder, so bear this in mind in your planning.

In the first stage of the exercise, we will move through seven distinct evolutionary stages, spending five to seven minutes in each. After this, you will share your experience with a partner according to the directions given for that part. Finally, we will repeat the actual movements of each stage, this time bringing a greater degree of consciousness to the whole and focusing attention on the *connections between* the stages, putting in, as deliberately as possible, those patterns of integration.

THE EXERCISE

Begin by sitting on the floor or on a lawn that is free of burrs. Allow enough space around you initially so that you can move freely.

Get as deeply as you can into each evolutionary stage; the more deliberately and fully you give your consciousness over to the movements and sensations, the more complex and precisely authentic these movements will become and the more beneficial you will find this exercise. Remember that neither fish nor reptiles are likely to say "Excuse me" to another member of their species. Speech did not evolve for a very, very long time and we are trying to recover connections to much older parts of the brain.

Stage 1

THE FISH   Lie flat on the floor on your stomach with your arms at either side, and roll gently from side to side. Make sure that your body rolls as a *single unit,* the head and torso and lower body all together. Notice your perceptions as you roll like a fish. How does your world look, feel, sound, smell, taste? Notice your sense of direction . . . of distance . . . of gravity. Continue the rolling movement, knowing that by doing this you are engaging the ancient fish structures of your brain.

Continue this for five to seven minutes.

THE AMPHIBIAN   You are now evolving into an amphibian. Slowly begin to use your forearms to drag the lower part of the body along. Pull with the left and the right together. Notice the greater differentiation of the spine and the activation of the head. As you move in your amphibian being, you are activating the amphibian structures of the brain.

If you happen to find yourself crawling over or under others, know this to be a normal part of amphibian life and continue to pull yourself along. This stage and movement correspond to the period in which you, as an infant, pulled yourself along on your forearms.

If you tire, stop and continue the movements kinesthetically until you are rested enough to continue doing them physically. Allow your mind to be open to the brain's remembrance of amphibian life and experience.

Notice how your senses have changed as an amphibian. How does your reality look now? . . . Sound? . . . Taste? . . . Smell? . . . Feel? What do you desire? . . . And fear?

Continue this for five to seven minutes.

THE REPTILE   Gradually evolve now from an amphibian to a reptile. Although you are still crawling on your belly, you will experience greater movement of your legs, which will be coordinated with your arms, moving first to one side and then the other. As you experience the greater mobility of the reptile, know that you are activating the reptilian structures of your brain and those parts that have to do with your movements as an infant when you started to crawl with all fours on your belly with greater coordination of your arms and legs.

Allow yourself to fully remember being a reptile and notice how your environment seems to be changing. Let these early memories rise to consciousness. If you should become tired, continue the movement with your kinesthetic body for a while before actively performing it again.

Continue this for five to seven minutes.

The fish

The amphibian

The reptile

The early mammal

The early monkey

The great ape

Exercises in Evolutionary Memory

THE EARLY MAMMAL   You will make a radical leap as you evolve into being an early mammal like a lemur. Your belly will rise off the floor as you begin to crawl on all fours. At this stage the early mammal and the growing baby discover that sound can be used deliberately to communicate both pleasure and danger to others of its species. Explore now the sensations of the early mammal. Know that as you are doing this, you are activating the old mammalian structures in your brain. Notice how your head wants to move . . . your shoulders. See how your relationship to others begins to change.

Continue this for five to seven minutes.

THE EARLY MONKEY   Now the early mammal becomes a monkey, leaping and climbing, experiencing a greater lightness in regard to gravity and a greater freedom in the flexibility of the spine and movement of the head and neck. Listen to and make the sounds of the monkey. Notice your increasing playfulness and curiosity.

This corresponds to the period in your life when you began to romp around and occasionally stood erect for a few seconds. Actively explore your world and use your hands to bring things to your mouth and reach for brightly colored objects. Notice the change in your emotional state and the increasing use of your visual field. Know that as you do this you are activating the brain memory and structures that relate to the early monkey. And for this time live as fully as possible the life of the early monkey.

Continue this for five to ten minutes.

THE GREAT APE   The early monkey gradually evolves now into the great ape. The body becomes more massive and there is a development of powerful muscles. Now you can stand erect with ease but will move to all fours for rapid movement. Let yourself become the great ape and make the appropriate movements and gestures and sounds. Again, become aware of the change in your perceptions. How does the world look and smell? Notice your relation to distance and gravity, and to the other apes. These movements and perception are thought to relate to acquiring greater strength and surety of movement and to the ability to maintain balance as you swing from side to side.

Let the memories and muscles and brain structures corresponding to this period of evolution be activated as you enact the movements and experiences of the great ape.

Continue this for five to seven minutes.

THE EARLY HUMAN   Gradually, gradually, you are becoming now the early human being, losing your protective furry covering, standing on your two feet, vulnerable and immensely inventive and adaptable. Know now that this early ancestor of yours was able to master an alien and frequently cold environment, discovering language and art and music and tools. Jaws are thrust forward, and the body fully remembers the ape it has been so recently. And yet there is an ever-increasing intelligence and capacity to plan, driving the early human to move away from the apparent immediacy of animal life into a whole new experience of being alive in the world.

As you fully experience the early human coded within you, both male and female, let your brain be filled with the experiences of the reality that was and is encountered and the challenges that were met and overcome. Know that in doing this your brain is stimulated to remember the early stages of your own development, approximately the period from the twenty-eighth to the thirty-sixth month of your life.

Continue this for five to seven minutes.

THE MODERN HUMAN Gradually, the early human evolves into the human of the late twentieth century. Notice how your senses become more or less refined. How do your movements change? And your questions? And your relationship to people and your environment? Become more aware of the yearnings of the developing and evolving human, wandering and moving into villages, beginning to trade and build cultures, telling stories and discovering the written word, building civilizations, and other civilizations on the ruins of civilizations, using increasingly complex tools and becoming increasingly specialized. Keep going, coming closer and closer to the present era, to yourself, with all the levels of awareness that you possess in this time and space.

This corresponds to your development from the age of three to the present time. Take some minutes to become as aware as possible of yourself in your environment in the present.

Allow seven to ten minutes for this experience.

THE EXTENDED HUMAN BEING Allow yourself now to move fully into the next stage of your own evolution, into the evolving extended human being. Discover—with your body, with movement, with sound, with your voice, with gestures, and with others—what this stage might be like. You may explore this stage with others or alone. Whatever emerges from your exploration is appropriate. If you wish to dance, sing, make music, write, or draw, this is fine. But allow yourself a range of exploration into the nature and beingness of the possible human that is coded within you.

Allow seven to ten minutes for this experience.

Stage 2

Find yourself a partner and lie down on the floor or ground with that partner ear to ear so that your heads are together and you can easily hear one another as you talk softly. Now you will bring conscious verbal reflection to the process you have just been through, with full presence and without

Exercises in Evolutionary Memory

judgment. Do not worry where the memories or images come from—whether from books or films or your own activated evolutionary memory. Just allow these images to rise and express them to your partner as fully as possible, in the following way:

Taking turns, ask one another: "Tell me what you remember about being a fish." The respondent will begin the answer with "I am a fish and I remember . . ." Alternate roles between respondent and asker, always beginning the response with "I am a fish and . . ." Allow about five minutes for this experience.

Now say to each other: "Tell me what you remember about being an amphibian." And the respondent will answer: "I am an amphibian and . . ." Continue this for five minutes, taking turns asking and responding.

Now say to each other: "Tell me what you remember about being a reptile." And the respondent will answer: "I am a reptile and . . ." Continue this for five minutes, taking turns asking and responding.

Now say to each other: "Tell me what you remember about being an early mammal." And the respondent will answer: "I am an early mammal and . . ." Continue this for five minutes, taking turns asking and responding.

Now say to each other: "Tell me what you remember about being an early monkey." And the respondent will answer: "I am an early monkey and . . ." Continue this for five minutes, taking turns asking and responding.

Now say to each other: "Tell me what you remember about being a great ape." And the respondent will answer: "I am a great ape and . . ." Continue this for five minutes, taking turns asking and responding.

Now say to each other: "Tell me what you remember about being an early human." And the respondent will answer: "I am an early human and . . ." Continue this for five minutes, taking turns asking and responding.

Now say to each other: "Tell me what you remember about being a modern human." And the respondent will answer: "I am a modern human and . . ." Continue this for five minutes, taking turns asking and responding.

Now say to each other: "Tell me what you remember about being an evolved human being." And the respondent will answer: "I am an evolved human being and . . ." Continue this for five minutes, taking turns asking and responding.

Stage 3

Without further talking or disruption, you shall recapitulate these stages, using the same movements as in the first part of this exercise, but with the greater consciousness that has resulted from having completed the entire process and shared it with another person.

As you more quickly re-enact these stages, you will focus on the integration of each stage with the previous *stages,* thus putting together what evolution left asunder and consciously making these connections in your brain-mind-bodies.

Begin now by lying again on your stomachs and making the rolling movements of the fish for two minutes. Bring as much awareness as possible to this experience.

Slowly and consciously the fish evolves into the amphibian, gills are replaced by lungs, limbs emerge, you leave the gravity-free field of the water and move onto the land. Be aware of the fish you have been as you enter into the amphibian stage, fully activating the amphibian brain. Do this for two minutes.

The amphibian finds itself more and more at home on an increasingly dry land and evolves into the reptile, acquiring increasing freedom of movement yet remembering the fish and the amphibian that have come before and carrying their strength within. Be now this creature of land patterns, moving warily on arms and legs with your belly low to the ground and remembering the waters that had been your home. Do this for two minutes, consciously building the connections.

The reptile now becomes an early mammal as you begin to crawl on all fours, aware of your young and each other, remembering the fish and the amphibian you have so recently been. Experience the fullness of your early-mammal stage and feel the strength of the fish and reptile within you at the same time. Do this for two minutes.

The early mammal now becomes an early little monkey, feeling its integration with previous stages and reveling in its new freedom and possibility for exploration. Do this for two minutes.

The early monkey gains in stature and strength, evolving into the great ape, yet a great ape that remembers fish, and amphibian, and reptile, and early mammal as well as the little monkey so recently within. Be aware of the new perceptions and the faculties gained and experience them, integrating with the whole of your development. Do this for two minutes.

The great ape now evolves into the early human, bringing with this process all the stages since fish, fully integrating them into the early human. Moving now as early human, experience as actively as you can all this integration taking place and know the world through the perceptions of the early human. Do this for two minutes.

The early human evolves into the contemporary human. This time, however, you are a human being whose humanity encompasses far better connectedness with the developmental stages of your evolutionary process, so that fish, amphibian, reptile, early mammal, little monkey, great ape, and early human being are far more present and available to you than they ever have been before. Also, having just reflected on this with a partner, you have a better understanding of the meaning and possibility of these stages. Be now in the present stage of human development for three minutes, fully aware of having harvested the past that lies within you.

And now you are becoming the extended evolved human being—the one who is the harvester and agent of the evolutionary process. Be now the

Exercises in Evolutionary Memory

emergent and evolved human being. Explore this stage, now fully integrated, in any way you wish—in meditation, creativity, and community. Be now the next stage of human development. Do this for ten minutes.

Coming together now with others—or, if you are doing this alone, stopping to reflect on your new understandings and feelings—share these understandings by talking, writing in a journal, or drawing. What do they mean to you? How do they affect your inner understanding? How do they affect your outer perceptions? What could you now do for and with others that you could not do before?

DISCUSSION

What seems to be happening here? In Part 1 of the exercise you go through a series of movements. To the extent that you are able to quiet the inevitable yackety-yak of the buzzing neocortex and keep your awareness focused in your body, you may become aware of major shifts in sensory awareness, in perspective, in emotional tone.

In Part 2 of the exercise this awareness is made explicit as you consciously reflect on the process. In beginning each statement with "I am . . . ," you are making a conscious identification with these older parts of yourself and acknowledging the connection. This is quite different from saying, "I am a . . ." Try it for a while and you will see what I mean. Doing it with a partner enriches the experience and keeps you from generalizing from your own experience. It also keeps you from getting lazy!

In Part 3 you are bringing this conscious awareness back into the body, reinforcing the body-mind connection. *And,* simultaneously, you are consciously integrating these different stages so that they are no longer discrete events. In so doing, you will recognize that the preparation for each stage is inherent in the stage before. If there is some stage where you found yourself stuck—and this may manifest itself in a number of ways, including fatigue—go back and work on the previous stage, as it is in the previous stage that the development of the later stage is subtly prepared. As you do this, pay close attention to the sensory experience of the particular stage—eating, moving, and eliminating waste. Ask yourself such questions as What does the ground look like, feel like? What part of the body is in contact with the ground? What does the world look like? How far can I see? What is my tongue doing? What do things smell like? What do things taste like? How do I experience darkness and light? What is the nature of time and space? What is seeking to grow within me? What, within me, is not content with this stage? What is trying to change in my spine? What are the new movements that are attempting to create a greater differentiation in the head and neck?

Notice the new understandings and possibilities that are trying to grow within and beyond this stage, and allow yourself, with great awareness, to make the transition to the next stage, recognizing that it has become a question of grow or die, evolve or become extinct, because physically and psychologically you have outgrown the old stage, thrust forward by the evolutionary desire within.

One becomes enormously restless and restricted in the old stage, just as the full-term fetus does in the womb. To successfully complete the emergence into the next stage during this exercise is to accomplish a therapeutic event of considerable consequence.

Each of us has stages that we find particularly pleasurable, and others we find particularly distasteful. There is enormous variation among individuals in this, but very few people seem to choose the modern human as their favorite stage!

After the exercise, people have reported results as various as improved body image and integration; the remediation of certain psychophysical dysfunctions, such as nearsightedness; the acquisition of latent skills and capacities; and the disinhibition of physical, mental, and emotional blocks. Certain individuals will isolate themselves from the rest of the group at different stages. In the process of reflection upon this and other patterns that quickly become apparent, many people experience new insights into their own behavior.

Many feel themselves to be part of the emerging evolutionary process, strongly motivated to go forward as committed and concerned participants now that they have experienced their deep connections with the past. They express themselves as experiencing their spiritual dimension incorporated in a flesh that has become luminous and their physical selves as being the embodiment of their spiritual evolution. Some express a sense of profound integration with the stages of evolutionary development as well as unusual feelings of freedom and structural integration.

In the discussion following the exercise, it is often useful for the guide to initiate with the participants a series of reflections in which they are led to consider the possibility of acquiring the meta-level of each of the earlier stages. For example, what is the genius, or meta-level, of the fish when acquired on the human level? Participants often respond that, by virtue of this exercise, they are able to move in a more open environment. They also perceive a fluidity of opportunity in the various environments in which they now operate.

The question as to the meta-level of the amphibian (a creature in transition from water to land) brings forth responses about gaining the ability to operate "amphibiously" in different contexts and through many different styles of behavior and modality.

The genius of the reptile brings forth the old survival mechanism raised to the level of "stick-to-it-ive-ness." "I feel much more capable of follow-through as a result of having gone through this stage of the exercise," said one participant. Another added, "It is as if I've now gotten a momentum going to accomplish both ordinary and extraordinary tasks,

Exercises in Evolutionary Memory

which I didn't have before. I feel that I don't have to automatically opt for laziness."

The meta-level of the early mammal produces responses having to do with greater abilities to socialize and be gregarious. Sexual behavior becomes operative at this stage, as does the tendency to nurture and care for infants as well as other creatures. Women participants, especially, refer to being able to see their nurturing roles extended to a much larger social base as a result of acquiring the meta-level of this stage.

The genius of the early monkey invariably evokes the sense of high play and curiosity, finding almost everything of interest. The higher monkey gives as its meta-level a sense of power.

The genius of early man is felt as a cornucopia of resources, ranging from the ability to acquire skills and crafts to the capacity to take risks and explore one's reality more widely.

The meta-level of the modern human involves the endeavor to think speculatively as well as concretely and to join the vast resources on one's interior space to the creation of more complex and beautiful forms of manifestation in the external environment.

Finally, the achievement of the extended human is to have access to all of these earlier stages and to become a co-partner in the evolutionary process, able to see infinity in a grain of sand and eternity in an hour.

The experience here is often unitive, mystical, and open to an extraordinary abundance of creative energy. In this stage, one becomes a partner in evolution, the co-trustee of the emerging process on personal, planetary, and cosmic dimensions.

Having led and observed this exercise hundreds of times, I have become aware of constant patterns. Throughout the exercise, there is increasing vertical movement as the human struggles to become erect; one senses the organism reaching for the sun, gaining ever expanding perspectives. The movement of the head becomes increasingly differentiated from the rest of the spine, and the use of the eyes relative to the other senses becomes more and more important until the final stage, when the sensorium seems to be once again fully extended throughout the body.

The various stages, too, have their constants. There is relative silence in the worlds of the fish, the amphibian, and the reptile. The lack of emotional sexuality as we know it makes the inevitable clambering over one another that is a part of these stages a very impersonal experience. With the early mammal there emerges an increasing differentiation of sexual roles and perceptions. With the great ape there is often a struggle between males for the control of the female population—quite reminiscent of a fraternity party! The early human, vulnerable and flexible, wanders around, lost and wary until someone in the group starts tapping a rhythm or begins a chant. Quickly tribes form and the transmission of culture begins.

As increasing evidence from MacLean and others suggests, much of our behavior stems from the preverbal areas of our brain not usually modified by verbal therapies or suggestions. Therefore, it seems that this exercise may begin to reach and integrate these areas, allowing us to have access to these subconscious levels and bring them to the light of consciousness.

All kinds of fascinating material emerges from this exercise as you begin to listen to what people say. One woman misunderstood the instructions and did the entire exercise with her eyes closed. This had the unexpected effect of profoundly changing her sense of time. She had no sense of time past or time future, living always in the particular instant. Her evolution took a very different form from that of the rest of the group. While none of this *proves* anything, it does suggest many provocative areas for exploration.

This is an exercise I always include in a basic workshop of three or more days, and in any advanced workshop, so a number of people have done it several times with me. They report that in the repetition of the exercise there has been a great deepening of understanding; new levels— emotional, symbolic, and physical—appear to make the experience increasingly rich. A subtlety of awareness develops that is often missing from the initial experience. The novelty of the first experience, as well as its global intentions, often masks awareness of the very subtle processes that are actually happening.

EXTENSIONS

Children enjoy this exercise very much, extending it by making masks for each stage and creating skits through which they can share the wisdom and the conflicts inherent at each level. They can choose their favorite stage and act it out. It is a treat to watch the fish trying to escape from the mammal and the early human retreat before the advancing reptile. Adults have been known to enjoy this too.

As you work with this exercise, variations will occur to you. You will also become more aware of your own behavior, noticing when the amphibian starts to take over, or the little monkey. Over time these different aspects of your evolutionary history will become your allies, to be called forth at the appropriate times. Intention and action need no longer be at odds as more of yourself is fully remembered.

Exercises in Evolutionary Memory

CHAPTER **6**

To be alive is to be fortunate, Roderick. Of course, in the morning, when you first awake, it does not always seem so very gay. When you take your hair out of the drawer, and your teeth out of the glass, you are apt to feel a little out of place in this world. Especially if you've just been dreaming that you're a little girl on a pony looking for strawberries in the woods. But all you need to feel the call of life once more is a letter in your mail giving you your schedule for the day—your mending, your shopping, that letter to your grandmother that you never seem to get around to. And so, when you've washed your face in rosewater, and powdered it—not with this awful rice-powder they sell nowadays, which does nothing for the skin, but with a cake of pure white starch—and put on your pins, your rings, your brooches, bracelets, earrings and pearls—in short, when you are dressed for your morning coffee—and have had a good look at yourself—not in the glass, naturally—it lies—but in the side of the brass gong that once belonged to Admiral Courbet—then, Roderick, then you're armed, you're strong, you're ready—you can begin again.

JEAN GIRAUDOUX
The Madwoman of Chaillot

6

The Art of High Practice

There are two Yiddish archetypes that merit a great deal of consideration. The first, and all too familiar, is known as the Nebbish, the exemplar extraordinaire in the encyclopedia of archetypes of the Artist of Low Practice. This universal character type rambles through the byways of our lives like a cow in the middle of the road, stopping the traffic and diverting all the possibilities. There is not even a detour sign.

Although the Nebbish absorbs more psychological energy than any complex or neurosis, never do you find reference to it in psychology textbooks. But then that's typical of the Nebbish. To define its character would be a singular feat, for there is really nothing, or no one, to grab onto. One classic description goes: "When a Nebbish leaves the room you feel as if someone came in." Hapless and ineffectual, the Nebbish falls on its back and breaks its nose.

Many people stay in Nebbish for great chunks of their day-to-day lives, feeding it like a drug habit, coddling this addiction to their own inertia. This involves a willed passivity and a dedication to be in sync with nothing.

An old Yiddish proverb says, "Better ten enemies than one Nebbish." This is unfortunately true, for staying in Nebbish erodes our potential, deranges our human ecology, and saps our hopes. Enemies at least challenge us to hone our survival skills. They provoke our pluck and resourcefulness.

To research the nature of the Nebbish, I have been known to ask large gatherings in a Yiddish accent: "So tell me already, what is it like when you're stuck in Nebbish? Tell me some of the mishegoss statements you make in Nebbish." Here is some scientifically gleaned essence of Nebbish:

"If I tried it wouldn't happen, and if it happened it would cost too much."

"Why go to the movies? If it's any good you can't get in; if they let you in, it's a flop."

"I had all those babies and for what? They just grew up and left."

"Nobody really wants me. It's just that I'm the only one around."

"If I could do what I wanted, I probably wouldn't anyway."

"Don't look back on your life. It's too sad. Don't look forward. It's too horrible. You could die at any minute. Just stay in the now where nothing ever happens anyway."

"I love music but so what. I can't sing."

"So don't learn too much. The less you know about what you're missing the better off you'll be, but probably not. You'll be wondering anyway."

"I think I'll go home and eat cookies."

"They always told me to act as nice as I looked. Now I don't look so good."

"So why are you phoning me? Are you trying to avoid the ironing?"

The Nebbish is not tragic and does not have enough energy for real despair. Rarely does he rise to the pathos and the wisdom that comes of suffering. Swilling in bathos, his hurts have sensuous edges, the ready comfort of complacent hopelessness.

Jolts and crises, the gifting by another, or unexpected grace can sometimes dislodge the habit of Nebbish, but it is persistent. After months of being free of this character, you can awaken one morning to find the Nebbish alive and well, waiting on your doorstep, spaniel eyes drooping, jaws beating on gum, and whining, "I know you don't love me. Nobody does, but I have no other place to go. So would you mind if I rested for a few days in a corner somewhere? I'm such a nothingness you'll never notice I'm there." And in the Nebbish moves like the man who came to dinner.

In 1 million A.D., when all present human characterological types have gone the way of evolution and transmutation, the Nebbish will probably remain along with the cockroach and the termite—mankind's representative of the second law of thermodynamics, the entropy principle incarnate. And all the cathexes and catharses, the abreactions, auditings, and primals, the entire armamentorium of kosher and hokey therapies, not one will uproot the *perennial Nebbish*. There is, however, one thing that will—the laugh.

Let me demonstrate with a little experiment. Put yourself in Nebbish. Slouch. Slump. Hunch your shoulders. Drop your jaws. Let your eyes glaze over. In short, get into whatever position you generally assume when the Nebbish is at home. Think what a pain it is to be holding this book. You're clearly not getting any edification and you're probably ruining your eyes. Soon you will find that your mood and perception will take on a Nebbishy cast and you won't feel so hot, but then why should you? Now, staying in Nebbish, read or have someone read to you (preferably with a Yiddish accent) the following story:

> Hymie is so orthodox. He says the morning prayers; he says the afternoon prayers; he says the evening prayers. All day nothing but pray, pray, pray. So would you believe that nobody wants to marry him? Even to the shadchen (the marriage broker) he goes, but no girl is

interested. Finally the shadchen tells him, "Hymie, look, I'm sorry, but a wife for you we cannot find. Better you get another kind of companion. Better you should get yourself a talking bird."

So Hymie agrees and shops around until he finds a most intelligent parrot. He names the parrot Nathan and gives him a little yarmulke to wear on top of his head feathers. One day as Hymie intones the prayers, Nathan suddenly joins in. A quick study, Nathan is soon saying the prayers along with Hymie in perfect Hebrew. All day Nathan sits on Hymie's shoulder and together they daven and pray. Comes the first big Jewish holiday, Rosh Hashanah, Hymie takes Nathan to the Temple. News of the praying bird has spread. People are skeptical. Up comes Felice Finkelstein saying, "So Hymie, I hear you have a bird that's going to pray."

"That's right," says Hymie, "my bird is very religious and says the prayers perfectly."

"A bird you make soup out of. A bird doesn't pray."

"This bird prays," Hymie insists.

"Ten dollars says your bird won't pray."

"You've got a deal," says Hymie.

Along comes old Meyer, nodding and snuffling, his eyes rheumy from so many hours spent in the study house. "So-o-o, Hymie," he singsongs, "you have a bir-r-d that's supposed to pra-ay?"

"Yes, my parrot Na-than says the pra-yers," says Hymie, singsonging back.

"That's im-poss-ible," says the learned Meyer, "for no-where in the Talmud, not in the Mishna, not in the Halakah, not in the Haggadah, in no commentary, in no commentary upon the commentaries, not in the commentary upon the commentaries upon the commentaries, not even in the three hundred and sixteen debates of the rival schools of Hillel and Shammai is there one single reference to a praying parrot. Therefore it is im-poss-i-ble."

"My bird prays," Hymie insists.

"Twenty-five dollars says your bird doesn't," says the scholar.

"You've got a deal," says Hymie.

All of a sudden everybody wants to bet with Hymie. Before it's time to go into the synagogue, he has made six hundred dollars in bets that Nathan the parrot will pray aloud during the service of Rosh Hashanah.

Inside the synagogue Hymie begins to pray. Nathan, sitting on his shoulder, is silent. Hymie prays louder. Nathan is silent. "So Nathan, pray already," says Hymie.

"Sqwaaaaak!" says Nathan.

Hymie continues the prayers, davening and weaving back and forth. Nathan looks solemn but says nothing.

"So Nathan, please *pray*," says Hymie and pulls at Nathan's tail feathers.

"*Sqwaaaaak!*" says Nathan. "*Sqwaaaaaaak!*" he replies to all of Hymie's requests. "Sqwaaak! Sqwaaaaak!" Nothing but "*sqwaaaaak!*"

Comes sundown, the service is over, and Hymie has lost six hundred dollars. As he leaves the temple he tries to shake Nathan off his shoulder.

"So Nathan, so fly away already," Hymie growls. "Every day for the last six months, every day you've been praying in perfect Hebrew. Today of all days you talk parrot. So leave me already before I turn you into soup."

"So Hymie, so why are you so mad?" Nathan screeches as he struggles to keep his perch, "come Yom Kippur we get five-to-one odds!"

What's happening? Many of you are laughing, and not only laughing, but your posture has changed, your mood is lighter, colors are brighter and the Nebbish has vanished. All this from "the coordinated contraction of fifteen facial muscles in a stereotyped pattern and accompanied by altered breathing." And more, for when we laugh we dramatically alter our existence on the grid of space and time. At the height of laughter the universe is flung into a kaleidoscope of new possibilities. High comedy, and the laughter that ensues, is an evolutionary event. Together they evoke a biological response that drives the organism to higher levels of organization and integration. Laughter is the loaded latency given us by nature as part of our native equipment to break up the stalemates of our lives and urge us on to deeper and more complex forms of knowing.

What Nathan, that Jewish bird, did for us was bring the sacred and the outrageously profane together, causing us in our laughter to live on several planes of existence at once. Previously unconnected matrices of experience were thrown together: the High Holy Days, the sacred temple, a parrot who prays in Hebrew, and the betting world. All these elements put together create the world of the absurd, which is another name for creative instability—which is another name for evolution.

In humor we move away from the world of stale and habitual associations. We part company with the Nebbish and its world of withdrawal and dissociation. The pattern underlying all varieties of humor is bisociative—perceiving a situation or event in two habitually incompatible or unlikely associative contexts. The resulting paradoxical synthesis fools our expectations, unlatches our reason, and we start to notice new connections that surprise, alert, and make reality juicier than it was.

That is why humor and laughter are the kissing cousins of creativity. As Arthur Koestler, a scholar of the creative process, has observed, "The history of science abounds with examples of discoveries greeted with howls of laughter because they seemed to be a marriage of incompatibles . . . until the marriage bore fruit and the alleged incompatibility of the partners turns out to derive from prejudice."[1] The *Aha!* of discovery is next of kin to the *ha ha!* of paradoxical synthesis.

In both, I would suggest, an evolutionary physiology comes quite literally into play. At the height of both laughter and creativity you enjoy a cortical emancipation from the blind urges and ancient dreads of your archaic and conditioned mind. You are again as a little child, withholding judgment and, convulsed with laughter, understanding without formal instruction the topsy-turvy glory of things.

One hundred and eighty degrees removed from the Nebbish on the Yiddish characterological scale is the second great archetype we are going to consider, the Mensch. And what is a Mensch? Here are a few of the responses I have received to that question:

"A Mensch is a full person."

"Golda Meir was a Mensch."

"A Mensch is not a hero. A hero is a one-shot deal while a Mensch is forever."

"A Mensch lives on all levels."

From an eighty-five-year-old Jewish woman: "Mein Mama was a Mensch. Such power, such pizzazz she had you wouldn't believe. But how did she use it? Like an angel already."

"A Mensch loves to take his children to the zoo and doesn't mind doing the income tax."

"A Mensch can give with grace and receive with the same. When a Mensch scrubs the toilet bowl, he's cleaning up the world."

"When a Mensch walks down the street even the sidewalk feels good."

"When you are with a Mensch, you grow a little."

"A Mensch celebrates life."

"A Mensch has leaky margins."

"A Mensch loves to learn, loves to laugh, loves to listen."

"A Mensch knows how to cry."

"A Mensch sees the Mensch in you."

"A Mensch, when the Nebbish comes to the door, tells him a joke."

The Mensch is the human possibility in all of us. Along with laughter, the Mensch is the antidote to Nebbish and deserves at least as much practice. Indeed, the Mensch is the ultimate musician, the Artist of the High Practice. The Mensch is ourselves whenever we go into High Self. And having experienced ourselves as High Self, we are enchanted by the beauty and the wonder of this memory, by this glimpse of the possibility within. While the Nebbish may have enormous survival power, the Mensch, once invited in, is here to stay.

As I have mentioned, the Nebbish can be banished by the gifting of another, by a deep recognition of the dynamic potential hidden beneath posturings and masks. And so we, as the Mensch, have the power to restore to one another the glory of who we are. While learning this lesson was profoundly painful for me at the time, the empowerment and understanding I received at a crucial moment in my life has shaped my teaching and provided the grounding for this book.

The Art of Acknowledgment

I was eighteen years old and I was the golden girl. A junior in college, I was president of the college drama society, a member of the student senate, winner of two off-Broadway critics' awards for acting and directing, director of the class play, and had just turned down an offer to train for the next Olympics. In class my mind raced and dazzled, spinning off facile but "wowing" analogies to the kudos of teachers and classmates. Socially, I was on the top of the heap. My advice was sought, my phone rang constantly, and it seemed that nothing could stop me.

I was the envy of all my friends and I was in a state of galloping chutzpah.

The old Greek tragedies warn us that when hubris rises, nemesis falls. I was no exception to this ancient rule. My universe crashed with great suddenness. It began when three members of my immediate family died. Then a friend whom I loved very much died suddenly of a burst appendix while camping alone in the woods. The scenery of the off-Broadway production fell on my head and I was left almost blind for the next four months. My friends and I parted from each other, they out of embarrassment and I because I didn't think I was worthy. My marks went from being rather good to a D-plus average.

I had so lost confidence in my abilities that I couldn't concentrate on anything or see the connections between things. My memory was a shambles, and within a few months I was placed on probation. All my offices were taken away; public elections were called to fill them. I was asked into the advisor's office and told that I would have to leave the college at the end of the spring term since, clearly, I didn't have the "necessary intelligence to do academic work." When I protested that I had had the "necessary intelligence" during my freshman and sophomore years, I was assured with a sympathetic smile that intellectual decline such as this often happened to young women when "they became interested in other things; it's a matter of hormones, my dear."

Where once I had been vocal and high-spirited in the classroom, I now huddled in my oversized camel's-hair coat in the back of classes, trying to be as nonexistent as possible. At lunch I would lock myself in the green room of the college theater, scene of my former triumphs, eating a sandwich in despondent isolation. Every day brought its defeats and disacknowledgments, and after my previous career I was too proud to ask for help. I felt like Job and called out to God, "Where are the boils?" since that was about all I was missing.

These Jobian fulminations led me to take one last course. It was taught by a young Swiss professor of religion, Dr. Jacob Taubes, and was supposed to be a study of selected books of the Old Testament. It turned out to be largely a discussion of the dialectic between St. Paul and Nietzsche.

Taubes was the most brilliant and exciting teacher I had ever experienced, displaying European academic wizardry such as I had never known. Hegel, gnosticism, structuralism, phenomenology, and the intellectual passions of the Sorbonne cracked the ice of my self-noughting and I began to raise a tentative hand from my huddle in the back of the room and ask an occasional hesitant question. Dr. Taubes would answer with great intensity, and soon I found myself asking more questions.

One day I was making my way across campus to the bus, when I heard Dr. Taubes addressing me: "Miss Houston, let me walk with you. You know, you have a most interesting mind."

"Me? I have a *mind*?"

"Yes, your questions are luminous. Now what do you think *is* the nature of the transvaluation of values in Paul and Nietzsche?"

I felt my mind fall into its usual painful dullness and stammered, "I d-don't know."

"Of course you do!" he insisted. "You couldn't ask the kinds of questions you do without having an unusual grasp of these issues. Now please, once again, what do you think of the transvaluation of values in Paul and Nietzsche? It is important for my reflections that I have your reflections."

"Well," I said, waking up, "if you put it that way, I think . . ."

I was off and running and haven't shut up since.

Dr. Taubes continued to walk me to the bus throughout that term, always challenging me with intellectually vigorous questions. He attended to me. I existed for him in the "realest" of senses, and because I existed for him I began to exist for myself. Within several weeks my eyesight came back, my spirit bloomed, and I became a fairly serious student, whereas before I had been, at best, a bright show-off.

What I acquired from this whole experience was a tragic sense of life, which balanced by previous enthusiasms. I remain deeply grateful for the attention shown me by Dr. Taubes. He acknowledged me when I most needed it. I was empowered in the midst of personal erosion, and my life has been very different for it. I swore to myself then that whenever I came across someone "going under" or in the throes of disacknowledgment, I would try to reach and acknowledge that person as I had been acknowledged.

I would go so far as to say that the greatest of human potentials is the potential of each one of us to empower and acknowledge the other. We all do this throughout our lives, but rarely do we appreciate the power of the empowering that we give to others. To be acknowledged by another, especially during times of confusion, loss, disorientation, disheartenment, is to be given time and place in the sunshine and is, in the metaphor of psychological reality, the solar stimulus for transformation.

The process of healing and growth is immensely quickened when the sun of another's belief is freely given. This gift can be as simple as "Hot dog! Thou art!" Or it can be as total as "I know you. You are God in hiding." Or it can be a look that goes straight to the soul and charges it with meaning.

I have been fortunate to have known several of those the world deems "saints": Teilhard de Chardin, Mother Teresa of Calcutta, Clemmie, an old black woman in Mississippi. To be looked at by these people is to be gifted with the look that engenders. You feel yourself primed at the depths by such seeing. Something so tremendous and yet so subtle wakes up inside that you are able to release the defeats and denigrations of years. If I were to describe it further, I would have to speak of unconditional love joined to a whimsical regarding of you as the cluttered house that hides the holy one.

Saints, you say, but the miracle is that anybody can do it for anybody! Our greatest genius may be the ability to prime the healing and evolutionary circuits of one another.

How tragic, then, that this genius, which has the greatest, most incalculable value, should be relegated through cultural ignorance and neglect to the status of attic memorabilia. We have concentrated on the successful appearance of things to the starvation of the roots of who we are. Our world of appearances is a marvel of technological expertise while our hidden world of meaning droops, languishes, and becomes moribund for lack of attention, lack of acknowledgment. We have unwittingly put a false face on the nature of things and placed a high value on their maintenance. Transient matterings—how much we make, how much we bought, what grade we got, who won—leave us finally as atomized masses, deodorized, sanitized, camouflaged, scented, and sunk in the bamboozlement that if only we could *quantify* happiness (in dollars, degrees, and domains), then surely all the others would know who we really were and there would be an end to heartache.

We have no choice but to leave the places of our psychic disaffection. When we do so we move from an exclusive consideration of quantity to one that includes quality, and from this we move inevitably to a consideration of the nature of meetings.

It is all a matter of the meeting. We spend our lives *not* meeting people. Weeks, months, and years can go by when nothing happens between ourselves and others. This nonhappening exaggerates our longing for a "meaningful relationship" with *the other*. Should "the other" appear, we often closet ourselves together in an intensity that excludes the rest of the world, thus committing and compounding the folly of *the two*. Then there are the static two, living together in closest proximity but as island universes, functioning and maintaining themselves in the home for years on end yet never meeting.

Not having met ourselves, we project our unmet selves upon those we encounter as we also become the screens for the projections of others. We project to others our stale, habituated expectations, so that we have little choice but to "live down" to a tragically limited projection of ourselves. How often have you thought, or perhaps even said to someone you've known for a long time, "Don't tell me what you're going to say. *You* I know. You *couldn't* surprise me. I can predict everything you're going to say. And if you behave differently, I'll *know* something's wrong with you!"

We imprison others in these projections, isolating them in a containment of sameness and stagnation. In our presence they become caught in a nausea of eternal return, with little hope of breaking out of the circularity of our settled expectations.

The marvel of life and its varieties outside the expectations, the élan vital that shapes, spices, calls forth, and gives form to the new, that sees the possibilities of growth in our latency, is cut off at its root for want of fertile soil and friendly sun to receive and give nourishing haven to its tentative gropings. When tender shoots of personal growth are refused the nutrients necessary to their continuance and flowering, they wither and die.

Earth plants, animals of the earth, birds, fish, and creeping, crawling things all need food, shelter from the wild and harsh weather, and a climate that is congenial, or to which adaptation can be made, for the continuance of life. No less than any one of these is the human person. Yet, unacknowledged and made a screen for constricted projections, we become less. People leave home, jobs, friends, spouses, and even life itself to get away from the stale projections and disacknowledgments that are laid upon them and that they in turn lay upon others.

It is an old and dishonorable tale, this mutual incarceration of personhood. Hegel found its historical form grounded in the nature of the negative dialectic of the projections inherent in the social hierarchy, especially in the mutual expectations of the master and the slave. Similarly, other role pairings have inhibited the possibilities of those incarcerated within them: man-woman, white-black, adult-child, governor-governed, priest-congregation, rich-poor, haves-have nots, lover-beloved, ruler-subject, teacher-student, therapist-patient, helper-helped, creator-creature, the All-Perfect God-sinful lowly man. Add your own.

As a consequence of this lack of nourishment, companionship on almost any level or of almost any kind ceases to be sought and is instead scorned because it is misunderstood. It is let go—its treasures disregarded, its provision of infinite life lost to creation. Meaning is destroyed and, in essence, essence is denied.

For all the current political and economic readings of man's difficulties, I suspect that much of history's trauma and turmoil comes from the deep-brewed resentments rising out of the lack of recognition between projecting pairs. Only in those isolated societies where the static traditions of hundreds of thousands of years assure the maintenance of prescribed expectations between people can human existence continue without the major upheavals that occur as a result of a radical demand for acknowledgment. However, virtually all of these "primitive" societies have seasonal rituals and rites of passage in which the sacred is evoked into space and time and in which the people, both individually and as a whole, are congregationalized, renewed, deepened, and acknowledged.

America today is especially prey to the pathologies attendant upon resentment and projection. So much of the American self-image was woven in simpler times when the style of our nation was to see itself as the "first" and the "best" and "*the* goodest." The enormous power we gained after World War II, and the apparent magnanimity with which we used this power (the Marshall Plan, the Peace Corps, foreign aid), reinforced our notion of America as the nation sanctioned by history, and quite possibly by God, to provide leadership and answers in all directions and to all questions.

Again the Greek tragedy: hubris rises, nemesis falls, and we find ourselves compromised in all arenas. It is not the difficulty of obtaining fossil fuels that is the source of our decline. It is our failure to recognize the genius and value of other cultures and peoples. We do not acknowledge them on their own terms. We make short shrift of their potential by immediately investing them with our own. Colonialism, whatever guise it currently wears, is no longer merely a question of subsidies, Coca-Cola, multinational corporations, or teams of experts bearing gifts in aluminum-plated, atomic-powered Trojan horses.

The effect of latter-day colonialism is far more insidious, for it involves now the colonizing of the psyche of those from whom we could learn so much if only we would listen. Instead, we export a very limited psychology, imposing, along with our technology and inherent in it, a rather primitive and extroverted blueprint of what constitutes an adequate human being. The resulting resentment is not just the resentment of the neglected and repressed psyches of peoples and cultures, but may well be the resentment of the planet itself in reaction to our inhibition of the necessary exchange, balance, variety, and cross-fertilization of perspectives so necessary to the maintenance of an evolutionary ecology.

Necessarily we fail, the dollar diminishes, we are no longer taken seriously. We have failed to acknowledge.

The next revolution in humankind will quite possibly not be in the form of contending political and economic ideologies but of a vast planetary and populist movement demanding recognition and real equity between people. The present rise of the transnational religions, of Islam in its present political form as a populist reformation, of Buddhism subtly influencing Western psychologies, of evangelical Christianity—these are the indicators of the rising of the depths and the need to recognize and be recognized in these depths.

It is all a matter of the meeting. We can no longer afford to meet each other so seldom. In human meeting, real exchange and refreshment takes place. Something happens. A door opens. A vitality is given and received and given again. Meaning blooms in the most unlikely places. And this meaning, sudden and unexpected, seems to be part of an autonomous life force in itself, a luminous third aliveness. Some feel it as Presence and call it so—the Holy Spirit, the Goodly Being, the Soul of all quickenings, the One. It renders the partners in the meeting present to all their content, and they discover themselves broadened, deepened, nourished, known. And so the meeting engenders a field of living reality that lights and connects both the core and the corners of our lives.

Quite simply, the meeting invites a larger ecology to enter in and join the relationship. We become larger than the old dialectic of pairs. We know that in harming the other we harm ourselves and the universe, while in acknowledging the other, not just the other but the cosmos grows.

It is an art form that has yet to be learned, for it is based on something never before fully recognized—deep psychological reciprocity, the art and science of mutual transformation. And all the gurus and the masters, all the prophets, profs, and professionals, can do little for us compared to what we could do for each other if we would but be present to the fullness of each other. For there is no answer to anyone's anguished cry of "Why am I here, why am I at all?" except the reply, "Because I am here, because I am."

Exercise 1

The Art of the Mensch

TIME: 30 minutes

Before you enter into the High Practice of the Mensch, let your imagination call forth all the Mensches you have known in your life and, just as you imaged the superb athlete with the kinesthetic body, let their way of being flood into you. In some very real sense, you are giving their qualities life as you fuse them into your own being, subtly seeding the world with the possible human.

PREPARATION

Stand now and stretch. Fully remember the feeling you have had when you have been a Mensch or in the presence of a Mensch. Let this feeling flood your body and grow as you do the exercise.

THE EXERCISE

To the accompaniment of Pachelbel's *Canon in D* or some other Mensch-provoking music, close your eyes, and say to yourself slowly some variation of the following evocation. Feel free to dance or move to this celebration of the Mensch.

I am getting strong and healthier.
A process of rejuvenation is taking place in me.
Any toxins or negative intentions are leaving me as quickly and in as large an amount as is best for me.

I am coming to have more and more freedom.
I am coming to function better and better in all the ways.

I will continue to function better and better as time goes by.

I will use more and more of myself until eventually I'll be able to use a much fuller range of my own potentials.

I am becoming harmonious and whole.

I experience great zest for life.

I am coming to enjoy life more and more.

I will be able to enjoy all kinds of relationships, even those that may be difficult and challenging.

I will be able to take interest in and make something creative out of any kind of challenge.

My senses are becoming more acute.

My brain—my good friend—is functioning better.

My memory is functioning better and I am able to harvest the seeds of my life.

The rhythms of life flow through me, making me more creative, imaginative, wiser, more caring and compassionate and increasingly present both in what I do and what I believe.

Beauty shines through me.

I am becoming more and more able to heal myself and others.

Life flows through me.

I will be able to heal with words.

I will be able to heal with touching.

I will be able to heal by looking.

Healing and becoming whole are a vital part of my being.

I will be able to heal others because I will be able to see myself whole.

Loving, healing, growing, I am moving more and more to that natural and extraordinary way of life that is my own Higher Self.

Great nature, great heart, great soul; I am the microcosm of the universal love, creativity, and mindfulness that is.

I am Mensch.

DISCUSSION

As you continue to work in this book, stay in this state. When you feel the Nebbish knocking at the door, laugh with him or her. This is not to suggest that you become a Pollyanna or a mindless bliss ninny, oblivious to the complexity of the world, for the Mensch knows tragedy and pathos, bitterness and frustration. *And* the Mensch knows the art of High Play.

This is an exercise in the self-fulfilled prophecy, in recognizing and remembering your possibilities and allowing yourself to be open to their development and training. If you proceed through life with the attitude that these things are not possible, then they will not be, and you will have chosen to diminish your own reality and, inevitably, the reality of all that you touch. On the other hand, if you are willing to allow for a greater possibility, you open yourself and others to the creator within.

EXTENSIONS

If you lose your sense of the possible, your sense of Mensch, you can follow the advice followed by William James, who finally fought the profound depression and suicidal tendencies of his youth by acting "as if" a greater reality were possible. Rather than giving in to all the obvious difficulties in a particular situation, he committed himself, as a discipline and as an "experiment," to acting "as if" a desirable outcome might be achieved. In the apparent playfulness of the "as if" attitude, he tapped into deep reservoirs of courage and commitment. This changed his life and allowed him to profoundly enhance the lives of many others, directly and indirectly.[2]

Exercise 2

Dyads of Acknowledgment and Communion

TIME: 45 minutes

This exercise allows two people to acknowledge and empower the essential humanity, the High Self, in each other. Then, joined in this recognition, you traverse the universe together, coming back at last to the totality which is the other.

This is not an exercise in "instant intimacy" or an invasion of the integrity or privacy of the person in any way. Here the personal particulars are, for this time, laid aside so that there may be a meeting at a deeper level. Whether your partner is a daily intimate or a total "stranger" is no longer relevant. In either case, habituated expectations can be safely dropped.

Such a dropping of masks and persona is unfamiliar to most of us, and so you may experience momentary anxiety. Savor this discomfort for a bit, as it is an indicator that you are embarking on a new experience—and call forth the Mensch within.

When you look into the eyes of another person, you are indeed looking directly into the brain of that person, for the pupil of the eye provides unshuttered access to that mystery. Allow yourself, therefore, to experience this mystery with awe and wonder, freed of the habituated training of social discourse.

You can do this exercise with another person or in a group that will be divided into couples. Ironically, this exercise can be more difficult with someone you know well, as we all have established ways for avoiding real meeting. Ultimately, however, this is the most rewarding, because once those patterns are dropped and each is truly and deeply empowered by the other, any old patterns that had become shackles tend to dissolve.

The first few times you do this exercise you will need a guide or a tape recording of the instructions.

PREPARATION

At the end of this exercise you will need some music. Baroque adagio movements are especially suitable, as is, of course, the Pachelbel *Canon in D,* or you can make your own selection.

Choose a partner and sit facing each other, touching fingertips lightly. Close your eyes and make yourselves as comfortable as possible. If you want to change your position during the exercise, feel free to do so, but try to keep your fingertips together.

THE EXERCISE

Put your consciousness now into that point of contact between the two of you at the fingertips . . . all of your consciousness there in the fingertips. Breathe deeply and rhythmically, with your total awareness focused in the fingertips.

At first you will feel heat, muscular sensations, and the pulse of life. Keep your consciousness there at the point of contact . . . feeling the flow of life, the electrical flow of life from your fingers to your partner's, and from your partner's fingers to you.

Just feel the flow of life, the energy flow from one to the other, so that after a while you no longer really know where your fingers leave off and where your partner's begin.

Continue this for two minutes.

In a moment, but not yet, open your eyes and receive the eyes of your partner. What you will be receiving will not be the everyday person, not John Jones or Susan Smith, but rather the essential humanity residing there in the other. You will receive the Eternal Human who is there in your partner and you will be so received.

Continue to keep your fingertips together and feel the flow of life. Now, open your eyes and, without speaking, receive the universal humanity of

the other, the High Self who is there to be recognized and know that you are being similarly recognized. Now open your eyes and receive.
Continue this for two or three minutes.

Now close your eyes and, continuing to keep your fingertips together, feel the flow of life between you as the circuits of an extended being. Together—plugged in, as it were—you are extended and amplified. You have become together a powerful receiving station, an antenna on reality. Together now receive all the things going on in this room right now—all the sounds, breezes, emotions, feelings, thoughts, moods present in the room passing through the antenna which is the two of you.
Continue this for one or two minutes.

Become now receiving stations for the entire neighborhood—receiving the reality happening throughout the place.
Continue this for thirty seconds to one minute.

You are antennas now on this entire region, receiving now the total reality of this country.
Continue this for thirty seconds to one minute.

Receive now together the sights and sounds and feelings and anguish and pleasure and pain and thoughts flowing through the life stream of the western hemisphere.
Continue this for one minute.

Together now tune in to the planet Earth.
Continue this for one minute.

And now you are receiving stations on everything that is happening in the solar system.
Continue this for thirty seconds to one minute.

You have become antennas on this particular spiral turn of our galaxy, receiving together this corner of the galaxy.
Continue this for thirty seconds.

Receive now the galaxy, the galaxy passing through you.
Continue this for one minute.

Together, receive now the universe.
Continue this for one minute.

Receive now the mind of God.
Continue this for one or two minutes.

Dyads of Acknowledgment

In a moment, but not yet, I will ask you to open your eyes and receive your partner. But this time you will receive the everyday self of the other, the eternal, universal humanity that resides in the other, and also the other as the repository for All that is, that other who has traveled with you to the limits of reality, and who in some sense contains that reality.

Now open your eyes and receive that All, knowing that you are also being so received. Open now and receive.

Continue this for two minutes.

Now, close your eyes and bring your foreheads together. Let a deep acknowledgment of one another quietly pass between you—a feeling-blessing of celebration: Thou Art! Let the mutual blessing and empowering flow between you.

Continue this for one minute.

Now, drawing your heads back and opening your eyes, let the same things you have sent to the other be sent through your eyes.

Continue this for thirty seconds.

If you are doing this in a group: Quickly and quietly, holding your partner's hand, join with other dyads to form circles of four or six people. Sitting as a circle together holding hands, close your eyes and sense the flow of humanity around the circle.

If there are only two people: Take your partner's hands and move into a comfortable position together.

Start the music. As you hear this music, let yourself flow and unite with the confluence of beauty that is the universal humanity in which we all become One.

After three or four minutes, open your eyes and acknowledge with your eyes alone the High Being, the Universal Self, in the other or others.

When the music ends, stay in your circles or with your partner and share together what you have experienced.

DISCUSSION

Reactions to this exercise are often profound and moving. Once you have met another at this level, you will continue to do so and be empowered to empower others. It is as though a door that may have been hidden before is permanently opened and you are free to meet and be met by the other, whether the other is a student huddled in the back of your class, a dying parent, or a casual acquaintance.

CHAPTER 7

Whenever we refuse to be knocked off our feet (either violently or gently) by some telling new conception precipitated from the depths of our imagination by the impact of an ageless symbol, we are cheating ourselves of the fruit of an encounter with the wisdom of the millenniums.

HEINRICH ZIMMER
The King and the Corpse

Creative Realms

The Creative Realms of Inner Space and Time

To restore the balance of nature between inner and outer worlds and to evoke the creator within, we must cultivate the vast untapped resources of the psyche. The key to the depths lies in the world of imagery—in the development and understanding of *inner* space and *inner* time.

Lewis Carroll recognized this a century ago when his Alice stepped through the looking glass and things got curiouser and curiouser. Who and what she met in the Looking Glass World provided the correctives to the excessive proprieties of the world of Victorian England. In the language of the Jabberwock, the logic of Tweedledum and Tweedledee, and the shrieking of the White Queen, who cries before she pricks her finger so that she will not have to do so afterward, we have a delicious recovery of the Other Side of Things. Culturally determined concepts of time and space stand on their heads only to do the splits and find that they have been incarnated as a Mad Hatter.

Without inscapes, our world, and Alice's, becomes a series of barren and flattened landscapes. The wonder of the land of Alice is that she gives us a marvelously nonsensical visionary anthropology with which to explore the realm of the *non* senses. These are the images of our inward life, whose cavortings, to be productive, must be viewed in their own terms, which defy the reality of outer logic.

We do this by knowing that the human being has a natural capacity to think in images as well as in words. This capacity is very widespread, and perhaps is universal in young children. An emphasis in education and elsewhere upon verbal process inhibits this capacity, but it can be reactivated. In some artists, scientists, mathematicians, and others the inhibition has been less effective. By his own statement, Einstein's most important thought was accomplished with visual and kinesthetic images, not with words and numbers. He described himself in an important letter to the mathematician Jacques Hadamard as someone in whom visual and muscular or kinesthetic thinking was predominant.[1] Similar statements have been forthcoming from other highly creative people. By thinking in images, ideas emerge that are otherwise impossible.

The Process of Imagery

The present state of brain research suggests that thinking in images may involve areas of the brain where the thought process is more passive and receptive, and also more susceptible to patterns, symbolic processes, and constellational constructs. In verbal-linear thinking, for example, the thinking process tends to go 1–2–3–4–5 or a–b–c–d–e, one specific thing following another. So your sequential verbalizer knows that "the ankle bone's connected to the shin bone, the shin bone's connected to the knee bone, the knee bone's connected to the thigh bone," and *hears* the *word* of the Lord. Your imagizer, however, will *see* the *way* of the Lord, and so perceive and conceive of the skeletal frame as a connected, functional whole.

Thus, in imagistic thinking the pattern is more often 1 through 5, 5 through 20, *a* through *m*, *m* through *z*—a patterning of ideas and images gathered up in a simultaneous constellation. And because the brain can process millions of images in microseconds, and images seem to have their own subjective time not related to serial clock time, a great deal can be experienced in imagistic thinking in shorter times and in ways that evidently cannot occur in verbal thinking. It is also important to note that whereas verbal thinking is largely bound to left-hemispheric processing and therefore to the left brain's time-specific nature, visual thinking is chiefly a right-hemispheric function, and the right hemisphere is not timebound. For all these reasons—in the dynamic inherent in coded symbolic imagery—more information is likely to be condensed in short time frames. The so-called "creative breakthrough" might then be seen as the manipulation of larger patterns of information that are part of the imaginal, symbolic process. When we look at the phenomenology of high-level creativity, we often note minds engaged in imagistic thinking, racing over many alternatives, picking, choosing, discarding, synthesizing, sometimes doing the work of several months in a few minutes.

Many children are natural visualizers; indeed, some are much more geared to visual thinking than to verbal thinking. Many of these children are cut off from their visualizing capacity by the verbal-linear processes imposed on them by the educational system. Such children may subsequently do poorly in school and suffer a sense of inferiority. Bright and talented as they may naturally be, they quickly lose a sense for their own capacities and intelligence, not only in school and among their peers but throughout their lives. The strong emphasis on verbal-linear processes appears to have grown out of the medieval scholastic system of educating clerics in such a way as to weed out the high-sensory types from the more austere students given to conceptual, verbal thought (who would be less trouble in the monastery). This was fine for medieval Catholicism, but its long arm is still felt in modern education to the detriment of the many natural nonverbal thinkers.

Take, for example, the case of Billy. About twelve years ago, I kept getting letters and phone calls from a woman who *insisted* that I address a women's club in northern Michigan. The lecture had to be on one of the days I was teaching college, and the other circumstances surrounding the event were similarly unpersuasive.

Still, the woman persisted, until finally I went. After my lecture she took me to her home for tea and cake. As we entered her living room, she indicated that I was not to sit there but to follow her to the basement. This was a little strange, but I made my way down the almost perpendicular wooden steps and stumbled into a room filled with . . . very peculiar machines. At least they looked like machines. When the reticent little boy who showed them to me threw switches it seemed that Rube Goldberg was alive and well and living in a basement in northern Michigan. Water ran down chutes, throwing Ping-Pong balls into sockets, which caused bells to ring and a miniature pig to spin, turning an alligator's head in which you stuck your pencil to be sharpened. Other machines did practical things in similarly innovative ways.

"Who made these?" I asked, marveling at their wild originality.

"Me," said the boy, and looked away.

I turned to his mother and exclaimed, "You must be very happy having such a brilliant kid."

"Well, I'm happy," she said, "and I'm glad you are. But teachers are *not*. Billy is flunking out of school."

"How is that possible?" I sputtered.

"Well, I'm glad you asked that, Miss Houston," she said, smiling, with a note of triumph. "You thought I brought you here just to speak to my ladies' club."

"No, Madam," I demurred. "I was beginning to suspect that you did not."

"Well, you're right," she said. "I've been making quite a study of Billy and the way he thinks. And I *know* that there are thousands of other children like him who are being labeled as unintelligent, and are made to feel worthless in school. And I *know* that if we can get our act together and make the proper scientific studies there are wonderful things we can do at home and in the schools to encourage and develop people like Billy. That's why you're here."

"How do we start?" I asked, knowing that this lady had a lot of good ideas.

"Let me show you something," she said, pulling a tape measure, a pad, and a pencil from a drawer. "Now, Billy, you know how you learned in school last week how to figure out the area of a room?"

"Oh, Ma, do I have to?"

"Yes, Billy, now you go ahead and do it."

Billy made the measurements, clenched his jaws, and started figuring with pad and pencil. After many erasures, he sulkingly handed his mother the answer. It was an area about the size of a football field.

"Now, Billy, do it your own way," she advised him.

Billy grinned, shut his eyes, and made little rhythmic movements with his head, as if he were listening to an inner song. After a while he jotted down something on the pad, closed his eyes for some more internal business, opened them, jotted something else down, and gave us the correct answer.

By this time I was on to him. "Billy, what were you doing when you closed your eyes? Were you thinking in pictures?"

"Yes," he nodded, "but it's other stuff too."

"What kinds of stuff?" I asked.

"Well, when I close my eyes to figure something out, it's like a cross between music and architecture."

"That does it!" I exclaimed, and called up Sister Margaret Mary, head of the philosophy department at Marymount College, where I was then teaching. The good sister agreed to teach my courses in existentialism and Whitehead for the next week while I pursued the case of Billy. (It was wonderful teaching in women's Catholic colleges in the 1960s. The nuns had just leaped out of the fourteenth century and were heading faster than anyone into the twenty-first. They were enormously supportive of all my experiments and investigations.)

I took Billy to the testing department of a nearby university and had him given a standard IQ test. He didn't do very well. He tested at about 85, which is below normal intelligence. Then I told him we would take another test—but this time he was to use his imagery and musical thinking to answer the test questions.

"It's not allowed," he complained.

"I'm the one giving the tests, Billy, and I say that it is."

"Okay, but you've got to change the way the test is given," he said. "You'll have to ask those questions so I can answer them by doing the special kind of stuff I do in my head."

"Then you'll have to help me, Billy," I responded. "We'll have to redesign the test together."

And that's just what we did. Together we took each question and wherever possible translated it into a visual form and even sometimes into "a cross between music and architecture."

It was an extraordinary experience. Here was a child, deemed below normal by the standard intelligence test, rewriting and reconceptualizing this test and then, more often than not, giving the correct answer to the questions where previously he had failed. Even when he scored a wrong answer, his responses were unusually creative, and on some more enlightened test would have been acknowledged for their brilliance and originality. As it was, he tested at an intelligence quotient of 135, fifty points higher than his previous score.

So absorbed was I in this remarkable process, so boggled before the event I was witnessing and helping to elicit, that I have no clear memory of the specifics of what we actually did. All I can assure the reader is that I never prompted him; indeed, he prompted me, helping me to look at a question in an entirely different way. The baffled psychologist who scored both of Billy's tests said it was unique in his experience.

Armed with *truth*, armed with *scripture*—the IQ score—I showed up in Billy's classes the next day, pulling behind me some wagons filled with his inventions. I had Billy show his teachers how his inventions worked (they had never seen them or known that he did anything like that). When they were properly astonished, I brought out his IQ score.

"IQ scores," they exclaimed. "Then it must be true."

"Of course," I said, looking heavenward.

For the next week I stayed at the school, working with the teachers to figure out ways of presenting information and questions to children like Billy so that their special styles of imagistic thinking could be encouraged. Billy offered many brilliant suggestions on how we could do this, and the teachers agreed to incorporate these methods into their classrooms, not just for Billy's sake but also for the sake of other children like Billy. Out of the five teachers who taught Billy, all but one consented to go along with this program. The one who refused said it was "so much baloney," and he had never heard of visual thinking in his Master's degree program in education. I'm sure he hadn't.

We explored other related areas. For example, after encouraging a child like Billy to use his own innate style of thinking, how then to build bridges in the child's mind between his visual modality—in which he felt strong and confident—and the orthodox verbal modality so that he would ultimately be able to think in both images and words?

I kept up with Billy's progress and, as his mother noted, he moved within the year from flunking out to a B average. Just as important was the fact that he ceased to be the withdrawn, almost autistic child he had been before and became much more outgoing and involved with school and friends. As of this writing he is twenty-four years old and is well on the way to becoming a brilliant design engineer and inventor. Interestingly enough, during most of junior high and high school, his grades never rose above a B average because, he said, the test questions only allowed for limited answers. In multiple-choice questions, especially where he had to answer *a* or *b* or *c* or *d* or *e*, he would often answer *f* and give reasons why he saw possibilities for a much more complex and interesting answer. Teachers sighed and marked him down.

Billy's case is legion. He is an extreme example, of course, for by the age of twelve he was a highly developed visual thinker. But there are so many children whose natural dominance is toward visual or kinesthetic or even auditory thinking and who are penalized because of brain dominance. How many thinkers and creative spirits are wasted, how much brain power goes down the drain because of our archaic, insular notions of brain and education? The numbers are undoubtedly horrendous. But what happens when a child is encouraged to pursue his or her own mind style? Margaret Mead, for example, frequently thought in images. In her unschooled childhood, imagery was natural and normal. As she once told me, "You moved from watching clouds and seeing images in them to closing your eyes and seeing images without clouds." Stimulated by memorizing vivid poems, she soon began to use imagery to solve problems as well as to entertain herself. Here, for example, is a sequence she related to me as it unfolded before her closed eyes. She was thinking about women's occupations in preparation for a paper she had to write.

> I see women bending over, winnowing in the rice fields, women carrying burdens, women following the plow, women driving tractors in World War II, and then men looking down from the plane, seeing that the lines weren't quite straight, which was one of the things men used to say they saw when they looked down. . . . I think about the Benitez family in the Philippines, the enormous house where they lived and where they started the first women's college in Asia—and what the consequences were of Helen Benitez having perpetuated an interest in home economics that had status in the Philippines when it didn't have status anywhere else. And there was a paradigm in this. I see a girl who is working on the History of Nursing in the Philippines, and that goes off into an image of a mother superior bringing in a great bowl of soup in a Paris hospital, and the fight between her and the secular doctors because they objected to her kind of nutrition and to her feeding the people. And the image of hospitals in Algiers, where prostitutes were the only people who would take care of the sick; and horrible images that are rather like Hogarth's drawings of the hospitals in England, where there were only prostitutes to care for them after the nuns were thrown out. This intervenes with some pictures of closing the monasteries, and the nuns and brothers disappearing and the churches being completely silent and the monasteries being empty. And then coming back to Florence Nightingale with a lamp. . . .

Most people doing this kind of experiment allow their minds to wander all over the place. With Margaret, the experienced visualizer, this was rarely the case. She stuck to the point, even in the interior world. The images are organic but organized, providing a coherent flow of memories, ideas, contexts, metaphors, and information that can then be fed into a paper or the solution of a problem. In this way, and utilizing multiple styles of thinking, she could enrich the scientific, objective data that most concerned her.

It is significant that Margaret Mead, an exacting scientist, employed such potentials in discovering new things. By the use of vivid daydreams and imagistic thinking she would explore alternative scenarios to problems and programs. She might begin by thinking, "If this should happen, what would follow?" She would then sit back and watch the images and the story unfold in her head, a very effective technique in eliciting the creative process.

The one fairly large-scale effort to preserve the imaging capacity of children was the experiment of the Jaensch brothers in special schools in Marburg in the 1920s; the results were most encouraging. Children taught to use the image-thought process were, by the time they reached their teens, more creative and better able to draw. Also, they scored higher on intelligence tests than comparable children whose imagery was allowed to meet the usual fate of atrophy and inhibition imposed by educational processes too oriented to the verbal.[2] In our own programs with participating schools, we are able to prevent the inhibition of this faculty in children by allowing education to be a training in images as well as in words. We are also able to effect a disinhibition in adults so that they have access alternatively to both verbal and visual thought processes. This results in the ability to consider more alternatives and solutions, and, in general, to think more creatively. Depth levels of patterning and information become available because imagistic thinking leads inevitably to dimensions of the imaginal and archetypal realms.

Activating Imagery

In our laboratory we have been able to facilitate access to the imagery process through a variety of means by using both instrumentation and methods involving induced or self-induced altered states of consciousness. Imagery can be stimulated by activating ideoretinal patterns with stroboscopic light, allowing the subject to see the form-constants of his or her own eidetic perceptions.

A sensory-deprivation chamber allowed us to study the image-making processes because subjects, deprived of visual and auditory reference points, began to hallucinate and project their own internal visual and auditory structures. We also created audiovisual overload chambers, which had the effect of stimulating imagery centers in the brain; after a while the subjects entered into an unconscious partnership with the forms and colors flowing in front of them and began to project onto the screen their own previously internal imagery. At this point, the subject might shut his or her eyes and discover that the "show" was continuing in the form of eidetic imagery seen with the eyes closed.[3]

We once developed an instrument to facilitate basic research into visual imagery that won us a certain notoriety. The Altered States of Consciousness Induction Device—ASCID—was suggested by our study of historical accounts of a variety of devices said to have been employed by "witches" for the purpose of traveling to the "witches sabbath." From these accounts we surmised that individuals employing the device experienced altered-states-of-consciousness phenomena and especially vivid visual imagery, as well as imagery in other sensory modalities. These instruments, typically referred to as "witches' cradles," differ in varying degrees, but all include the feature of an immobilized person moving within a kind of pendulumlike supporting enclosure. The ASCID is essentially a metal swing or pendulum in which the research subject stands upright, supported by broad bands of canvas and wearing blindfold goggles. This pendulum, hanging from a metallic frame, moves the subject forward and backward, side to side, and in rotating motions generated by involuntary movements of the subject's body.

The vestibular system of the subjects is affected (a condition known by tribal shamans and NASA technicians to induce altered states of consciousness) and they tend to lose their spatial as well as their temporal referents, experience some somatopsychic dissociation, and gradually (in anywhere from about two to twenty minutes) enter a trancelike state in which a wide variety of phenomena occur. Typically, many subjects feel as though they are flying through whorls, vortices, and mists. The mists then take on coloration and gradually dissolve, and the subjects find themselves in a world of their own internal imagery that is not just visually seen behind their closed eyes but is also subjectively felt in other sensory modalities, so that the inner realm is heard, touched, or even tasted. Often, the imagery is initially regressive— scenes of childhood or other early memories may be vividly experienced. ("Why, here I am at my fifth birthday party. And there's Dukie, and Susie, and there's Mary Ellen. Hi, Mary Ellen! Whatcha bring me?")

Frequently, the subjects then move into a realm that could be described as employing a kind of visionary anthropology (not unlike

Alice's), experiencing subjective realities in which detailed fantasies unfold: fairy-tale kinds of narratives, myths, archetypal figures, visits to "other worlds" and to "other dimensions" and similar science-fiction-like schema ("I am traveling at enormous speeds to the other end of the galaxy. I arrive at a planet where everything is made up of iridescent cubes of intelligence . . .").

Sometimes, religious and mystical experiences have occurred in these undirected ASCID experiences. As an example of a very largely undirected and mythic-religious type of experience, a young college graduate experienced herself as dying and then being reborn as the mythic Prometheus. After "an eternity of death," she experienced "a tremendous cosmic life force entering my body through the feet. . . . The force then traveled up my body. I had superhuman strength and powers and experienced myself as the mythic Prometheus. I was chained to the side of a rock on a mountain. The chains did not bother me because I knew I had the strength to free myself at will." She then had the powerfully emotional experience of bringing fire to mankind and to various individuals, in each case the fire being symbolic of a gift of great importance to the respective persons. With each gift, she felt a more and more intense personal fulfillment, culminating in an experience of being "in an active connection with the harmony and unity of nature and the cosmos through a force I guess you'd call love."

The subject's experiences—which may also be guided—have demonstrated possibilities of problem solving and varieties of artistic work that have sometimes led us to refer to the device as a "cradle of creativity."

At this point it should be noted that this work with instruments and machines characterized our research in the 1960s and has largely been discontinued. Since 1972 most of our techniques to elicit altered states of consciousness and imagery are verbal, inducing hyperalert states, trance states, and states employing what are essentially "active-imagination" procedures, several of which are described at the end of this chapter.

The question then arises of why we used machines or equipment at all. The answer derived from cultural necessity. We live in a time when many of the ontological and mythic supports of our given reality structure have been demythologized. The moral mandates and structural givens of the "reality" sanctioned by the establishment began to crumble. This crumbling gained momentum in the 1960s, and with it the mythic scaffolding that once assured the acquiescence of person and culture. There is no such thing, however, as a mythopoeic void. Some potent and potentiating newly emergent myths of transformation are standing in the cultural wings. In the interim, we have had the spectacle of a last-ditch remythologizing process occurring in terms of the vistas of a sacramentalized science.

After the successful epiphany of the industrial revolution, many people attached a kind of *mysterium tremendum et fascinans* to the machine. It was a case of the old deus ex machina coming back to haunt us. Thus, in the 1960s we often found that subjects who would not immediately respond to mere humanity and its verbal procedures *would* respond with alacrity to those "sacred machines" when they felt it was the machine that was affecting their consciousness. Once they felt this alteration, it was easier to deliver them from the mechanistic mysta-gogue and reacquaint them with the human element. By the 1970s this kind of fascination had run its course, and subjects were happier with human inductions and evocations.

The remythologizing of the terms of science was brought home to me very curiously one day in 1968 when I said to a class of Catholic college girls: "Tell me, observe your own internal reaction and find out what turns you on. I will give you some words and I want you to discover which ones you automatically respond to." I then said: "Mother of God . . ." No reaction. "Holy Ghost . . ." No reaction. Somebody popped a piece of bubble gum into her mouth. Then I said "DNA . . ." Many girls tensed up. "RNA . . ." Breathing was perceptively faster. "Intergalactic nebulae . . ." A chorus of echoing *Oh wow's* was heard. Such an experiment provided a remarkably accurate index as to where the power of the myth resided. In this case, "oh wow" was the modern liturgical equivalent of "amen." And if you wanted the entire liturgy it would undoubtedly have been *Oh wow, far out!*

Thinking in images is very easy for some people, quite difficult or almost impossible for others. Sensory dominance is the determinant as well as the mode of thinking adopted in childhood. For example, my husband is an extraordinary imager. If I were to say to him, "Bob, close your eyes and tell these people what you see," he might say, "I find myself in ancient Egypt and I am the pharaoh." (He is always the pharaoh, never the serf!) "And they are building the great pyramid to me, Cheops. The falcon God, Horus, comes down and plucks me up to the top of the pyramid, where there is a huge emerald. I enter the emerald and find myself in a world of writhing serpentine forms glowing from within. I enter the eye of the goddess whose temple this is and pass out through the yellow maw of a crocodile basking on the banks of the Nile and . . ." And so it goes, on and on. In seventeen years of marriage we've seldom been to the movies together. He asks, "Why should I go to the movies? All I have to do is close my eyes and it's the greatest movie ever made . . . costs billions!"

As for me, until recently whenever I closed my eyes all I ever saw was the tile on the bathroom floor—and that with cheating by pressing my eyelids! In childhood and throughout all my schooling I was reinforced by teachers for my ready skills as a verbalizer to the point of an almost total inhibition of any visual facility I may have had. Since this culture rewards verbal-linear thinkers, I was fortunate. In a visual culture I might have been considered retarded.

Imagery can be developed, however, in most nonimagizers, although this gets more difficult with age. It takes regular and devoted practice since it literally involves an activation of latent electrochemical circuitry in the brain. You might begin, for example, with a simple observation of your own eidetic after-images by staring at an object for a minute or so and then closing your eyes and trying to continue to see that object. After a while you can begin to direct that object into other internal visual patterns or movements. If you have been looking at a chair, for instance, you can try to put a lion in that chair. (For some reason outrageous imagery is easier to elicit than normal and expected imagery.)

Here is a directed sequence starting with an after-image, which then engages related imagery and is extended to involve kinesthetic and tactile imagery. We find that the more styles of internal imagery we can employ, the easier it becomes to activate visual imagery:

> Begin by looking for a few seconds at a candle flame. Close your eyes and look at the bright after-images. Now see this ball of light you are looking at behind your closed eyes turn into a sunflower with bright yellow petals, a brown seeded center, and a long green stalk. Move closer to the sunflower. Now dive through the center, feeling the rough seeds fall away as you swim through them. Enter now into the heart of the sunflower and find there a golden sun. Swim amidst the bright gases of the sun for a while. Feel the heat all over your body. Now dive deeper into the sun until you find a sunflower. Take one of its seeds and eat it, wishing yourself home. The seed has magic powers, for you open your eyes and find yourself back.

In another technique, you may enter the world of imagery through the sensory modality of hearing. Listening to music—with its capacity to evoke tactile sensations all over the body—you can "bridge" to visual as well as to other imageries in a fusion of senses that enhances each sense. (Exercise 3 in Chapter 2 deals with synesthesia and music.)

A Review of Our Research

Let me now review a few of our findings resulting from our imagery studies with hundreds of subjects.

First, the visual-imagery process appears to be essentially creative, tending to gather meanings and seek out solutions. For example, images observed long enough will cease to be random or disconnected and will organize into symbolic drama, narrative, or problem-solving processes. Fiction and drama could be manifestations of this inherent tendency. We could almost say that if novels didn't exist, the brain would have to invent them. Tantric Buddhist and Sufi spiritual disciplines as well as some of the proliferating image therapies may be indebted to it for their efficacy.

Second, prolonged, vivid narrative imagery, especially if it is repeatedly experienced, increases motivation to do creative work and also sometimes breaks through creative blocks, which may basically be blocks within the imagery process. The old chestnut suggests that genius is composed of 98 percent perspiration and only 2 percent inspiration, a conundrum that still leaves us with the question: Where did all those geniuses get the wherewithal to perspire so much? Could it be that imagistic thinking (a frequent occurrence among geniuses and highly creative persons) is bonded in neurophysiological terms with psychic energizers and hormonal enthusiasts? The state of brain research is still too primitive to answer that one, but phenomenological evidence points in that direction.

Third, there are imagery experiences that, liberating and serving the needs of an entelechy or self-actualizing tendency, not only enhance creative motivation and enable breaking through creative blocks, but also lead to a higher order of creativity as a consequence of maturation and growth that apparently occurs when the entelechy factor is operative.

A Four-Level Typology

Our studies before 1965 with LSD and our later nondrug investigations suggest a four-stage typology of imagery corresponding to a descent into four major levels of the psyche. We termed these the *sensory*, the *recollective-analytic*, the *symbolic*, and the *integral*.

On the most surface level—the *sensory level*—imagery is initially perceived as random color patterns, checkerboards, vortices, and other ideoretinal form constructs. Imagery may then become more specific, with pictures, scenes, and faces, but is disconnected and without any particular meaning.

On the second level of imagery—the *recollective-analytic level*—

the subject begins to explore his or her own psychological inner space. At this stage imagery tends to be more reflective or analytic. Subjects study their past, problems, and potentialities, somewhat as in psychoanalysis. Memories, both verbal and visual, are more than ordinarily accessible, providing a greater quantity of materials with which to work. The visual thought on this level seems to promote a greater concreteness of thought and also a more than usual free flow of imagination and fantasy. Further, the combination of visual thought and its symbolic codings of patterns of information provides considerably more data and variant views of this data to work with, be it for personal reflection or problem solving of any kind.

On the third level—the *symbolic level*—which is deeper than the second and may require prior experience of the second level, there is a development of a rich mythopoeic symbolism, in which one's own life may be seen in terms of guiding patterns or goals, symbolized, as in a myth-making process, so that the concrete symbol can stand for personal life and its context. The development here involves a movement beyond the personal-particular of the second level and toward broadening contexts and more universal formulations. The symbolic images are predominantly historical, legendary, mythical, ritualistic, and archetypal. Subjects may experience a profound and rewarding sense of continuity with evolutionary and historic process. Or they may see images of rituals in which they participate with all their senses and with profound emotion, so that the rite of passage can have the same effect as an actual rite, significantly advancing them toward maturity.

Others may encounter images of the archetypal figures of fairy tales, legends, or myths, and perhaps discover the broad patterns of their own lives as they identify with Prometheus, Parsifal, Oedipus, Faust, Don Juan, or some other figure. Lately, the Wise Old Woman has been emerging with astonishing frequency in the imaginal levels of both male and female subjects and seminar participants, suggesting a profound change in the psychodynamics of the present historical situation. In these mythic and symbolic dramas, too, the sense of participation may be strong as the images emerge in a meaningful and purposive sequence and the symbols appear in undisguised relevance to the person's life and problems.

The granting of reality to a geophysical realm perceived in an altered state of consciousness has an ancient and honorable tradition. The Sufi mystics, for example, speak of the *alam al-mithal* or *mundus imaginalis*, an intermediate universe that is thought to be as ontologically real as the sensory empirical world and the noetic world of the intellect. It exists in a metageography that possesses extension and dimension as well as figure, color, and other features perceived by the senses. However, this world can be experienced only by those who exercise their psychospiritual senses, and through this special form of imaginal knowing gain access to a visionary world that is not unlike the *mundus archetypus* of Carl Jung. There dreamers and visionaries return again and again, extending consciousness and reality at the source level of *gnosis* and creative process, a place where the self moves freely amid archetypes and universals, listening to the pulse and dynamic coding of the transforming patterns of the Dromenon.

Finally, there is the *integral level* of the experience, in which the subject feels a kind of subjective "descent" to a level of awareness apprehended as Essence, Ground of Being, or even God. When experienced, it is felt as an entelechy—a kind of structuring, dynamic energy rising up from the depths and informing and energizing the other three levels. What this four-stage typology suggests is that this energizing fundamental reality (the entelechy) rises first to the third level and there assumes its universal paradigms, reinforcing and invigorating the mythic structures, and then, moving upward, energizes the personal, historical, and psychological structures of the second level, and finally intensifies the sensory levels by cleansing the doors of perception both within and without. The tendency throughout, as in the religious experience, is a flooding into the world at large of this experience, giving the person a sense of new communion and commitment to the social and ecological orders. Thus does the imaginal descent into the ecology of the inner world remythologize and energize the ecology of the outer world.

In such experiences it is possible to traverse the inner realms of ourselves in much the same way as the archaeologist unearths the treasures of the planet's history. The gold of Troy, the mask of Agamemnon, the iconic beauties and mysteries of ancient pantheons, the inscrutable sphynx, the divine bestiary—all are there for the having, but the techniques for the digging and the sifting must be learned. You must gain familiarity in these realms in order to reap their rewards.

Time and Time Again

Critical to these realms is the world of inner time. When we learn to evoke the imagery process and then join this capacity to an ability to excavate the terrains of time, we have the basis for a flowering of the creative process as exuberant as it is unsuspected.

Consider the nature of time. It is one of the greatest of our untapped potentials. We know and explore so little of this world, caught as we are in the tyrannies of clock time, which, truth to tell, is more Euclidian space than time, with the hands of the clock moving in arcs around a circle. And yet there are so many kinds of time. It is not just "a nonspatial continuum in which events occur in irreversible succession from the past through the present to the future." After we leave the periodicities of twenty-four-hour-around-the-day time or the astronomer-measured passages of star time, we enter into the plenum of the temporal kaleidoscope: atomic time, galactic time, relativity time, biological rhythms, body time, being-in-love time, being-in-rage time, wasting time, fear time, anxiety time, pain time, pleasure time (do you have long pains and short pleasures or long pleasures and short pains?), a five-year-old's time, a seventy-five-year-old's time, borning time, dying time, creative time, meditation time, focusing time, timeless time. Ecstasy and terror have their own temporal cadences and, in mystical experience, the categories of time are strained by the tensions of eternity.

Unfortunately, we live in an era in which time has been traumatized by technology and by too much of an involvement by too many in the peculiar time zone of the radical *Now*. The tyranny of clock time and the rule of the machine over the rhythms of our daily life have served to fragment and dissociate the flow of living time and natural rhythms. The times become abstracted from the primary orderings of life. Abstract time becomes a new milieu, a new framework of existence.[4] It is a framework that aids efficiency but brings an accompanying loss of a sense of past and future. With abstraction of space and time, and with the loss of a sense of the stages in any operational process, there is an inevitable loss of a sense of duration. When the rule of life is "no sooner said than done," the whole temporal fabric of existence becomes warped. Warped, too, becomes the necessary lag in duration between wants and the satisfaction of those wants. Recent studies show that over the past twenty years many people, especially adolescents, have become less future-oriented, less able to defer gratification of their wants, indicating a loss of the sense of duration and of the time flow necessary to make critical choices.[5] This may also account for the recent widely noted lessening of people's attention spans. The ultimate negative form of this phenomenon may be in depriving language of meaning and value, since so much of grammatical experience and the logic of language is grounded in the interrelationship of grammar, logic, and duration.[6]

One of the best ways of reclaiming and exploring the powers of time is to begin by reflecting on the extraordinary range and capacities of temporal experience. Most of us, for example, have had unusual experiences with time, especially with events that occur in regard to accidents. The experience I will relate is not so unusual, and many have told me of similar episodes.

It began in June 1972, when I awoke in the middle of the night with the matter-of-fact feeling that I would be dying within the next months. I thought the notion absurd. I was perfectly happy with this life, everything was going quite well, and I had no intention of dying for the next fifty years. Still, the sense of impending death stayed with me as a rather mild-mannered irritation in the back of my mind. To be on the safe side, I made a will and attended to a few other matters normally of no concern to anyone barely past thirty. The notion persisted: I was going to die soon and that was that.

Later in 1972 I visited my father in Los Angeles. We were to have dinner one evening with Ray Bradbury, and my father was anxious to get started. As we got into the car, I *knew* that this was it: my death would be that evening. I got out of the car, announcing that I didn't think we should go to the dinner.

"Whaddya mean, not go to the dinner?" my father hooted. "Why, Ray Bradbury is my ideal. Get back in that car!"

I continued to argue against going, using, I confess, very foolish reasons, such as how I preferred Isaac Asimov, and since we had had such a large lunch at the Chinese restaurant, who needed dinner? But my father was insistent, and eventually we took off down the Ventura Freeway. It was crowded and the cars were all hitting seventy miles an hour, none of them more than twenty feet apart. And my father's driving hardly inspired confidence, since he'd learned some of his motoring skills from watching old Mack Sennett movies. For a while nothing happened. The crowded freeway hummed along with a seemingly automatic positioning of cars and drivers. Surely I was wrong. Even my father's driving was unremarkable.

Then, with an unmistakable clarity, I knew it was happening. I looked around. Everything was fine. We were in the fourth lane by the rail of a four-lane highway, driving close to the car in front of us. I glanced to the second lane on my right. There a yellow Cadillac suddenly pitched into a 90-degree swerve, crossed the third lane horizontally, and was hit full in the side at seventy miles an hour by the car in the fourth lane, directly in front of us. Instantly I was yanked into another time zone. The two cars moved with ponderous slowness but with great grace up into the air. I marveled for the longest time at their balletic grace—they hovered up there like two elephantine Nijinskys executing a pas de deux in the Los Angeles air. I thought of all the premier danseurs I'd ever seen, and compared them unfavorably with the lyrical dance before me. Somewhere in my being I knew that we were in a lot of trouble and about to crash into this spectacle. A cool (my father told me later, steely) voice found its way out of me. I said, "Dad, swerve to the left, now to the right, and accelerate."

In my time-slow state I seemed to *see* the way through that crash, as if we had been driving leisurely through an obstacle course on a deserted country road. My father did exactly what I told him to do, and we made it through or under or past the crash in some astounding way. The two cars smashed down *behind* us, spraying our rear fenders with broken glass. We pulled over to the side and raced out to see what we could do. It was by far the worst accident I have ever seen.

The two cars were a blazing shambles, and there was no way to reach the passengers within. A huge pile-up stretched down the free-way (twenty-four cars, we later learned). We went back and tried helping there. Helicopters, ambulances, fire engines all arrived in record time, but there were six deaths in the two cars, and many minor injuries among the passengers in the pile-up. Ours was the only car in the line of the accident that had completely avoided it.

I had no wish to go on to dinner but my father did and, since I was scheduled to give an after-dinner talk, we resumed driving. I became aware that I was still in a different time zone, although it was not as pronounced as it had been during the accident. Further, my body was filled with phantom achings and shadowy amputations that, while not unpleasant, gave me the odd feeling that if I had been in that crash these were the injuries and mutilations I would have sustained. The theme of ghostly trumpets that recurs throughout the movie *Patton* best de-scribes the phantom wounds that echoed through my body. During the dinner that evening, and for the next forty-eight hours, I was haunted with the notion that, in some other close temporal dimension, I had been severely wounded, probably killed. True, the notion could have been influenced by the presence of Mr. Bradbury and the science fiction conversation that circled the table, but, more remarkable than the notion, the sense of my coming death left me from that time on, never to return. It was as if in some other time realm I had completed "the death" and was therefore no longer obligated to die in existential space and time.

Or perhaps, more practically, I had been provoked by crisis to utilize an innate human capacity to accelerate time in the external world while greatly slowing it down in the internal one. This capacity had given me the "presence" of mind to perceive and act in ways of which I would ordinarily be incapable. What, then, would be possible if I could activate and use this kind of capacity at will? Our studies in this area indicate that when the orchestration of inner time is added to the process of imagery it is possible not only to greatly expand and free the processes of thought, but also to increase and deepen the amount of subjective experience that would have normally occurred within the boundaries of clock-measured time. There is simply more "inner time" available to consider the dimensions of "inner space." With this, subjec-tive experience becomes imbued with meanings it had previously lacked. And beyond even this we observe the emergence, in many of our research subjects and seminar participants, of a growing sense of well-being attended by an ever-increasing sense of their own power to orchestrate the forces within them.

Techniques developed by Robert Masters and me for entering these realms demonstrate that, under certain conditions of accelerated consciousness, a wealth of ideas and images can be experienced, extending in consciousness for hours, days, weeks, and yet all occurring in objective (clock) time within only a few minutes. The change takes place on the level of subjective, experiential time, and the explanation lies in the phenomenon we used to call AMP, accelerated mental process.

We are uneasy with this term since we cannot, at this stage of the art and science of mind-brain research, be certain whether mental processing is actually accelerating or whether, in getting beneath the surface crust of consciousness through altered states, there is a widening and deepening of the person's own knowledge, an opening into an awareness of the more that is always happening. It is likely that other areas of the brain are being engaged during this phenomenon. This alone would account for the experiences of intensification and amplification, in some cases of going beyond the usual categories of time and space. For these reasons I have changed the term to *alternate temporal process* in the interest of our present ignorance, and use the letters ATP.

It has long been known that ATP occurs spontaneously under conditions of dreaming sleep (the hours-long dream that lasts only a few seconds or minutes of clock time). There is the telescoping of time in situations of great emotional stress such as my near automobile accident when death appears as a certainty. For example, a man who falls from a great height and expects to die but somehow survives, later recounts the scenario of his lifetime that appeared before him during his fall. This kind of an experience is one of images in which the person participates as a dreamer does in some of his dreams. The Swiss Alpine Club has recorded hundreds of cases of this kind of experience reported by mountain climbers who have fallen, expecting to die, but survived to testify to the scenario that is relived without any haste, events seeming to happen at a normal, everyday rate of speed.

At age nineteen during my salad days I had a parachuting experience that confirms this phenomenon. Once, having pulled the jump cord after a jump, I fell for an exceptionally long time. Before the emergency chute opened (a few seconds) it seemed to me as if the main events of my life (though not every little pork chop and candy bar) up to the age of nineteen went by as images at their own natural pace.

Such experiences, as I've noted, were once considered to be mere crisis hallucinations deserving no consideration. Today we take them more seriously because we know that the brain can process an enormous number of images in fractions of a second. In near-death situations such as those I have mentioned, the significant events of a lifetime present themselves for review in an instant. There appears to be an adrenalin rush to the brain that triggers images patterned in a life review. Linear time as we know it is suspended and we enter an atemporal eternal present in which years of experience unfold at their own pace.

Imagery is central in experiences of ATP because imagistic thinking is apparently not bound by the mechanisms that retard that flow of verbal thought. Most thinking is geared to speech and to the movements of the body in work and play, an additional cause of the slowness of most thinking. But thinking need not be limited by the slow pace of the physiological being or by the inhibitions of linear-verbal thought. It is worth repeating that in many instances of creative process, especially when "it" all comes together, the mind enters into a different temporality, and thinking that, sequentially, would take weeks, months, even years, is done in hours, minutes, and seconds.

Pioneering work with ATP using induced trance to alter and accelerate thought was described in 1954 by Dr. Linn Cooper and Dr. Milton Erickson in their book, *Time Distortion in Hypnosis*.[7] Cooper and Erickson identified the phenomenon I am calling ATP as "time distortion." Cooper emphasized creative work and problem solving while Erickson explored the psychotherapeutic applications. Upon publication, the Cooper-Erickson book was acclaimed as a breakthrough of major importance, presenting "the first new hypnotic phenomenon discovered in well over 100 years," according to *Scientific Monthly*. But this work reached only a limited audience, and little subsequent effort was made to explore the potential investigated by the authors. Almost no effort was made to go beyond work that had already been done until we at the Foundation for Mind Research began to pursue this fascinating area of research.

In teaching the potentials of ATP we begin by telling subjects that their usual thought process and their subjective experiencing is much more restricted than it need be. Some previous experiments are described, and it is made clear that subjective events are not bound by the laws of time or motion that apply in the objective world. For example, a subject in an altered state of either trance or hyperalertness can re-experience a football game or movie he or she has seen. It can be experienced as it was originally experienced in all its details and at its same pace, and yet in terms of clock time only three minutes will have passed. During this subjective experiencing of the game or movie, perceptions and awareness will be of a reality often no less objectively real than when he or she actually attended the event.

A subject's experiencing does not have to be of something that really happened in past time. It can be of events that are entirely imaginative but that impress the subject with their own validity as he or she becomes aware of them. Subjects' ability to experience ATP may be developed, for example, by enabling them to experience a fairly elaborate adventure within a brief unit of clock-measured time. The process given in Exercise 3 in this chapter, "The Archaeology of the Self," makes use of this phenomenon.

In our developmental experiments using ATP, a trance is usually induced and the subject is instructed in somewhat the following words: "Now I am going to give you considerably more time than you need to do this experiment. You will have one minute of objective, or clock-measured, time. But with special time alteration, that one minute will be just as long as you need to completely live out a very interesting adventure. This adventure may seem to take a minute, a day, a week, a month, or even years, but you will have all the time you need although only a minute of clock time will have passed. I am going to start the stop watch and I will tell you to begin! You will start at the beginning of your adventure and will continue through to the end of it. You will have all the time you need to do this. If you understand completely and are ready for the experiment to start, please nod your head. Now begin!"

Of the approximately five hundred subjects who have participated in these ATP experiments, only twenty-seven have had subjective experiences they thought lasted one minute or less. Most subjects have felt that their experiences lasted from about five to forty minutes. A smaller number of subjects have experienced the ATP factor as a day, a week, or longer. A few have said that time was meaningless.

In these experiments we are deconditioning subjects from their usual temporal referents in the objective world by taking them beneath the surface crust of consciousness and introducing them to the more fluid categories of space and time that are operative in the depths of the psyche. In our earlier work we tended to use trance as the mode of entering this inner realm, but we have found that the state of consciousness conducive to these journeys varies from person to person and from time to time. Sometimes the hyperalert states involving trance and meditation forms are more appropriate. At other times, and for certain temperaments, the hyperalert states are more helpful. Subjects can also use active imagination in this deconditioning if it will help to deepen and focus inner awareness. It is the process of going inward, of activating imagery, and of paying attention to the unfolding of internal content that generally results in an altered state of consciousness and an experience of expanded time.

By developing and practicing the techniques that are described later in this chapter it is possible to focus psychic processing so that it seems as if a pathway is being cleared to formerly hidden knowledge. In extensive experimentation with techniques for tapping inner resources, we have come to know that subjects can, with practice, effect desired attitudinal changes within themselves, rehearse previously learned skills (tennis, speaking a foreign language, playing a musical instrument, etc.), and participate in a depth transformation that results in greatly expanded creativity.

For example, one of our subjects, a priest, felt that he had been traumatized by his failure to realize the objectives of a thirty-day spiritual retreat. After an induction that prepared him for the experience, he was given three minutes of clock time to relive the retreat. Using ATP, he relived the entire thirty days, but this time he "paid very close attention" and completed the spiritual exercises successfully. He was relieved of what he considered to be trauma symptoms and felt more self-assured, more at ease with people, and more creative. He was able to produce and have published a series of papers he had long planned but had been unable to write.

In one of our most unusual cases, a young concert pianist, a woman of twenty-four, was faced with the prospect of giving a recital for which she felt almost totally unprepared. For some weeks she had been unable to bring herself to play at all; or, if she forced herself to play, her fingers became stiff and awkward. After several hours of hypnotic training, a good trance was induced. She was told to find herself in a cavern and to proceed into the cavern until she met a very wise person who would tell her something important about practicing the piano and about concentrating on the practice. After about a minute the subject spoke with considerable emotion and said she had been told that she must do her practicing with very great love and passion. She also said that she now remembered she had noticed herself becoming extremely fatigued before she experienced the total inability to practice. She realized that this was the first symptom in a developing cluster of symptoms that had finally obstructed her altogether. This disclosure led to further trance exploration of her creative block. What emerged from this exploration was that the piano had become a sexual object for her and her playing a sexual act, which she found extremely distressing. She then understood that the advice of the very wise one in the cavern was to accept the sexual implications of the piano playing, and that the erotic energies thus generated could be expressed in a highly acceptable and creative way through the music. The subject was assured that sexual and creative energies are closely linked in many persons, and in fact that works of art have often been understood as expressions of sublimated sexual drives.

With these understandings, the young woman was able to experience herself in a subjective reality consisting of an empty concert hall and a piano at which she sat down to play. She was given two minutes of clock time and told that this would be sufficient for her to have a full practice session. At the end of the two minutes she was asked how long she had been playing. She replied an hour and a half, during which she had done an extensive rehearsal of the Bach and Chopin pieces to be played at her recital. She was then given brief periods of time in which to memorize pieces of music that she had previously been unable to commit to memory. At one point, and within thirty seconds of clock time, she felt herself to have spent two hours memorizing music by Stravinsky that she had been unable to memorize. This memorizing was done with the help of sheets of music that she imaged as appearing before her closed eyes. At first the pages were vague and blurry and she could not make out the notes. Upon instruction from the experimenter to "bring it into focus," however, she was able to read the notes and memorize the music. After the trance ended, she went to a piano and was able to play the Stravinsky piece she had memorized in trance quite well and with only a minimum of stumbling. She experienced similar training in musical imagery rehearsal using ATP on two subsequent occasions. Her typical comments as to what she had been doing while in trance were: "I've just changed some phrasing in the Bach and made it longer. . . . The Mozart sonata was very clear, the first movement especially good. Dynamically very good. In the first movement I felt very excited. The phrasing went very well. . . . The Stravinsky first movement was much better, everything seemed faster."

After leaving these hypnotic sessions, she would go home and practice for another hour or so on her own piano. In the later experiments she reported experiencing as much as two weeks of practice time in about thirty minutes of clock time through the use of ATP. In addition to these prolonged rehearsal periods, her subjective reality was altered by suggestions of an increasingly large audience before which her practice was taking place. During her final ATP practice, she went through her entire recital before a large audience in a few minutes of clock time and reported happily that she had received an enthusiastic ovation at the end of the concert! During this last session she also was given two minutes in which to create an original musical composition. She wrote this down while still in trance and described the piece as "quite contemporary, polychoral. It's not in any key but goes chromatically through several key centers till it hits A. It starts on a center around B and goes through B flat, A, and G." She informed us that it would ordinarily take her several hours to compose such a piece. Curiously enough, the piece was totally unlike anything she had ever composed before. She had done very little composing before, and it had been of a lyrical and melodic nature.

As the rehearsals progressed, she became less aware of a specifically sexual element in her playing, although she experienced herself as playing with unusual passion and energy. She accepted this, however, as being a sublimated version of the original sexual energy.

Eleven days from the time this young woman first came for help she gave her recital with complete confidence, and with the feeling that she had never played so well. The audience and the music critics responded to the performance with enthusiasm, and her teacher commended her, saying that her playing was not only technically better but that it was also more inspired than he had ever heard from her before.

The techniques described depend for their success on a subject's having had previous training, preparation in the skill to be rehearsed. Someone who has studied Beginning German cannot expect to learn Intermediate German by means of this process. The actual input of information must have previously taken place even though knowledge of it may be very faint in ordinary consciousness. The techniques seem to activate the retrieval system of the brain so that dormant learnings are brought up to consciousness, which then charges and "teaches" the sensory-motor base of the skill so that real change and real improvement is effected. (In the case of the pianist, even in trance one could observe subtle yet intense muscular fibrillation occurring, evidence that sensory-motor learning was taking place.) There is also in the use of these techniques a disinhibition of blocks, and a gaining of confidence regarding the skill. By shifting levels of operation, the "block" loses its field and simply does not have access to the necessary amounts of time and emotion for its usual obstructiveness.

An example of this would be the case of a noted American medieval scholar who was asked to direct a large international conference on medieval theology to be held in France and Italy. The scholar had a good reading knowledge of French and Italian, the languages of the conference, but had had little experience speaking them. A week before the trip, he found himself terrified and unable to speak either language. I asked him to give me a word in French that was to him the essence of the French language. "No question about it. It is *tendresse,*" he replied, and lovingly savored the word as it rolled off his tongue. "Good," I said. "Now what I want you to do is to allow that word, *tendresse,* the essence of the French language, to flow through your entire body so that the very heart of the language is flowing through every part of you. In a sense you are becoming the French language."

The professor indicated that this was happening. I induced a light trance and said to him, "I am going to give you thirty minutes of clock time but, in that period, I want you to drive through France for an entire week, talking to everybody—the baker, the gendarme, the old lady who sells flowers, the theologian. At the end of this time you will probably find that you have had so much experience speaking French that your blocks will be no more."

At the end of thirty minutes with ATP, he came back smiling and talking a very lively, if somewhat ungrammatical, French. He was certain now, and indeed it was true that his block had disappeared. He requested that I follow the same procedure for his Italian. We began just as we had for the French. "What is the word for the essence of the Italian language?" He laughed and replied, "It's two words this time, *mange bene!*" "Splendid!" I said (I was recalling all those exhortations by my Sicilian relatives at all those Sunday dinners). We then repeated the entire experience, except that the professor's one-week traveling time was directed to Italy. As with his trip through France, he came back speaking the Italian language with great gusto although with considerably better grammar. He maintained these improvements because once he had overcome his fear of speaking the languages he created opportunities for himself to speak them, and now gives papers every year in both France and Italy. Upon renting a car in Europe the following week, he found himself driving to many of the same places he had visited in the ATP experience, and, of course, *talking to everybody.*

Time and the Automatisms of the Creative Process

Many of our research subjects and seminar participants who have become proficient in the time-expansion process begin creating their own works of art, music, literature, or poetry. Subjective time is critically related to the creative process for, as we have already discussed, in alternate-temporal-process (ATP) there is simply not the "time" to mobilize the usual creative blocks. People who had previously demonstrated little creativity find themselves engaged in the automatisms of the creative process with self-creating works of art emerging from their minds and demanding expression.

For example, musicians who have a knowledge of the history of music can readily be "taken" down into the Realm of Music and there go to the place of some specific composer, perhaps Johann Sebastian Bach. They can be told that they have two minutes of clock time, equal to all the time they need, to dwell in the realm of Bach and there to learn a new composition in the style of Bach, a composition that is being played in that realm for the first time. They are also told to learn the piece and come back and play it for us. In most cases, these musicians will come back at the end of the several minutes with a rather decent second-rate Bach or, in a few cases, even a first-rate Bach. Musicians can be sent "down" again and again to the realms of other composers they know or have studied and come back with more compositions in the style of those composers. They can then be sent to the realm of their own music and bring back complex and intricate compositions of their own making that they will have experienced as self-creating. At the conclusion of such successful experiments some people have even felt a little bit guilty, in spite of their pleasure and fascination with what has happened. "It's as if I have just been eavesdropping on some other reality and didn't really create anything," one young composer said. "But if I didn't create that music, then who did?"

Who indeed? For when you enter into a durative time field beyond the militant beat of past-present-future, you seem to enter into a field continuum that contains many answers and patterns of possibility. (I explore the "where" and the "how" of this creative field continuum in the final chapter.) Seen under the rubric of extended time, the creative process becomes a participant in realms of synchronicity, where everything is ultimately related to everything else. In the creative act, the world becomes selectively illumined by remarkable and remarkably creative correspondences—larger-storied, as it were—that one did not see before.

Art and story are the essence of all living form. Everything is storied, from the unfolding tale of the DNA molecules to the precession of the equinoxes. Story contains the potencies through which space/time materializes in the creative act. This leads me to speculate on the relationship between story, creativity, and the metaphysics of time. As I have suggested before, clock-conditioned knowing inevitably impedes the flow of creative thought because it habituates the thought to the serial beat, which usually leads to little stories, routines, or banal probabilities. God or Creation never harkened to the call of Big Ben or were subject to the limitations of a digital watch.

Historical and anthropological literature attests to the prevalence of this kind of creative process in probably all times and places. And it was because of the experiential *given-ness* of important ideas and images that the ancients often believed them to be gifts of the gods, or of creative daimons possessing the poet or artist or thinker.[8] The recipients of the vision often concurred, declining to take credit for the production, and so regarded themselves as nothing more than channels through which a supernatural force flowed. This was particularly likely to be the case when the emanation into consciousness was accompanied by high emotional intensity that carried with it the sense of an irresistible manifestation. In such cases it was customary to speak of the poet's "divine madness," or of inspiration.

Descriptions of the creative process by artists, authors, mathematicians, inventors, composers, and others give voluminous accounts of creations arising into an awareness that passively receives these productions from a source "outside" of consciousness. In this often hypnoidal or trance state, they experience these "self-creating" inventions, works of art, or whatever as images—visual, auditory, kinesthetic, or some combination of all three. Olfactory and gustatory images, though less common, may also be part of the experience.

It was a force of this kind that Friedrich Nietzsche experienced when he was writing *Thus Spake Zarathustra*, of which he has provided a powerful account of in *Ecce Homo*. His description includes the elements of given-ness, imagery, ecstasy, and other intense affect; the paradoxical sense of complete freedom while at the same time being "utterly out of hand"; a certainty of the profundity, beauty, and truth of what floods into consciousness; an acceleration of the mental processes—all of it illustrating, among other things, the similarity of such experiences to those of mystics and other recipients of revelations and theophanies. Concerning Zarathustra's creation, he writes:

> Provided one has the slightest remnant of superstition left, one can hardly reject completely the idea that one is the mere incarnation or mouthpiece or medium of some almighty power. The notion of revelation described the condition quite simply; by which I mean that something profoundly convulsive and disturbing suddenly becomes visible and audible with indescribable definiteness and exactness. One hears—one does not seek; one takes—one does not ask who gives: a thought flashes out like lightning, inevitably without hesitation—I have never had any choice about it. There is an ecstasy whose terrific tension is sometimes released by a flood of tears, during which one's progress varies from involuntary impetuosity to involuntary slowness. There is the feeling that one is utterly out of hand, with the most distinct consciousness of an infinitude of shuddering thrills that pass through one from head to foot;—there is a profound happiness in which the most painful and gloomy feelings are not discordant in effect, but are required as necessary colors in this overflow of light. There is an instinct for rhythmic relations which embraces an entire world of forms (length, the need for a widely extended rhythm, is almost a measure of the force of inspiration, a sort of counterpart to its pressure and tension). Everything occurs without volition, as if in an eruption of freedom, independence, power, and divinity. The spontaneity of the images and similes is most remarkable; one loses all perception of what is imagery and simile; everything offers itself as the most immediate, exact, and simple means of expression.[9]

Nietzsche attributes no specific identity to the source of *Zarathustra*, and neither does he grant that source absolute ontological status. However, his work is scriptural and aspects of his experience are reminiscent of those of Mohammed, Joseph Smith, and Joseph Caro, to whom were "dictated" their respective scriptural volumes by "supernatural beings." Even as compared to those men, however, Nietzsche's creative process was an extreme case—extreme in terms of its emotional intensity and, even more so, in terms of the extent of his possession by the process. *Zarathustra*, an extremely long work, was composed in three separate ten-day bursts of inspiration, and Nietzsche asserted that one would have to go back "millenniums" to find its counterpart. But apart from these extremes, which few men or women could sustain and which may have been fatal for Nietzsche's own constitution, other aspects of the creative process have been experienced by a great many other persons.

For example, a contemporary author, the late Enid Blyton, wrote numerous children's books that came into her awareness quite as much the products of automatisms as *Zarathustra* came to Nietzsche. In a letter to psychologist Peter McKeller she gives a brief summary of the emergence into consciousness of her "self-creating" works:

> I shut my eyes for a few minutes with my portable typewriter on my knee. I make my mind a blank and wait—and then, as clearly as I would see real children, my characters stand before me in my mind's eye. . . . The story is enacted almost as if I had a private cinema screen there. . . . I don't know what is going to happen. I am in the happy position of being able to write a story and read it for the first time at one and the same moment. . . . Sometimes a character makes a joke . . . that makes me laugh as I type it, and I think, "Well, I couldn't have thought of that myself in a hundred years," and then I think: "Well, who *did* think of it?"[10]

In a somewhat comparable manner J. R. R. Tolkien believed he was doing more than inventing a story when he wrote of the tales that make up *The Silmarillion*: "They arose in my mind as 'given' things, and as they came, separately, so too the links grew . . . yet always I had the sense of recording what was already 'there,' somewhere: not of 'inventing.'"[11]

Similarly, Jean Cocteau has related how, waking from a fitful sleep, he witnessed as from a seat in a theater the performance of a three-act play, later written and produced as *The Knights of the Round Table*.[12] Amy Lowell described poems occurring as spontaneous auditory images that she then wrote down.[13] Many composers have reported experiences of auditory musical imagery, complete or fragmentary in nature, original and equal in quality to compositions created by other means. This musical imagery is literally heard just as visual images are literally seen. The imagery may be of a voice or voices singing, of a single instrument or a combination of instruments, even of an entire orchestra.

In vividness the imagery may range from faint and barely audible up to a painful loudness, comparing again with visual imagery, which may range from barely illuminated up to a painful "blinding light."

Beethoven, Berlioz, Mozart, and Wagner are among the noted composers who have experienced these automatisms, or self-creating compositions. In some cases the simple recording of such autonomous and given imagery is the method of composition. E. T. A. Hoffman, for example, often remarked to his friends, "When I compose I sit down at the piano, shut my eyes, and play what I hear." And Mozart remarked of his compositions: "Whence and how do they come? I do not know and I have nothing to do with it." He noted some very interesting alterations of time and imagery that occurred in these states:

> All this fires my soul, and, provided I am not disturbed, my subject enlarges itself, becomes methodised and defined, and the whole, though it be long, stands almost complete and finished in my mind, so that I can survey it, like a fine picture or a beautiful statue, at a glance. Nor do I hear in my imagination the parts *successively*, but I hear them, as it were, all at once (*gleich alles zusammen*). What a delight this is I cannot tell! All this inventing, this producing, takes place in a pleasing lively dream. Still the actual hearing of the *tout ensemble* is after all the best. What has been thus produced I do not easily forget, and this is perhaps the best gift I have my Divine Maker to thank for. . . . For this reason the committing to paper is done easily enough, for everything is, as I said before, already finished; and it rarely differs on paper from what it was in my imagination. At this occupation I can therefore suffer myself to be disturbed; for whatever may be going on around me, I write, and even talk, but only of fowls and geese, or of Greta and Barbel, or some such matters. But why my productions take from my hand that particular form and style that makes them *Mozartish*, and different from the works of other composers, is probably owing to the same cause which renders my nose so large or so aquiline, or, in short, makes it Mozart's, and different from those of other people. For I really do not study or aim at any originality.[14]

In other creative forms, William Blake, Gustav Moreau, Paul Klee, Ernst Fuchs, and countless other artists have painted images that simply appeared to them in hypnagogic trance and dream states. From dreams alone have been taken poems, musical compositions, works of fiction, paintings, mathematical and scientific discoveries, inventions, and solutions to military, political, and many other kinds of life's problems.[15]

These creations have often been preceded by conscious effort, but other products of automatisms appear to consciousness as novelties, and this increases the receiving mind's sense of itself as passive and invaded, possessed by the creation. In my own research I have witnessed creative productions arising complete into the conscious minds of subjects in every one of the above categories, with the exception of solutions to military problems.

Certainly some of these creations have been preceded by conscious effort, and those creations that have made a lasting impact on our culture were made by those who had developed a high degree of skill in their medium. Amy Lowell was not an illiterate and Mozart was not tone deaf! And yet there is a critical quantum leap between consummate skill and the inspiration that illumines. Brewster Ghiselin in *The Creative Process*, Arthur Koestler in *The Act of Creation*, Jacques Hadamard in *The Psychology of Invention in the Mathematical Field*, and Stanley Krippner in many papers concerning the phenomenology of creative work are among the numerous writers who have documented the importance of automatisms and altered states of consciousness for creativity.

Commonly, the spontaneous creative process surfaces in trance and trancelike or hypnoid states that come upon the individual unintended. Some recognize clearly that their work is accomplished in trance or in an altered state. Others, not recognizing this specifically, still describe practices that doubtless serve as self-hypnotic induction processes. These would include such consciousness-altering procedures as prolonged immobilization of the body, focused concentration on some particular object before beginning work, or working in a dimly lit place.[16]

The use, or abuse, of alcohol to this (creative) end has taken an incredible toll among creative individuals through the centuries.[17] Enhanced creative capacity has also been observed to result from the body-mind states engendered by tuberculosis,[18] the late stages of syphilis,[19] and the onset of schizophrenia.[20] However, I am not suggesting that you try these methods! What is true, however, is that as more knowledge is gained, and as techniques are refined, it ought to be possible to more effectively use those aspects of the creative process that, in the past, have tended to be random and uncontrolled even in the most highly creative persons. Then, perhaps a Byron would not have to court "waking dreams" with strong drink or a Socrates have to wait for a word from his daimon.

The history of genius and of high-level creativity in art, in science, in mathematics, in religion, in philosophy, and sometimes even in statesmanship testifies abundantly to alterations of consciousness and unusual modes of perception and knowing that enter into the creative process. Much of what is best in humanity's accomplishments and progress, therefore, has been the result of randomly occurring, and little if at all guided, transgressions of the bounds of normal consciousness. With what we know now, far greater accomplishment in creativity and discovery, and even just in personal amusement, ought to be possible under conditions of controlled, self-volitional regulation of consciousness. The research we have done suggests that this can be true not only with the naturally gifted but also with people in general if they learn to avail themselves of these innate faculties and capacities.

Thus the question arises: *Can we all begin to tap into these levels and evoke the creative process in ourselves and in others?*

Obviously, it is not enough merely to alter consciousness or have access to inner dimensions of imagery and time. F. W. H. Myers cautioned long ago, in the course of his own investigation of genius, that "Hidden in the deeps of our being is a rubbish-heap as well as a treasure-house; degenerations and insanities as well as beginnings of higher development; and any prospectus which insists on the amount of gold to be had for the washing should also describe the mass of detritus in which the bright grains lie concealed."[21] My own work with psychedelic drugs abundantly confirms the extent of the rubbish heap and the potential for the treasure house.[22] The likelihood of finding treasure is enormously enhanced when the individual already has well-developed skills of expression of mind and body and is sensitively guided in the exploratory process.

What are we to say, finally, about the source of these automatisms of the creative process? Do they stem from muses, secondary personalities, archetypal realities, or even aesthetic programmers existing at deeper levels of the psyche? The literature of creativity attests to this phenomenon in all times and places, and the literature of psychiatry attests to the fright that some medical minds feel before it, often putting creativity on a continuum with madness. To relegate these creative happenings to the restrictive labelings of either godlings or complexes is to reduce the manifold splendor of the psyche in its infinite connections with the universal narrative. I no longer find it a source of wonder that, given certain psychological conditions, novels and sonatas, inventions, paintings, and architecture flow out of us with such abundance as from a cornucopia of cosmic craft.

The news from the deeps is very good. It suggests that creative work and expression are the *natural activities* of the human being who is able to release, at least temporarily, the inhibitions of habituations and culture. To be meaningful, the connection to the extant cultural forms must, of course, be present! There must be a common language or symbol system if the expression is not to be purely personal or perversely autistic. Although, traditionally, few have been able to penetrate the surface crust of environmental conditioning, as this crust cracks around us and more of us learn to fish in the deeps, the creative potential within each one will be heard.

Those who have explored these realms with me repeatedly validate the relationship between the inner cosmos of the psyche and the outer cosmos of the universe as a whole. They tell of the resonance and sustenance of patterns within and without. If your personality is, in some sense, the universe in miniature, then the generic images of the depths are as much a part of nature as the wind, the sands, and the stars. Great nature is contained within and without, the planes of our inner life demanding differing frequencies of consciousness for nature's manifest forms, but offering perhaps equal ontological reality. The work of men like Jung and Teilhard de Chardin confirm our findings that the individual psyche opens up to the Psyche of Nature. Images and archetypes are perhaps the very structural forms of our consciousness that reflect the wider reality. What we perceive in the creative imagination of our interior world may be the reflections not only of the movements of the innerverse but also the movements of the outer reality as well.

The ecology of the wider life affirms that all is resonance, and that we can do much to become conscious and creative participants in this resonance. In so doing we become world-makers, the instruments through which creative evolution can enter into time.

Exercise 1

Becoming Units of Time

TIME: 45 minutes

We live on a planet on which space is stationary and time flows through it. Imagine, instead, that we live in a reality where time stands still and space flows through it. Even the thought boggles the mind. Nevertheless, since space and time are the coordinates of the grid upon which we plot much of our reality, we can choose, as we play with our reality, to say that time will be the constant and space the variable. In this model you can view the world from the perspective of a unit of time rather than as a body occupying space.

PREPARATION

Before you begin, practice moving into a hyperalert state by making a z–z–z–z–z–z–z–z–z sound like a very large bumblebee and allow this buzzing to resonate throughout your body. We will use this sound and its resonance to carry us from one unit of time to the next, so, as you practice, allow your focus to be fully present in the z–z–z–z–z–z–z and yet relaxed.

THE EXERCISE

Sit down in a comfortable and supported position. Now you are going to travel *to* time, becoming on the journey different units of time. You will be looking at reality through the eyes of a person whose being is structured by units of time.

Keep your eyes open or closed, as you choose. Now sound the z–z–z–z–z–z powerfully throughout your being and, continuing to sit, allow your body to move slightly with this resonance and be carried to specific units of time. As you travel on the z–z–z–z–z you will stop for some small space, or large, but it will be all the space you need, at various stations on this journey into time.

Now z–z–z–z–z–z–z–z–z–z. (Allow thirty seconds to a minute for this.)

You are now one second! Look at reality from the perspective of being one second. (Allow fifteen seconds to a minute for this.)

Now z–z–z–z–z–z–z–z–z–z. (Allow thirty seconds to a minute for this.)

You are now one minute! Look at reality from the perspective of being one minute. (Allow fifteen seconds to a minute for this.)

Now z–z–z–z–z–z–z–z–z–z. (Allow thirty seconds to a minute for this.)

You are now one hour! Look at reality from the perspective of being one hour. (Allow fifteen seconds to a minute for this.)

Now z–z–z–z–z–z–z–z–z–z. (Allow thirty seconds to a minute for this.)

You are now one day! Look at reality from the perspective of being one day. (Allow fifteen seconds to a minute for this.)

Becoming Units of Time

Now z–z–z–z–z–z–z–z–z–z. (Allow thirty seconds to a minute for this.)

You are now one week! Look at reality from the perspective of being one week. (Allow fifteen seconds to a minute for this.)

Now z–z–z–z–z–z–z–z–z–z. (Allow thirty seconds to a minute for this.)

You are now one month! Look at reality from the perspective of being one month. (Allow fifteen seconds to a minute for this.)

Now z–z–z–z–z–z–z–z–z–z. (Allow thirty seconds to a minute for this.)

You are now one year! Look at reality from the perspective of being one year. (Allow fifteen seconds to a minute for this.)

Now z–z–z–z–z–z–z–z–z–z. (Allow thirty seconds to a minute for this.)

You are now a hundred years! Look at reality from the perspective of being a hundred years. (Allow fifteen seconds to a minute for this.)

Now z–z–z–z–z–z–z–z–z–z. (Allow thirty seconds to a minute for this.)

You are now a thousand years! Look at reality from the perspective of being a thousand years. (Allow fifteen seconds to a minute for this.)

Now z–z–z–z–z–z–z–z–z–z. (Allow thirty seconds to a minute for this.)

You are now ten thousand years! Look at reality from the perspective of being ten thousand years. (Allow fifteen seconds to a minute for this.)

Now z–z–z–z–z–z–z–z–z–z. (Allow thirty seconds to a minute for this.)

You are now a hundred thousand years! Look at reality from the perspective of being a hundred thousand years. (Allow fifteen seconds to a minute for this.)

Now z–z–z–z–z–z–z–z–z–z. (Allow thirty seconds to a minute for this.)

You are now a million years! Look at reality from the perspective of being a million years. (Allow fifteen seconds to a minute for this.)

Now open your eyes and look around. What are you aware of? What is it like *being* a million years? Share your experience with others or take some time now to write or draw in your journal.

DISCUSSION

Reports of this journey range as wide as time itself, although most people report a mystic or universal sensibility in being a million years. The horizons of space seem to expand with the endurance of time. One woman who was a "a needleprick, a bee sting, an eyelid blink, the thought of a stutter" at one second found herself knowing at ten thousand years: "The seas and their mountains, the rivers and their hills, the brooks and their wooded banks, the deserts, the tropical forests, the ice lands, all these have entered me."

In a world that often seems to be divided between those with "time on their hands" and others with "no time to say hello—goodbye," this exercise goes far in shifting and extending locked perspectives and restoring an appropriate sense of fluidity to the experience of time. When you look at some problem that appears overwhelming from the perspective of a millennium, it certainly looks different.

Exercise 2

The Yardstick of Time

TIME: 30 minutes

As the work of Dr. Humphry Osmond, Dr. Bernard Aronson, and others have shown, when you change time, you change reality. In this exercise, you will learn how to orchestrate your experience of the categories of time past, present, and future to help you control your mood, perception, and understanding. This is not meant to determine your temporal dominance, but to give you some sense of where you *feel* yourself to be on the time spectrum.

PREPARATION

To begin, seat yourself comfortably.

THE EXERCISE

Close your eyes and imagine a yardstick thirty-six inches long. The first twelve inches will represent the category of time past, the next twelve inches will represent the category of time present, and the last twelve inches will represent time future.

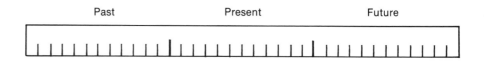

Try to determine where you generally exist on this yardstick. Are you right in the center of the present at eighteen inches? Are you a little into the future at twenty-six inches? Or are you living somewhat in the past at nine inches? Some people who live a great deal in the past or future have even been known to say that they are existing at around six inches or even thirty-four inches!

Now, sitting in a relaxed position with your eyes closed, breathe deeply. Observe your breath and with each exhalation, let go of time. Breathe deeply—inhale. Exhale and let go of time. Inhale and exhale, letting time go. Continue this for several minutes until it feels totally natural and relaxed.

Now imagine that same yardstick with its three twelve-inch divisions into time past, present, and future. But now shorten the number of inches allotted to time past and present time so that you have only eight inches of time past, eight inches of time present, and *a full twenty inches of time future*.

The category of future time is greatly expanded to occupy twenty inches of the yardstick so that your consciousness is under the dominance of time future.

And you have a greatly expanded sense of future time . . . twenty inches of time future and only eight inches of time past and eight inches of time present.

You are living now in the realm of the expanded future. Sense yourself fully in this expanded future realm, moving in it, thinking in it, seeing and hearing.

Now open your eyes and look around. Move, still sensing yourself as living in time future. You can either share your perceptions and experience with another person or write in your journal now or after the entire exercise is finished.

Close your eyes again and breathe deeply, again letting go of the categories of time on the exhalation.

Returning now to your yardstick, discover that it is restored to its original divisions, with twelve inches each representing time past, present, and future.

Now you are going to greatly *expand the sense of time past* by extending that division all the way *to twenty inches* so that you have twenty inches of time past and only eight inches of time present and eight inches of time future.

Past time is greatly expanded and your consciousness is under the dominance of time past.

A greatly expanded sense of past time . . . twenty inches now of time past and only eight inches of time present and eight inches of time future. You are living now in the realm of time past.

Sense yourself fully in this expanded past realm, moving in it, thinking in it, seeing and hearing.

Now open your eyes and look around. Move, still sensing yourself as living in time past. You can either share your perceptions and experience with another person or write in your journal now or after the entire exercise is finished.

Close your eyes again and breathe deeply, again letting go of the categories of time on the exhalation.

Returning now to your yardstick, discover that it is restored to its original divisions, with twelve inches each representing time past, present, and future.

Now you are going to enormously *expand the sense of present time* by expanding the middle way over to the left part of the yardstick and way over to the right so that you have thirty inches of present time and only three inches of past time and three inches of future time.

You are living now in the loaded present, with thirty inches of time present.

The category of present time is becoming fuller and fuller so that your consciousness is under the dominance of the expanded present . . . thirty inches of time present and only three inches of time past and three inches of time future. A full, deep, powerful experience of present time.

Now open your eyes and look around. Move, still sensing yourself as living in time present. You can either share your perceptions and experience with another person or write in your journal now.

DISCUSSION

Needless to say, this exercise draws a great variety of reactions and differences of perception. In the expanded future, for example, many have felt a great sense of relaxation and even euphoria, for they have all the time they could ever need. Asked about problems, they generally respond happily, "What problems?" Depth perception changes and colors may seem to be pastel. The room seems larger. An easy sense of confidence in what they have to do is characteristic of the consciousness of participants in the expanded future.

On the other hand, the expanded past gives most people a heavy and even morose feeling. This may be related to the future-orientation of our culture, which leaves us unprepared to deal with past time. People typically feel space contracting and oppressing, colors darkening, and experience an agitated concern over details of things left undone. Others, however, love the expanded past, feeling that it gives them a real sense of roots and growing up out of the depths of things. Thus they have a vision of a "webbing of interconnections" of people and culture, remarking on the almost tribal sense of relatedness they feel to others in the room. The sharing of this perspective introduces others to a new and creative way of dealing with past time. On the second time around with this exercise many of those who had hated the expanded past grow to appreciate it and find all kinds of useful applications for it in their own lives.

Surprisingly, another beneficial use of this procedure has to do with motivating the unmotivated, since the reacquisition of the past provides the person with more substance and more temporal momentum to get going. They are not just stuck in the revolving door of the here and now. Or, as one previously unmotivated person said to me, "Now I feel that I'm coming from somewhere. I am shooting out of the past, through the present, and into the future." In gaining your temporal dimensions, you apparently gain a greater sense of reality as well.

The expanded present is for many an extremely energizing experience. Depth perspective becomes intense, as does figure-ground configuration. Everything is loaded with presence and life, even inanimate objects. It is easy to focus in this state and to perceive more perspectives on things at both the sensory and the conceptual levels. However, for some, the vividness of this experience is painful. It is certainly not recommended for those who are suffering from acute mental or physical distress because it will tend to accentuate these feelings.

EXTENSIONS

Infinite variations are possible, and you will discover many of them for yourself as you begin to work with this exercise, particularly as you do it with others.

Some find that the yardstick is a very arbitrary and fallacious symbol to use for time. Perhaps, but there are all sorts of corrective extensions of the metaphor. You can resume the basic exercise as follows:

Breathe again the breath of releasing time.

Now recall in front of your closed eyes the yardstick, but this time it is made of rubber. You can bend it so that the beginning of time past is joined to the thirty-sixth inch of time future and have past, present, and future in a circle. Breathing deeply and spinning your head, feel the categories of past present and future spinning and flowing together.

Pastpresentfuturepastpresentfuturepastpresentfuturepastpresentfuture pastpresentfuturepast presentfuturepastpresentfuture, etc. And time, spinning as in a spaceship, spinning in space and time, traveling through the universe. Pastpresentfuturepastpresent futurepastpresentfuturepast

presentfuturepastpresentfuture. The future is behind you. The past is in front of you. And all the categories of time are flowing together . . . .

Allow this to continue for one minute.

Now come back. Open your eyes and look around. What do you see and sense and feel? How has your sense of who you are changed?

As always, responses vary enormously, and thus I hear "Jeez, am I dizzy!" and "I have become the moving image of eternity" in the same group on the same afternoon. There are no "right answers"! Many have spoken of getting from this an integration of the three orders of time, even leading to a sense of what infinite time is like.

Another variation is to allow a color to emerge that is attached to each of the divisions. As you extend each category, allow the color to change if it wants to, to move into specific symbolic form, to grow more intense or more subtle. Let go of the colors for a while. Restore the yardstick to its original configuration and see if the colors are changed.

You may also allow yourself to become very small and walk along the yardstick of time, experiencing it as a vast road with hills and valleys, mountain peaks and oceans. Notice the differences in the lands of the past and the present and the future. If you meet any creatures in any of these lands you can ask them to journey with you into the other lands. How does the past perceive the present and the future?

You may see the yardstick as the span of your own life and walk off the beginning or the end. Continue walking back and sense the connections to time beyond your own time. You may find that when you "go off the deep end" you are no longer walking but moving in a very different way.

Again, you may drill a hole through the yardstick at any point and explore the Underworld of Time, knowing time in this extended dimension and unearthing treasures that are not apparent on the surface.

All these suggestions are intended to stimulate you to recognize the possibilities that lie in the experiential exploration of a metaphor and to encourage you to do your own pioneering.

Exercise 3

The Archaeology of the Self

TIME: 45 minutes

The self is a layered entity. As the earth is known to us according to its strata, so have we come to our knowledge of the physiological and psychological world. As I discussed earlier, our research in taking depth probes of the psyche indicates that our interior world has four levels—the sensory, the recollective-analytic, the symbolic-mythic, and the integral-religious—each tending to have its own unique style of imagery and content, logic, happenings, psychologies, and even metaphysics. The psyche is not unlike a real archaeological dig in which different civilizations are revealed at each level.

Unlike the field archaeologist, however, we have living access within ourselves to the cultures and knowing of our various strata and therefore can learn "on site" how to tap our hidden treasures for the benefit of our existential lives. It is also possible to build sustaining bridges, networks to and among these strata, thereby encouraging an ongoing communication and exchange of content, a kind of commerce of the psyche. The exercise that follows aids awareness of the development of the depth levels of the self. It will help you begin to inhabit a larger domain of your own given reality.

PREPARATION

We will explore each of the four levels of imagery, pausing after each level to reflect upon and thus harvest the experience of the previous levels. You may, however, especially during subsequent sessions with this material, prefer to explore the levels without taking a break between them. See what works best for you and follow that route.

This exercise is best done with another person serving as a guide, timing the inward journeys and facilitating the sharing of experiences after you have finished. You can, however, read it onto a tape; if you do, include some signal that will let you know when the suggested time is up.

THE EXERCISE

The Sensory Level

Sitting or lying down comfortably, close your eyes. Breathe deeply. Keep your eyes closed through this deep breathing and the imaging process. As you inhale, hold an image of the air rising into your brain and energizing it.

On the exhalation, hold the sense of the brain's being aerated, gently brushed through, enlivened. Continue this breathing for about one minute. As you do this, feel yourself deepening into a place of discovery.

You are walking down a street. A large crocodile comes waddling toward you.

You have one minute of clock time, equal to all the time you need, to find out what happens.

Opening your eyes now, share what you have found on this journey with others or by writing or drawing in your journal.

The Recollective-Analytic Level

Again, breathe deeply, as you did earlier, and energize your brain. Continue to do this for one minute. As you continue the breathing, sense yourself deepening into a level of yourself where you have never been before.

You are standing in front of a full-length mirror that appears to shine with an inner light. This glow fascinates you and you reach out to touch the surface of the mirror. Your hand does not stop at the mirror's surface but goes quite easily through the mirror. You decide to follow your disappearing arm, and you step into the world that is on the other side of the mirror.

You have two minutes of clock time, equal to all the time you need, to find out what happens.

Opening your eyes now, share what you have found on this journey with others or by writing or drawing in your journal.

The Symbolic Mythic Level

Again, close your eyes and breathe deeply. Feel the inspiration ascending to your brain, giving it a great and wondrous life. Exhale and feel the wash of new invigoration, a marvelous energizing. Continue this for one minute, sensing as you do so a deepening within yourself as you allow yourself to travel to an excitement and clarity of adventure such as you have not known before.

You are walking in a forest and you hear behind you the sound of slow, measured hoofbeats. You turn and see a majestic black horse approaching you. Its rider is a distinguished and benign-looking skeleton in armor. He bows to you with great dignity and presents you with a golden chalice.

You have three minutes of clock time, equal to all the time you need, for this experience to unfold.

Opening your eyes now, share what you have found on this journey with others or by writing or drawing in your journal.

The Integral-Religious Level

Closing your eyes, breathe deeply again. Feel your brain activated, cleansed, energized, enlivened by the miracle of the air you are taking in, this great gift of life. Let your exhalation flood you with a heightened sense of life and energy. Continue to do this for two minutes, sensing as you breathe that you are going deep within yourself to a place of profound mystery, deeper than you may ever have been before.

You find yourself on a packaged bus tour of the Holy Land. The bus stops on the outskirts of Jerusalem. There is free time, so you get off the bus, noticing around you rampant commercialism, vendors of all kinds, Coca-Cola signs, postcards everywhere you turn, and candy wrappers underfoot.

Disgusted by all of this, you wander off by yourself toward the hills. Suddenly you notice that the sky seems different; the light has changed and there is a luminous quality to the air that is gently blowing through your hair. You look down and notice that the road you had been trudging on has disappeared. There are no longer telephone poles marring the landscape. The bus station has disappeared. There is no sound of activity anywhere, no planes in the sky. A strange and powerful silence envelops you.

You continue to investigate the area. Indentations in the sand at your feet, a shallow trench, lead you to notice a large stone pushed into the hill in front of you. You look carefully and see that the stone has been pushed to seal the mouth of a cave. You search about you for some means to pry the stone away from the entrance to the cave. Finding a large stick, you manage, with much effort, to move the stone away enough so that you can slip into the cave.

You go inside. There is a human figure lying there, wrapped in a shroud, lying still, quiet; the hands and feet have stained the shroud with blood. You know who this is. You lean over and say to the man lying there shrouded, "It is time to wake up now."

You have four minutes of clock time, equal to all the time you need, to experience what happens.

Opening your eyes now, share what you have found on this journey with others or by writing or drawing in your journal.

DISCUSSION

The responses and experiences evoked by this exercise range from the absurd and comical to the life-altering and sublime. The patterns lie within the individual as much as in the exercise. One person may report that the crocodile is a great mechanical beast with a wind-up key on his back and eyes that roll clockwise while "he," quite unexpectedly, gives birth to an endless train of miniature mechanical crocodiles as he lumbers along singing "zippity do da, zippity ay" over and over again in some sort of chromatic progression, while another reports that her crocodile gulped her down effortlessly while she stayed, in her words, "totally aware of where I am, sitting on my chair, hearing the ballgame on TV in the next room, and feeling the cloth of my slacks against my hand."

Taken as a totality for any person, this series of images often reveals the basic structures motivating and energizing his or her daily life. As you record these images through drawing or writing, or express them through music or dance, more and more aspects of these symbols will reveal themselves to you over time.

Often you will not "finish" some particular narrative in the allotted time. This may be a sign that the story symbolically referred to in these images is not yet complete in your own life. There is often much more power in those narratives that feel incomplete than in those that are all nicely tied up and finished. As you record these images in your journal along with your other experiences, the connections will begin to reveal themselves—often in very surprising ways.

EXTENSIONS

You can do this exercise every few weeks to take a depth sounding of your own psyche. You will find it helpful to develop other series of images for each of the four levels in order to explore further in the archaeology of the self. Here are some suggestions, but feel free to create your own.

Sensory Level

A bull frog jumps out of a pond and into your lap and croaks, "I am here."

You are driving down a highway when on your car radio you hear, "This is your car speaking. Let me take you on a trip." And suddenly the car begins to move in another direction from the one in which you had been going.

A bird starts to build a nest on your head.

You are visiting Australia and a giant kangaroo hops up and puts you in her pouch.

Psychological

You are walking down a street in an old town and pass an abandoned home of Victorian design, when from within the abandoned house you hear a baby crying.

You are invited to a party with people whom you have never met before and where stuffed mushrooms are served. You eat a mushroom and suddenly discover that all the characteristics of your personality, both favorable and unfavorable, become greatly amplified.

You wake up one morning at the house where you lived during your early childhood, in your parents' bedroom. Feeling yourself to be in an adult body, you go to the mirror and discover that you have become your own mother, and by the clock you know that it is time to wake up the child that is you.

You are walking in a meadow and see a very old and wise person approaching you. As this wise old one comes closer, you recognize that he

The Archaeology of the Self

or she looks like you might look if you were to be hale and hearty at a hundred years of age. The wise elder comes up to you and merges into you.

Mythic

A strong and beautiful hand emerges from a rock upon which you are sitting. You grasp that hand and it pulls you into the rock.

You are fiddling with your favorite ring while looking into a pond. Suddenly your ring falls off your hand and to the bottom of the pond, but the pond is so murky that you know you cannot retrieve the ring. Then a beautifully colored snake rises out of the pond and offers to retrieve your ring for you if you will help him find his true home. The snake warns that it will be a journey with many dangers and awesome challenges.

You are lost in the woods, in despair over your life and its meaning, when from behind an ancient oak tree there appears a man or woman of great knowledge and wisdom, dressed in classical robes, who offers to guide you through hell, purgatory, and heaven.

You climb a mountain and at the top you see a beautiful crater lake in which a naked woman is bathing. Her beauty and majesty are so great that you realize she must be a goddess. She is angry that you have seen her and says, "For what you have seen you must wander throughout the world for the next seven years blind and of the opposite sex." Immediately you find yourself of the opposite gender and unable to see with your eyes.

Integral

You are standing under an ancient tree when suddenly the weather changes. The wind begins to wail around you and through the branches, and you hear the wind say, "Now is the time to know the god." A bolt of lightning strikes the tree in the center and a part of the bark falls away, revealing a golden door.

A unicorn bearing six wings of many colors flies over to you, touches his horn to the ground in front of you three times, and says, "It is time for you to ascend to the heights."

You are walking in a forest and you see ahead of you a gleaming crystal palace. You enter the palace, which has no furniture, and walk through the great halls, seeing in each brilliant facet a reflection of the whole universe. Gradually, you feel your own powers and possibilities deepened and enhanced by the effect of the crystal and the shimmering light. Finally, you reach the center of the palace, where there stands a single crystal vase with a single flower in it. You look deep into this beautiful flower and see in its center a seed that you know contains the germ of all you are and can be. It is the seed of the unfolding of your capacities as well as the germ of that which, if allowed to grow in you, can restore you to the spiritual order of reality.

You are standing before an ancient temple at dawn at the time of the full moon. On the eastern horizon the sun is rising, on the western horizon the moon is setting, and in the center there is a falling star. Suddenly you understand and contain the universe.

Exercise 4

Skill Rehearsal with a Master Teacher

TIME: 45 minutes

In the final exercise of this chapter you will use many of the procedures you have worked with so far to enter into an inner realm. It is symbolic of all your unconscious knowledge concerning a skill you have learned but need to practice and perfect. You will evoke a "Master Teacher" to help you improve this skill. This teacher may be someone you actually know or a major figure from the past such as Leonardo da Vinci, Beethoven, or Einstein, or the persona of the teacher may emerge spontaneously into your consciousness. This teacher may be someone or even something you have never met before, but it will represent a symbolic personification of the knowledge and artistry of the skill you want to perfect. Using alterations of consciousness, imagery, the kinesthetic body, and alternate temporal processes, you will be able to achieve a deeper learning of material that has been incompletely learned, improve the fine motor connections between body and brain, and gain confidence and resourcefulness in the use of your skill.

PREPARATION

Choose the skill you wish to improve and rehearse. If the skill is one in which you need a special setting, such as a tennis court or swimming pool, it is helpful to do this exercise there so that you can actually rehearse at the appropriate time. However, it works almost as well to go through the motions of the skill wherever you may happen to be, although the results may be less apparent and less astonishing.

Actually go through the motions of your chosen skill, replicating "real conditions" as much as possible, rehearsing with as much attention as possible. Then stop and do them in your kinesthetic body. Go back and forth between doing them actually and kinesthetically several times.

Run around for a few minutes like a three-year-old, twisting and turning, going up and down, turning somersaults, climbing and crawling and jumping. This activity frees the motor cortex to learn new movements of the skill. When you are thoroughly exhausted, lie down and listen to the following instructions, which should be taped or read by another person.

THE EXERCISE

Feel yourself lying alone in the bottom of a little rowboat. You are being carried out into the ocean by gentle rhythmic waves. The ocean sparkles like a million diamonds in the sunlight, and you feel very relaxed and drowsy as the rhythmic, rocking, gentle waves carry you out and out and out.

Gradually you begin to notice that the pattern of the boat is now going down and around and you are being carried lightly into a vortex of water that is taking you down and around, around and down, deeper and deeper and deeper into the ocean.

The water does not close in on you, and you watch with interest how it rises above you, a wonderful circle of water through which you can see the sky. You are in a tunnel of spinning water, going down and around, and around and down. Finally, with a little bump, you land on the ocean bottom.

Getting out of the boat now, you discover on the ocean floor a circular bronze handle, which you pull. Sand falls away and a door opens on the bottom of the floor. The door takes you into a stone stairwell leading to a realm underneath the ocean floor. You begin to go down the stairs, which go down and down and down and down, deeper and deeper, down underneath the ocean floor—down and down and down. Finally, the stairs end and you find yourself looking out on a great cavern filled with the most gloriously shaped and colored stalagmites and stalactites.

You wander through this cavern admiring the mighty shapes and jeweled walls until you come at last to a stone corridor. Walking through this corridor you now continue on your journey until you come to a large oak door over which is written: *The Room of the Skill*.

Enter that room now and find yourself in a place completely imbued with the presence and spirit of your skill. Just being there is like osmosis, and you already begin to feel improvement. But there are more possibilities here, for in the room is a Master Teacher of the skill—perhaps someone you know or a historical figure or someone you have never seen or heard of before. Whichever it is, this person or being is your Master Teacher, and in the time that follows this teacher will give you deep and potent instructions to help you improve your skill.

The Master Teacher may speak in words or not. Teachings may present themselves as feelings or as muscular sensations. The Master Teacher may have you practice old skills or learn new ones. The teacher may be solemn or quite comical.

However this being works with you, the learning on your part will be effective and deep. And you will be feeling increasingly more free, more spontaneous, and also much more confident that the skilled person within you is emerging and developing and overcoming inhibitions and blocks of all sorts as well as undergoing some very intensive training and learning.

You now have five minutes of clock time, but with the use of alternate temporal processes this is equal to all the time you need—hours, days, or even weeks to have a rich learning session with the Master Teacher, rehearsing and improving your skill. *Begin.*

Allow a full five minutes for this.

Now it is time to leave your Master Teacher; you will thank this being for the help you have received and know that you can return here for further training and instruction as you need it. But before you go, notice the special light that is streaming down from one portion of the ceiling. That is the light of confirmation of you in your skill. If you wish, go and stand under that light. As you do so, you may feel a deepening and confirming of your skill throughout your mind and body. The skill becomes a natural part of you. You are being confirmed in your skill.

Allow thirty seconds to a minute for this.

Leave the room now, carefully closing the door behind you. Quickly go down the corridor and run through the great cavern, feeling the skill growing in you all the while. Go up the stone steps, up and up and up until you emerge on the ocean floor. Put the door back and get into the boat, pushing it into the circular column of water. The vortex reverses now, carrying you up and around and up and around, higher and higher and higher and higher. And as you rise you feel your skill continuing to grow into you, pervading your whole being, rooting itself in all your nerves and sinews, your neurons, your cells, and your synapses. The skill is streaming with felicity through all your conduits and making itself present in your whole being.

The boat reaches the surface of the ocean and heads toward shore. As it is carried by the waves, you feel your skill in you so that you are getting very excited about getting back and trying it out. The waves move faster now, up and down, and up and down and up and down and up on the last wave, and with a downward swoooosh your boat is carried to shore. Leaping out, you pull the boat to a mooring pier and tie it up. You are wide awake and full of your skill, and you get up as soon as you can and actually, physically, perform or go through the motions of the skill.

After you have rehearsed your skill physically for a while, stop and rehearse it in your kinesthetic body. This helps to deepen the sense of it and brings your body image into the skill performance as well. Now do it in the actual body for a while. Go back and forth between the kinesthetic rehearsal and the real rehearsal until you can feel the full integration of the two.

What do you notice about the improvement of your skill? and what do you particularly remember about your Master Teacher?

DISCUSSION

Once you become familiar with your Master Teacher and begin to trust and act on the advice and knowledge that is imparted, you will find it increasingly easy to have access to this kind of deep learning and will not need such an elaborate procedure for getting to it. You will begin to develop a body sense of your state of consciousness that allows you to retrieve knowings that were blocked by emotional trauma, inertia, or, most frequently, habit.

The Master Teacher is a potent reminder of our inner "allies" and may often provide much more teaching and wisdom than we had intended when we set off on this journey. And the exercise may also lead you to the discovery that the inner realms have their own subtle machinations for guiding you.

While we can use and orchestrate these inner realms, we must also listen to them, for they have urgent messages to send to us. If we *cooperate* with them—that is, *with our own deepest knowing*—we begin to notice an astounding change in our lives. Students who have gained access to this realm report greatly increased health, "amazing" synchronicities, increased motivation, improved production, and a sense of delight, for this world is akin to that of Alice, and we must laugh with it.

CHAPTER **8**

. . . a sense sublime
of something far more deeply interfused,
Whose swelling is the light of setting suns,
And the round ocean and the living air,
And the blue sky, and in the mind of man:
A motion and a spirit, that impels
All thinking things, all objects of all thought,
And rolls through all things.

WILLIAM WORDSWORTH
"Tintern Abbey"

Michael Samuels

8

Toward a New Natural Philosophy

Almost everyone wakes up at least once in a lifetime, and almost everyone goes promptly back to sleep again. But through the drowse of the rest of their days they still faintly remember that time of awakening.

I am going to tell you about the time I woke up. I will tell you this because what happened to me then influenced my whole life and does much to explain why I propose this particular natural philosophy.

It all began because my mother was a Sicilian Catholic with leanings toward Christian Science while my father was an Ambulatory Protestant. He had been born a Southern Baptist, which he had remained until he fell in love with Erma Mae McDermott, daughter of the Methodist minister of the east Texas town where he then lived, whereupon he became a Methodist. Then he fell in love with Maudie Bullock, who sang in the Presbyterian Church choir, so he joined up with the Presbyterians. Then he fell in love with Bethie Sue Schultz, a member in good standing of the Holiness Church, so he became a Holiness. This could have gone on indefinitely except that he went to New York and fell in love with my mother, a first-generation Sicilian born in Syracusa, with the name of Maria Graziella Seraphina Annunciata Fiorina Todaro. With those people there is no fooling around, so he had to become a Catholic in order to marry her. A young priest at St. Patrick's Cathedral gave him religious instruction. After six weeks of trading jokes instead of theology, the priest finally said, "Oh, the hell with it, Jack! You're just a natural-born pagan!" and gave him a learner's permit so he could go ahead and get married. From that time on my father made an inseparable connection between comedy and religion. Religion was where the jokes were. Religion was where the girls were. Religion was the source of all piquant and funny things. When, at about the age of four, I asked my father to tell me about "sweet Jesus, meek and mild," I was answered with a hilarious description of Christ the Comedian. When I turned five and was sent to Catholic school in Brooklyn, he would gag up my catechism and give me the most interesting questions to ask the nuns. Like . . .

"Sister Theresa, when Ezekiel saw the wheel, do you suppose he was drunk?"

"Sister Theresa, I counted my ribs and I counted Joey Mangiabella's ribs, and we have the same number of ribs. So if God took a rib out of Adam to make Eve like you said, how come . . . ?"

"Sister Theresa, how do you *know* that Jesus wasn't walking on the rocks below the surface when he seemed to be walking on the water?"

"Sister Theresa, when Jesus rose, was that because God filled him full of helium?"

You might think, perhaps, that the shy quaver of a small child's voice framed these questions after school to the little nun when she and I were alone in the hush of an empty classroom? Not at all. They were presented with all the delicacy of a circus calliope in the middle of a class, and generally when the Mother Superior was visiting. Poor sweet Sister Theresa. Convent life had not prepared her for the theological thrusts of my comedy-writer father's imagination. He had by that time written for Amos and Andy, Fibber McGee and Molly, Fred Allen, Bob Hope, and Abbott and Costello, and with these eminent credentials he was ready to raise the comic consciousness of the Catholic Church.

"Blashphemy!" the good sister shouted one day after I asked her whether Jesus ever had to go to the bathroom. "Blashphemy, Blashphemy, Blashphemy!" she raged. (Sister Theresa had a rather curious lisp.) "Sacrilish and blashphemy!" And with the zeal of one possessed she stormed over to the supply closet, took out a large sheet of oak tag and a bottle of India ink, marched over to the bulletin board, tacked up the oak tag, and, in large black letters, wrote: JEAN HOUSTON'S YEARS IN PURGATORY.

From that day on, any time I asked a question I shouldn't have, Sister Theresa took out the bottle of India ink, climbed up on a stool, and X-ed up more years in purgatory. Each X stood for a hundred thousand years! By the end of the first grade, when I turned six, I had three hundred million years in purgatory to my credit.

On the day of the great addition, when the X's were totaled up, I returned home crushed by the vision of spending eternity being barbecued on a spit with time off to be on the swallowing end of millions of miles of Italian spaghetti. (There was something about Sister Theresa's theology that led her to equate endless torment with eating. Perhaps that's why she weighed only ninety-five pounds.)

With *major crisis* plastered all over my face, I stumbled into the house and refused to look at my father.

"What's the matter, kiddo?" he asked, eyeing me from his typewriter. "You lost your Mexican jumping beans? No? Huh . . . ? Well, lemme guess. You were run over by a trolley car and the cookies in your pocket got mashed to crumbs. No? Oh, I know. You're growing leaves instead of finger nails, your toes are taking root, and now you're afraid you may have caught the chestnut blight!"

"Daddy," I blurted out, "I'm going to purgatory for three hundred million years, and it's all your fault!"

"Greeeeeat, Jeanie-pot-pie! You topped my lines! Keep that up and I'll put you on the air opposite Henny Youngman!"

"But it's true, Daddy! Sister Theresa added up all the years and says that because of the questions I ask in school I've got to go to purgatory for . . . why are you laughing? Stop laughing, Daddy! It's not funny!"

My father stopped howling long enough to swoop me up on his shoulders and start moving his feet to the sound of a train clicking along on the tracks.

"Watch out!" he hooted. "Here comes the Purgatory Special! Purgatorypurgatorypurgatorypurgatorypurgatory. Toot, toot!"

And gathering up steam, he raced with me out the door and down the block, keeping up his "purgatorypurgatorypurgatory" all the way.

High on his shoulders, I watched the amazed faces of the Sicilian neighbors as we sped by. Occasionally one would scream from a window, "Eh, dere goesa Crazy Jack! Eh, Crazy Jack, you betta watcha outa or yousa gonna fall ana breaka da bambina's head!"

As he leaped across the street, dodging motorists but never losing the beat, I shouted, "Where are we going, Daddy?"

"To the movies, honey-pot! To see how the real saints had it. You think you got troubles? Wait'll you see how they hogtied poor old Bernadette!"

Within minutes we were seated inside the Brooklyn Fortway theater watching *The Song of Bernadette*, a 1940s classic starring Jennifer Jones as the French peasant girl who saw a vision of Mary while praying at the grotto in Lourdes. We were surrounded in the darkness by good Italian Catholics, most of whom were watching this picture with the reverence accorded the Pope. When Jennifer Jones made her first appearance, the old lady sitting next to me murmured "*Cue bella questa santa*" (what a beautiful saint) and crossed herself.

I was spellbound, and identified with Miss Jones at every turn. When the spectral white vision of the Virgin Mary appeared to Bernadette I had to resist an urge to fall to my knees. Instead, I limited myself to a verbal outpouring of religious devotion: "Oh boy! Oh boy! Oh boy!"

The audience was entranced, the old lady beside me was muttering "*Ah Santa Vergine*" over and over again, when suddenly—a long, loud, whinnying laugh exploded our reveries.

"*Hyah . . . hyah . . . hyah* . . . hee hee hee ha ha ha *ha ha hyah* . . . *hyah . . . hyah* . . . hee hee hee ha ha ha ha . . . !"

Beside me, my father, the source of this eruption, was striving mightily and unsuccessfully to contain himself.

"Daddy! Shhh! This is the holy part!"

"Yeah. I know. *Ha ha ha ha ha*," my father brayed. "But that's old Linda playing Mary up there! You remember Linda, honey? Linda

Darnell? We met her at that party in Beverly Hills. Good old Linda. Hot dog! I told her she'd go far!"

And with that he sputtered and choked like an old Model T, only to dissolve helplessly into an unrelenting roar.

"Daddy," I ordered, desperate now. "Go to the bathroom!"

He obeyed, stepping over the knees of the old lady who stabbed the air in an evil gesture after him and hissed, "*Diablo . . . diablo!*"

He returned sometime later, semichastened, with only an occasional snort to remind us of his true feelings.

After the movie let out I began running home, heady with purpose. As I darted ahead of my father, he called out, "Hey Jeanie-pot, slow down. What's the matter? Are you mad at me? C'mon, take my hand—at least to cross the street. Where are you going, anyway?"

"I'm going to see the Virgin Mary," I replied, jerking my hand loose.

"Oh, izzat so? Okay. Let's go together."

With that, he grabbed my hand again and began skipping and singing down the street, trying to lure me into a Dorothy and the Tin Man routine: "We're off to see the Virgin, the Wonderful Virgin of Lourdes. We'll join the hordes and hordes and hordes and hoooooordes . . . The hordes to see the Virgin of Lourdes. We're off . . ."

"Quit that, Daddy! I've got something to do. Let me go."

With a fierce tug, I broke free and raced down the street, only to call back—"And don't follow me! This is serious!"

Back at the house I loped up the stairs to one of the bedrooms that contained a large deep closet with a wall safe in the back of it. The clothes had been removed from this closet since Chickie had recently chosen to have her eight pups there and had continued to lease the area as a dog nursery.

"No doubt about it," I thought as I squinted speculatively into the closet. "It could easily pass for a grotto."

I scooped up the puppies and dragged a protesting Chickie out of her nesting spot. The "grotto" cleared, I bounced down on my knees, clapped my hands together in prayer, and, with an eye fixed on the dial of the wall safe prayed, "Please Virgin Mary, please pop up in the closet the way you did for Bernadette. I'd really like to see you. If you come I'll give up candy for a month . . . two months. Okay?"

No Virgin Mary.

"Uh, Virgin Mary? Listen. I'm going to shut my eyes and count to ten and you be there in the closet when I finish counting. Okay? 1–2–3–4–5–6–7–8–9–10."

No Virgin Mary—only the dog carrying one of her pups back by the scruff of the neck to the site of my hoped-for Visitation. I indignantly pulled them out again and kneeled down for serious business.

"Look, Virgin Mary? This time I'm going to count to . . . twenty-three, and when I open my eyes you try to come down from heaven and get into the closet. Okay?"

I counted slowly, with my eyes closed, trying to imagine at the same time a picture of the Virgin Mary winging her way down from the skies like some great white bird and hovering over the Brooklyn Bridge looking for my house. At the count of twenty-three my eyes popped open. This time I was sure she'd make it.

No Virgin Mary. Just three more pups in the closet. I dragged the dogs away.

"Virgin Mary? Maybe you don't know where I live. It's 1404 Avenue O. It's the brick house with the stoop out in the front, where Etta Canzaneri is outside jumping rope. You go to the second floor and turn left. Okay? Now I'll count to . . . forty-one, so you should have plenty of time to find it."

Well, she must have gotten lost, for she never did show up. At least not in the closet. I kept on trying for a while, counting to even higher numbers such as 52 . . . 87 . . . 103 . . . 167 . . . but all I ever opened my eyes to was an ever-growing melange of puppies. Finally, I gave up, resigned to the fact that my efforts to lure heaven had failed. I gave up the ghost to the dogs, as it were.

Spent and unthinking, I sat down by the windowsill and looked out at the fig tree in the backyard. Sitting there drowsy and unfocused, I must in my innocence have done something right, for suddenly the key turned and the door to the universe opened. I didn't see or hear anything unusual. There were no visions, no bursts of light. The world remained the same. And yet everything around me, including myself, moved into meaning. Everything—the fig tree in the yard, the dogs in the closet, the wall safe, the airplane in the sky, the sky itself, and even my idea of the Virgin Mary—became part of a single Unity, a glorious symphonic resonance in which every part of the universe was a part of and illuminated every other part, and I knew that in some way it all worked together and was very, very good.

My mind dropped all shutters. I was no longer just the little local "I," Jean Houston, age six, sitting on a windowsill in Brooklyn in the 1940s. I had awakened to a consciousness that spanned centuries and was on intimate terms with the universe. Everything mattered. Nothing was alien or irrelevant or distant. The farthest star was right next door and the deepest mystery was clearly seen. It seemed to me as if I knew everything. It seemed to me as if I was everything. Everything—the fig tree, the pups in the closet, the planets, Joey Mangiabella's ribs, the mind of God, Linda Darnell, the chipped paint on the ceiling, the Virgin Mary, my Mary Jane shoes, galaxies, pencil stubs, the Amazon rain forest, my Dick and Jane reader, and all the music that ever was— were in a state of resonance and of the most immense and ecstatic kinship. I was in a universe of friendship and fellow feeling, a companionable universe filled with interwoven Presence and the Dance of Life.

Somewhere downstairs my father laughed and instantly the whole universe joined in. Great roars of hilarity sounded from sun to sun. Field mice tittered and so did the gods and so did the rainbows. Laughter leavened every atom and every star until I saw a universe spiraled by joy, not unlike the one described by Dante in his great vision in the Paradiso . . . *d'el riso del universo* (the joy that spins the universe).

Childhood kept these memories fresh. Adolescence electrified them and gave them passion, while first maturity dulled and even occasionally lost them. But even so, my life, both personal and professional, has been imbued ever since with the search for the unshuttered mind, the evocation and application of this mind in daily life and experience, and the conviction that human beings have within them the birthright of capacities for knowing and participating in a much larger and deeper Reality.

From this springs a search for the cosmic connection, a living sense of the nature of reality, a theology of the Way Things Work.

This search stems from the need to find a new natural philosophy that weaves the findings of physics, the recent research in physiology, the mysteries of consciousness, the call of the larger ecology, and memories of shimmering fig trees into a unity so profoundly felt that it inspires our growth, illumines our transitions, mobilizes our intentions, and gives us the courage to live daily life as spiritual exercise.

Perhaps this is why there is currently so much excitement about the hologram as a metaphor for integrating hitherto divided and distinguished realities. This emerging paradigm provides a scaffolding upon which can be built a reality at once both numinous and concrete, expanding the vistas of human possibilities by joining quantum physics to new research in brain function and the self-orchestration of neural patterns. Further, it suggests ways in which local and universal realities are related to each other and how extraordinarily available is our human instrument for receiving information from the primary order, allowing us to become co-creators with this order. Thus we may extend and deepen our reality and correct its pathology. What I am offering here is not "truth" but playful speculation, a way of seeing rather than a finished and formal system.

The hologram is an image in which all parts are co-tangent, and therefore the whole is resident in each of its parts. If you have a holograph of a bull in a barn and then excise the bull's nose and shine a laser beam of coherent light through the abducted nose, you will see a three-dimensional picture of the bull in the barn. This is to be expected when any piece of information—that is, the bull's nose—is equal to the sum of the parts, or the bull in the barn, the image being produced ubiquitously in interference patterns throughout every part of the hologram. Take this simple example to the level of its metaphysical implications and much in the Cartesian-Newtonian schema begins to sound like the stutterings of a failing computer.

This holonomic perspective is very ancient and has been known to mystics, magi, and other boundary-breaking folk for millennia. One of its earliest formal descriptions is found in the second-century Buddhist Avatamska Sutra:

> In the heaven of Indra there is said to be a network of pearls, so arranged that if you look at one you see all the others reflected in it, and if you move in to any part of it, you set off the sound of bells that ring through every part of the network, through every part of reality.
>
> In the same way, each person, each object in the world, is not merely itself, but involves every other person and object and, in fact, on one level *is* every other person and object.[1]

Similarly, the seventeenth-century philosopher Leibnitz declared the universe to be made up of "monads," which are tiny units of mind, each of which mirrors the universe from the perspective of its particular point of view. At the same time, each component, each monad, is interrelated with every other, so that, as in Indra's net, no monad can be changed without changing every other.

In Cabalistic lore the hologram finds its occult expression in the symbol of the Aleph, the point that contains all possible points in the infinite dance of space-time. Jorge Luis Borges accomplished a literary miracle in attempting to catalogue the containings of the Aleph in the short story of that title. The protagonist of the tale gains access to the Aleph as he observes the nineteenth step of a stairwell in a cellar in Buenos Aires:

> In that single gigantic instant I saw millions of acts both delightful and awful; not one of them amazed me more than the fact that all of them occupied the same point in space, without overlapping or transparency. What my eyes beheld was simultaneous but what I shall now write down will be successive, because language is successive. Nonetheless, I'll try to recollect what I can.
>
> On the back part of the step, toward the right, I saw a small iridescent sphere of almost unbearable brilliance. At first I thought it was revolving; then I realized that this movement was an illusion created by the dizzying

world it bounded. The Aleph's diameter was probably little more than an inch, but all space was there, actual and undiminished. Each thing (a mirror's face, let us say) was infinite things, since I distinctly saw it from every angle of the universe. I saw the teeming sea; I saw daybreak and nightfall; I saw the multitudes of America; I saw a silvery cobweb in the center of a black pyramid; I saw a splintered labyrinth (it was London); I saw, close up, unending eyes watching themselves in me as in a mirror; I saw all the mirrors on earth and none of them reflected me; I saw in a backyard of Soler Street the same tiles that thirty years before I'd seen in the entrance of a house in Fray Bentos; I saw bunches of grapes, snow, tobacco, lodes of metal, steam; I saw convex equatorial deserts and each one of their grains of sand; I saw a woman in Inverness whom I shall never forget; I saw her tangled hair, her tall figure, I saw a cancer in her breast, I saw a ring of baked mud in a sidewalk, where before there had been a tree; I saw a summer house in Adrogue and a copy of the first English translation of Pliny—Philemon Holland's—and all at the same time saw each letter on each page (as a boy, I used to marvel that the letters in a closed book did not get scrambled and lost overnight); I saw a sunset in Queretaro that bled and I seemed to reflect the color of a rose in Bengal; I saw my empty bedroom; I saw in a closet in Alkmaar a terrestrial globe between two mirrors that multiplied it endlessly; I saw horses with flowing manes on a shore of the Caspian Sea at dawn; I saw the delicate bone structure of a hand; I saw the survivors of a battle sending out picture postcards; I saw in a showcase in Mirzapur a pack of Spanish playing cards; I saw the slanting shadows of ferns on a greenhouse floor; I saw tigers, pistons, bison, tides, and armies; I saw in the drawer of a writing table (and the handwriting made me tremble) unbelievable, obscene, detailed letters, which Beatriz had written to Carlos Argentino; I saw a monument I worshipped in the Charcarita cemetery; I saw the rotted dust and bones that had once deliciously been Beatriz Viterbo; I saw the circulation of my own dark blood; I saw the coupling of love and the modification of death; I saw the Aleph from every point and angle, and in the Aleph I saw the earth and in the earth the Aleph and in the Aleph the earth; I saw my own face and my own bowels; I saw your face; and I felt dizzy and wept, for my eyes had seen that secret and conjectured object whose name is common to all men but which no man has looked upon—the unimaginable universe.[2]

There it is! The unimaginable universe—unimagined only because the lenses of our local imagination are too limited to contain it, and because, as Borges suggests, the successive nature of language trembles before the simultaneity of such an experience. But, as it was known in that revelation in the cellar in Buenos Aires, it can also be known when, in certain states of consciousness joined to quantum resonance, one gains access to any part of the universe.

The process philosophers of the early twentieth century pointed to all of this. In 1907 Bergson said that ultimate reality is an underlying web of connections and that the brain generally screens out the larger reality. He coined the term "cerebral reducing valve" to account for the lensing system. And in 1929 Alfred North Whitehead described nature as a great expanding nexus of occurrences beyond sense perception, with all minds, all things interlocking.

As we shall see, field theory and quantum physics gave further assent to the conjectures of these philosophers, especially Bell's 1964 theory, which presents evidence to connect all spatially separated events. It tells us that no theory of reality compatible with quantum theory can require spatially separated events to be independent, but must allow for the interconnectedness of distant events in a way that differs from ordinary experience.

Seen from this perspective, psychic phenomena are only by-products of the simultaneous-everywhere-matrix. And synchronicity—those coincidental occurrences that seem to have some higher design or connectedness—would seem to derive from the purposeful, patterning, organicizing nature of the primary order, the root system of the Farm, as it were. There is no such thing as coincidence if, following upon the holographic model, everything is in resonance and in patterns of interference with everything else. If the hologrammatic-Buddhist-monadic-Cabalistic theory is true, then you are literally ubiquitous throughout the universe and are being sent out as an interference pattern through the flow emulsion of the ether (a term that has been resanctified by high-energy physicists in recent years) to all possible places in the matrix of space-time.

Dennis Gabor's invention of holography made the metaphor concrete by objectifying in practical and useful terms the speculations of thousands of years. Suddenly the metaphor became accessible and provoked an "aha!" reaction across a spectrum of many fields of inquiry.

In neurophysiology, for example, evidence is mounting that, like

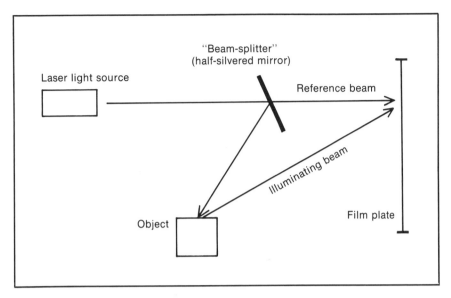

Holo-gram: whole message. Light from the laser goes through a maze of mirrors and "beam-splitters" to form two beams of light to make the hologram. A beam-splitter is a half-silvered mirror that allows part of the light ("reference beam") to pass directly through to the film while reflecting part of the light ("illuminating beam") toward the object from which it is reflected again onto the film. When the two beams meet, what is recorded on the film is the result of the interference patterns between the two beams. If the beams coincide, or are "in phase," there will be enough light to expose the film because the light energy is reinforced at the points of interference. If the beams are out of phase, they will cancel each other's energy and leave a dark place on the film. (Robert Satterlee, *Dromenon,* Spring/Summer, 1980.)

the hologram, memory storage is ubiquitous throughout the brain. Each neuron probably contains the totality of all your memories coded in interference patterns of waves. Thus each neuron may be viewed as a marvel of hologrammatic efficiency able to store billions of bits of information in a tiny space. (Some physiologists have begun to speculate that it is not just the brain which functions as a hologram but that perhaps other cellular structures in our bodies are functioning that way too. However, this cannot be proven at this time.)

Karl Pribram's genius was to take the hologram model of memory storage and suggest ways in which the brain performs complex calculations on the frequencies of the data it receives. Using the fluid mathematics of Fourier transforms, he describes the intricacies of nerve impulses traveling along between cells through a network of fine fibers on the cells—through what we might call the Indra's network of the brain. He speculated with great specificity on how, when the impulses cross the cell, the fibers move in slow waves that are then encoded throughout the rest of the brain in much the same way as the bells sound through every part of Indra's net.[3]

But now questions arise that have eternally haunted the speculative mind: Who rules in these realms of infinite lattices where a quadrillion different processes occur every second? Who garners the light and decodes its patterns into sounds and colors, tastes and smells, data and dreams, decisions and flights of conceptual fancy? Who does the actual knowing? Who in the brain is interpreting the hologram?

As St. Francis once put it, "What we are looking for is what is looking." Suppose for a moment that what is "out there" is isomorphic and of the same essential form as that which is "in here." Suppose that the universe is holographic and our brain-mind system is a hologram knowing a Hologram.

David Bohm, the Nobel physicist, provides an evocative quickening to this conundrum when he suggests on the basis of quantum theory that there are two orders of reality.[4] One is *the primary order, which is implicate, enfolded, harboring our reality in much the same way as the DNA in the nucleus of a cell harbors potential life and directs the nature of its unfolding.* This is an order of pure Beingness, pure frequency, consonant with the realm of Plato's Forms or Whitehead's Primordial Nature of God. Buddhist and Hindu philosophies have similar metaphysical systems and psychologies to account for this primary order of pure potentiality.

In this primary order there are no things and there are no movements as we understand them. It is a realm that transcends specification and knows neither here nor there.

Bohm refers to this primary order as the frequency domain. But as the concept of frequency remains an abstraction, I prefer to look for another metaphor to describe a realm that is at once the coalescence of all Pattern and the living Source of all caring. For I see it as a realm of Love and organicity, the lure of evolution and the Mind that is minding. It is the Place of the greening of reality. Thus I think of the primary order as the place from which the forms of reality are engendered, pervading all our processes and, potentially, totally available at any particular part of our reality.

The secondary order is second-generation reality and as such is explicate, unfolded, manifest in space and time, the decoded hologrammatic image of reality. All apparent movement and substance, then, are of the secondary order.

The secondary explicate order is an order of lenses, and we are saddled with many kinds, not least of which are the five major sensory lenses. We generally keep ourselves from knowledge of the primary order and its available abundance by means of these various lenses. The lenses of our brains mathematically construct secondary-order "hard" reality by interpreting frequencies from the primary order.

Additionally, many of the lenses we wear are cultural and are limited by the particular shutterings of tribe and nation. I think of a certain tribe in the Kalahari who "know" that the world ends about two hundred and fifty yards beyond their local area. It is reported that if you take them to that point, they will see nothing beyond it but a void. And if you tell them that you will prove to them that the world continues to exist beyond that point by stepping over the line of their so-called "world's end," they cry and beg you not to. If you persist in doing so, they are no longer able to see you and mourn your departure until you return across the line into the existing world.

Lest we feel superior to these people, let us remind ourselves that we do much the same thing, albeit in ways that are at once more subtle and more vicious. Think of the wars of ideology that have blackened our historical landscape, the many gatings of prejudice, the current ruling superstitions of scientism, the selective apertures of media.

Ask yourself where your acculturated lensing system shuts down and why. Is it at those points that lie beyond the physical, beyond what can be touched, measured, proved, beyond rationalism? How do your automatic shutterings react to the coming of a global civilization, to the sharing of all privileges and responsibilities by men and women, to the elevation of the qualities of mind, body, and spirit of the human race in the near future?

As children we have played the bittersweet game of the cracks in the pavement. Unwittingly we continue to play the game for the rest of our lives, fearing to approach the binding lines lest we lose what little reality we are able to sustain.

The most insidious of all lensing systems is that of the "I." The "I" is too often a little local camera with a ridiculously small capacity for picking up frequency. The modus vivendi of the "I" lens is to focus on those views that gain power for the "I." The unfortunate consequence of this focus is that it blocks the possibilities of larger realities.

By reorchestrating psychospiritual and neural functioning to by-pass the cerebral, cultural, and psychological reducing valves, we discover that we are naturally attuned to the source, or matrix, of reality. We discover at such times that we are both/and, implicate *and* explicate, uniquely our own and yet containing the information of the whole. We are citizens of two worlds that are One if we can but learn to see it.

Consider the mystical aesthetics of Thoreau, especially in those passages where he speaks of the occasional ability to see the higher order of reality behind the formed veilings of sensuous reality.

We get only transient and partial glimpses of the beauty
of the world. Standing at the right angle we are dazzled
by the colors of the rainbow in colorless ice. From the
right point of view every storm and every drop in it is a
rainbow. Beauty and music are not mere traits and ex-
ceptions; they are the rule and character. . . . I have seen
an attribute of another world and condition of things. It
is a wonderful fact that I should be affected, and thus
deeply and powerfully, more than by aught else in all my
experience—that this fruit should be borne in me,
sprung from a seed finer than the spores of fungi, floated
from other atmospheres! . . . Here these invisible seeds
settle, and bear flowers and fruits of immortal beauty.[5]

Visions of such illumined minds testify to the possibility that the brain is
a hologram interpreting a holographic universe.

As hologrammatic being, every part of you is a nexus of all possible
occasions that ever were and ever are. You are therefore the whole and
the part. You are who you are, a substantial being woven upon the grid
of space and time in the explicate order, and you are also the reflector of
all there is in the implicate order. Therefore you are both identity (who
you are in your developmental life process) and holonomy (of the order
of the whole). The structures of your being quite literally reflect the
ongoing structures of the universe.

As can be readily seen, there are many exciting implications growing out of this paradigm. One of the most important is that certain states
of consciousness are more conducive to those states of resonance that
allow for the opening to the primary reality. Harmonious, coherent
states of consciousness—love, unity, empathy, deep meditative states,
prayer, rapture—are more nearly attuned to this holonomic reality, a
reality of love, organicity, and the harmonics that are inherent in an
order where all Forms are interwoven.

In human relationships this can occur when strong feelings of love
and empathy allow the boundaries of the self to acquire what I call
"leaky margins" and so enter into resonance (perhaps in quantum terms)
with the other. Anxiety, doubt, and fear not only inhibit resonance but
add their toxic lenses to the lenses that already exist so that even one's
own identity becomes questionable. You may have recognized this
capacity as you did the dyadic exercise in Chapter 6.

When we consider the cooperative flow of the universe and ourselves that occurs in times of intense resonance (love, creativity, unitive
experience), we see how natural and seemly is the transfer of information from one dimension to the next. Suddenly the book falls open to
just the right page. The phone rings and out of "nowhere" the person

you needed to get in touch with is on the other end. The holoverse dances for your benefit in ordinary and extraordinary ways. New forms emerge as we tune into the resonant fields of an evolving reality.

Or, as the thirteenth-century mystic Meister Eckhart once said, "The eye by which I see God is the same eye by which God sees me." He got into a lot of trouble with the Pope over that one.

Max Planck may have begun the twentieth-century scientific inquiry into this phenomenon by suggesting that the brain may function on quantum principles. A series of cells starting to resonate will set millions of neurons firing in a quantum tunneling effect.

In those unitive states of consciousness associated with mystical experience, rapture, and meditation, there is often a stilling of the mind and an accompanying regularity and slowing of brain waves into synchronized alpha and theta patterns. Sometimes the coherence of the wave pattern reaches the proportions of macroscopic functioning. In psychological terms the phenomena of insight, of falling in love, of discovery and breakthrough may well find their physiological correlates in patterns of such resonance amplified in quantum terms throughout the brain. In our normal awareness, thoughts and perceptions move from one thing to another; the brain exhibits a great deal of variation in its different parts as well as a predominance of rapid beta waves.

Studying the brain-wave patterns of subjects in deep meditation, Lawrence Domash and his associates discovered that these patterns move to coherence in millions of cells, resulting in the transition of consciousness to another phase level. The focusing of attention that occurs in meditation appears to organize neural processes into coherently interacting patterns with a high degree of resonance and similarity of the EEG throughout the brain. Microphase patterns of ordinary attentional processes are transformed in meditation into macrophase coherence. This results in unbounded—unlensed—awareness, mystical experiences, and a genre of feeling and knowing that seems to belong to a deeper order of reality.[6]

Another way of looking at this is to consider the metaphor of superconductivity. In most electrical flow systems there is a resistance, analogous to a turned-on lightbulb impeding the flow of current, which creates the practical uses for the electrical current. But in superconductive states the electrons can flow unimpeded in perpetual motion through a flow loop.

This may be what is happening in the experience of deep meditation: neurons become superconductive flow systems, phase-coherent with other neurons by virtue of quantum tunneling. Resistance is overcome, the usual kinds of perceptual and psychological lenses are no longer operative, and the brain becomes a very different instrument, one that is available to receive messages from the primary reality.

Domash has suggested that there might be a permanent macrophasic coherent wave function deep in the brain, a realm of order and stillness. If this is so, then *original grace is indigenous to the brain and to our very being.* The signal is always calling, but we are rarely available.

The possible human hears the call, awakening to those processes through which the mind-brain system becomes "superconductive" and is able to enter into macrophase functioning. There can then occur the linking of consciousness and the extraordinary statement of Being that is going on all the time. But, and there is indeed a but, you have to find this linking with intentionality and commitment to learn from it. There are realities present here that can potentially transform the human condition.

How do we get beyond the shutterings of our cultural trance so as to have the courage and capacity to nurture the forms of the possible? How may we become co-creative with the evolutionary process?

We can find some guidance in the search for the answers to these questions in the work of the Nobel prize-winner Ilya Prigogine, whose work on dissipative structures in the field of nonequilibrium thermodynamics provides critical insights into that process of higher order emerging from fluctuation and instability. In his theory the great *bête noire* of natural science—the Second Law of Thermodynamics—is shown to be operating in the service of emerging structure. *Order emerges because of entropy, not despite it.*

It has been simply summarized as follows: "The more complex a structure, the more energy it must dissipate to maintain all that complexity. This flux of energy makes the system highly unstable, subject to internal fluctuations—and sudden change. If these fluctuations or perturbations reach a critical size, they are amplified by the system's many connections and can drive the system into a new state—even more ordered, coherent, and connected. The new state occurs as a sudden shift."[7]

This is true with molecules or theologies. Dissipative structures may model the way in which the implicate components of the primary order become explicate—that is, the way in which the timeless, spaceless realm of Essence moves into the manifest space-and-time-determined realm of Existence. As you may have noted, this corresponds exactly with what happens in the self-orchestration of consciousness in meditative states when the brain moves from local functioning to macrophasic wave functioning and enters the larger reality.

All of this suggests that the growth of consciousness is encouraged by a rhythm of dynamic input followed by coherence. The more complex a system, the more capacity it has for transformation. Its parts cooperate to reorganize it. Thus the more ideas you have, and the more information and accessibility to experience and reflections upon this experience, the more you are able to respond to the larger quantum resonance of the cosmos in such a way as to bring holonomic information back into the world of space and time. You enter into states of bliss-plus-knowledge, unitive reality plus specificity.

The high actualizers I have known, the pragmatic saints and world-making mystics, have been essentially of that genre: they have allowed their body-minds to become fields in space-time from which can be harvested the formings of the Farm. Their will and intentionality have become macrophase and consonant with the primary order. Of course they get the job done.

St. Francis returned from his raptures with very specific and practical ideas for changing the value systems of Europe. And consider the pragmatic genius of Teresa of Avila, whose unitive experiences left her with immense know-how in reorganizing the religious orders of Spain. There are countless other examples of highly honed minds entering into the mystical experience of the holonomic reality and returning with concrete plans to effect important changes in society.

Just so the seed crystal, dropped into a supersaturated solution, crystallizes into a larger and more complex pattern. You are that seed crystal when you are in a state of dynamic complexity and openness to interactive systems, people, and ideas. Then, when you enter into the supersaturated solution of the holonomic order, you are able to achieve a much larger quantum resonance with the whole. You are available to be seeded for new forms of action, formings, evolutionary strivings, co-creation. You become co-creative with the whole. When you return, there is rarely any question of knowing what you have to do because now you are the doer, the doing, and the done. Living now with the knowledge that you are both identity and holonomy, you become part of the universal nexus of creative occasions.

Potentially, this is true for all of us. Thus I am a zealous advocate of lifelong learning, growing, acquiring new and old ideas from many fields, recovering the cultural heritage that schools never gave us. We must think in multimodal ways—kinesthetically, in words and in images, and above all we must have sensuous bouts with ideas. For the more complex and interactive a creative nonequilibrium you have, the more "hooks and eyes" you develop to catch and bring back the forms of possibility when you enter into coherence with the whole.

The new forms of the possible human demand a mode of creative intention in which we bridge the chasm between the implicate and explicate orders and assume the coherence and consistency of the two. In so doing we open up our many latencies to become channels for co-creation in space and time.

What all this seems to mean is that we have to create miracles. And what are miracles? Miracles are *merely* the conscious activation of more patterns of reality than are usually seen in the linear-analytic Newtonian lens. William Blake exhorts us:

> May God us keep
> from single vision
> and Newton's sleep.

(Although to be perfectly fair to Sir Isaac, when he wasn't being Newtonian he occupied a great deal of his time with occult and alchemical endeavors!)

In many parts of the Eastern world miracles are called *siddhis* and are generally known by the terms in which they are described in the Yoga Sutras of Patanjali: knowledge of the past and future, telepathy, invisibility, and levitation.[8] Now, these are rather dramatic events when they occur, but in the form described do little to improve the human condition and a great deal to enhance human hubris. That is why religious teachers recommend that their acquisition (which may come spontaneously with enlightenment) be followed by their dismissal lest the adepts be distracted by their own dazzling displays and lose their way in the search for integral reality.

Rather than dismissing them, it may be time to look at the nature of *siddhis* in a more informed and productive way. If nothing else, they are telling proof that the laws of form in the explicate order are only a special case of the implicate order.

In the Domash work referred to earlier, twelve meditators were found to have had consistent experiences of unitive consciousness and were designated as "clear." This "clear" group reported the occurrence of *siddhis* as well as "witnessing sleep," a state of lucid dreaming and conscious awareness while sleeping. They also demonstrated greatly increased fluency of creative and original thought. There was a significant correlation between high creativity and the number of experiences of *siddhis*.

What is high creativity but the ability to look at things in terms of many other things and to process many different kinds of information at the same time? Hence, some of the exercises offered earlier in this book. On the physiological level there is evidently an extraordinary degree of resonance and cross-exchange of different neurological systems, driving the organism to systemic transformation and a new level of awareness and capacity. In such instances the brain seems to be a different instrument, one that can do different things and perhaps obey different laws.

Let us again examine high creativity in the light of this. There is an almost unimpeded flow of ideas, information, memories, and patterns that tend to move in organic groupings. Subjective time distortion with an accompanying acceleration of mental process is a frequent occurrence, and our brains process millions of these images in microseconds.

We could speculate that the potency of imagistic creative thought and its innate organicity of pattern is so powerfully desirous of expression that it recruits the entire matrix of the body-mind system to do its work. Quite possibly the human system, in a state of high creativity, sets up an organic phase-coherence with the surrounding fields of reality so that the very building matrices of reality begin to organize around the creative intention.

Like sunlight and the nutrients of earth and air organizing around the new buds of springtime, in creative states the budding intentions are in resonance with the holonomic reality, evoking from the primary order the proper nutrients needed to allow for the emergence of the physical expression of the creative intention, be it a novel, a symphony, a dissertation, a relationship, a business, or a community enterprise. During this process you discover that you are no longer identified with your personality; the local self becomes the "through which" the creative process finds form.

In neurological "recruitment" more and more parts of the brain are called into simultaneous action to accomplish more and more difficult tasks. In "miracle-making" (for which you may read high actualizing or creativity), the brain's recruitment system is used to its fullest.

In our study of religious and creative experience at the Foundation, we discovered that it is virtually impossible to have religious experiences without also having creative ideas. Similarly, it is virtually impossible to have intense creative experiences without their becoming religious or unitive.

In the past I had always understood this phenomenologically. Mystical or religious experience almost always yielded an increase in creative work. Creative endeavors yielded experiences of the knower, the knowledge, and the known enfolded in an undifferentiated unity. It was as simple or as complex as that. Now I am discovering that the physics and metaphysics of these experiences are the same.

In the most profound of these experiences you know that the farthest star lives in you and you are the stargate through which the world is seeded with new forms. You are identity and holonomy, the One and the Many. You are ubiquitous through space-time, existent in the Ultimate, and uniquely yourself in local reality. You are the hologram knowing the Hologram.

Or, in the words of the ancient Vedas, you are at the moment of understanding, *Purusha*, the cosmic Person whose being is a quantum coherence of body, mind, psyche, and the fields of life spanning the universe, animated by love and creativity.[9]

This total coherence is a state of pure potentiality. It is also a state of dynamic coherent nesting: the brain in macrophase is nested in the psyche, which is nested in the mind, which is nested in the fields of being, which are nested in the Mind of God. Upon this nest the Egg—cosmic or otherwise—can be laid.

Why must we have a passion for reality? Why must we love and desire and be filled with metaphysical ardor? Because these passions set up in us the momentum for bringing new forms into being. The process of realization primes us in all our parts to be in ecological resonance with more fields of reality, gives us the larger body—*Purusha*—which then acts at local levels to strengthen all possible neuronal networks lying at the basis of each type of motor and sensory performance, every level of mind-body coordination, raising the frequency and capacity of thought, evolving the self, and, finally, growing God-in-us.

Love is the form that gives life to the process and is itself increased by its own endeavor. Love becomes quite literally *all*. In states of coherence one is marrying oneself on all levels. Love then takes the next quantum leap and one loves all others in one's immediate reality. This then moves to an all-encompassing Love of all and everything. And so love becomes the most gentle and most powerful agent for the fielding and forming of reality. In love the lenses fall away. In love one forms all formings. In love one becomes generate in the Aleph.

In love one arrives home at last . . .

Exercise 1

Orchestrating the Brain and Entering the Holoverse*

TIME: 45 minutes

In this exercise you will again "talk" to the brain as you did earlier in the Left Brain/Right Brain exercise in Chapter 3, only this time you will be opening the lenses to the larger reality of the primary order—the ultimate source of the music within.

PREPARATION

Be seated in a comfortable position that you will be able to sustain for some time and close your eyes. Breathe deeply, following your breath all the way in and all the way out for several minutes.

---

*Adapted from an exercise of Robert Masters.

Orchestrating the Brain

THE EXERCISE

With your right hand explore the part of the skull where your brain is. Be sure that you follow your hand with your attention. Be aware of the sensations in your head and the sensations in your hand as it explores your head.

Now do the same thing with both hands, holding as much of your skull as you can with your two hands.

Gently move the skin up and down over your skull. Squeeze your head as if you were massaging it. Squeeze and release . . . squeeze and release . . .

Put your hands down a minute.

Now direct your attention to how your head feels as a result of what you did with your hands and the awareness you brought to this process.

Direct your attention now to the inside of your skull, to the space where your good friend, the brain, lives. Let your eyes look there also.

Look to the left side, the left hemisphere of the brain. Breathe freely.

Be aware of whatever you may sense, and look over toward the right side and the right hemisphere of the brain. See if you sense any movement, a gentle pulsing feeling or whatever it might be.

Now let your eyes and your attention roam around the space inside your skull where your brain is. Try to identify the place where the two hemispheres come together, the bridge that connects them—the corpus collosum. Mentally travel along that bridge, up and down, perhaps in your mind's eye climbing the bridge as you would climb a mountain and then sliding back down again.

Now imagine that you can walk through the labyrinthine convolutions of your own brain, traveling through the twisting, turning crevices, the great gray-pink walls of living brain tissue rising high on either side of you.

Inhale deeply and, as you do so, try to feel your brain inflating. And when you breathe out feel your brain deflating.

Inhale and expand your brain. Exhale and contract it. With each breath allow your brain to expand and contract . . . expand and contract . . . expand and contract . . .

Maintain your attention there in your brain and recall that your brain produces various kinds of wave patterns. The alpha waves are often associated with a diffused and serene state of consciousness as well as with meditation states. Your mind knows how to orchestrate the brain so that it produces a preponderance of alpha waves. Suggest now to your mind that it act upon the brain so that the brain will produce the long amplitude waves of alpha, the kind associated with meditation. Suggest to your brain also that it do this, your brain and mind acting together to produce predominantly alpha waves.

Breathe freely, just maintain your consciousness on your brain . . . alpha waves . . . alpha waves . . . alpha waves. With the alpha waves the brain becomes as quiet as placid waters.

And your brain can also produce theta waves that are slower than alpha and are often associated with creative reverie. Tell your mind to suggest to your brain that it produce the slow waves of theta . . . theta waves . . . theta waves.

And your brain can also produce delta waves to make you drowsy, to bring you close to a sleeping state. Let it now produce delta waves . . . delta waves . . . delta waves.

With the preponderance of the much faster beta waves you will be much more alert, so let your mind orchestrate your brain so that it produces beta waves and you become more alert, much more alert and awake than with delta, theta, or alpha. A preponderance now of beta waves . . . beta waves . . . beta waves.

See if you can discriminate differences among the four waves.

Your brain also produces substances rather like the pain-killing drug morphine. One of them, endorphine (endogenous morphine), is secreted by your brain as a painkiller and can also produce a kind of euphoria and pleasure. And suggest now to your mind that it tell your brain to produce enough of this internally manufactured pain-killing, pleasure-giving substance so that you can experience some of its effects.

If you are actually experiencing some pain, have your mind suggest to your brain that it knows how to send some endorphine to the site of the pain, bringing some relief, if not complete relief.

There are also in your brain pleasure centers that can give feelings of pleasure to your body.

Suggest now that these pleasure centers become activated, with one or more of your brain pleasure centers becoming more and more active, bringing sensations of pleasure to the body.

See if you can feel now that these centers have become more active, the pleasure centers evoking the body. And as you do this, feel the rush of pleasure, a kind of glowing throughout your body. You can feel it in your skin or deeper down as streaming sensations . . . the pleasure centers becoming more and more active.

Now concentrate on your breath and become quiet again.

Have your mind suggest to your brain that it produce alpha waves. Pay attention to your brain as it produces long amplitudes of alpha waves.

Now your brain is beginning to produce more and more theta, the waves of creative reverie. Theta waves . . . theta waves . . .

And then delta for a while, the drowsy waves so that you would easily drop off to sleep. Delta waves . . . delta waves . . .

Now have your brain produce beta waves . . . beta waves . . . and you are becoming much more alert and wider awake.

Now suggest to yourself that the parts of your brain involved with imagination and imagining become increasingly stimulated and activated so that pictures or images come into your consciousness.

As you speak to your brain about activating imagery, imagine that images and pictures are beginning to come—animals, architecture, faces, beings, landscapes or whatever it might be. Your brain is producing for you some of the contents from its vast storehouse of imagery.

And now suggest to your brain that your senses be stimulated and made more acute, your mind orchestrating your brain and, through your brain, the nervous system and your sensory system to give more to the intense experience of your senses.

First of all, ask your brain to extend your sense of hearing, so that you will hear more than you were hearing before. Extended hearing . . . extended hearing. Listen and note what you did not hear before.

Now allow your sense of touch to become more acute. Extended touch . . . extended touch. Touch whatever is around you—the floor, your clothes, parts of your body, whatever it might be—and see if your sense of touch is more acute and feels more than it ordinarily would.

Hold your skull, your brain cage, in your hands again. See how you touch your hair now, and the skin and the bones beneath the skin. Remember how it was when you touched your head at the beginning of this exercise and how you may more completely experience the top of your head as you hold it in your hands.

Squeeze and massage. Gently massage your scalp as you did before. Compare the sensations in your scalp as well as in your hands. See if your scalp now senses your hands more completely.

Put your hands down and continue to pay attention to your brain. Think about the waving turning convolutions of your brain.

Be aware of your corpus collosum, the bridge that connects your two hemispheres.

Be aware now of your whole brain.

Now pay attention to your spine and where it comes up to the top of your neck and the base of your skull and how it goes down and down all the way to the coccyx, or tailbone, at the end of the spine.

Take your awareness all the way up your spine again to the top of your head, and all the way down to your coccyx.

Paying close attention to each stage of the journey, travel up and down your spine several more times.

Focus now on the area just above your nose, inside and between your eyebrows. In that general vicinity is located the remarkable pineal gland, which, in some disciplines, is identified with the chakra of the third eye. Suggest to yourself that you stimulate that gland or chakra. And as you do so you are stimulating your visionary capacities and gaining access to subtler and deeper modes of perception.

Using the metaphor of the third eye, think of that eye as being there and as expanding and contracting . . . expanding and contracting . . . expanding and contracting. Think of the lid over your eye raising so that your eye opens. Open and close the lid over your third eye.

See what that eye looks like, if you can. What color is it? What kind of light shines from that eye? Does it sparkle? Is it gemlike? Is it shaped like your other eyes or is it different in some ways? Think about seeing with that eye. Look out with that open third eye at whatever you may see: images, colors, events, whatever.

Now once more have your mind suggest to your brain that it will become more and more alert, the whole mind and body becoming more alert and also more responsive to suggestions of better functioning of the whole brain and nervous system. Your brain, which is your very good friend, is helping to enhance all the systems of your body, extending your senses and bringing more awareness to all of your parts.

Now feel your body image entering your awareness. Although you still look at your brain, you now have a much greater sense of your whole body and the way that body is part of all that is.

The sense of your hands extending in space and time, your arms spanning the universe, your feet the ground of the universe, your pelvis the source of creation, your heart beating at the core of existence, your shoulders holding up the world, your neck containing the passageways of life, your head the continuum of totalities, your eyes all-seeing, your ears receiving all harmonies, your breath the breath of life . . . and in your brain, your dear friend begins a symphony within.

All waves becoming one wave, one song . . . the song of all being, the song of the holoverse, every part of your brain, every pulse and wave is in rapture with the whole. Open to the Source, enter the Source, receive now the holoverse, receive the totality, the primary level of all frequency, the source of all forms, the cradle of being, of God, of all that there is. Receive now all there is . . .

Allow five minutes for this.

Now begin to come back, but knowing that you can return to the Source. Suggest to yourself that you are becoming wider and wider awake, more and more alert, and have your mind and your brain working together to make changes throughout your body, to heighten awareness, increase alertness, helping you to truly wake up and be wider awake than you have ever been in the past, so that your previous existence may seem like sleep.

Become so awake that you begin to feel free from coercion from both within and without, feeling much more free in an awakeness that is freedom from dictation by impulses, be they social, biological, or processes of the unconscious.

Free now to make many more kinds of choices, free to recognize the subtle patterns that connect all existence, free to join and enjoy a larger ecology, free to know yourself as existing in the holoverse and having access to all that is.

The unconscious and conscious minds becoming increasingly one, your body and your body image becoming increasingly one and more and more aware.

Your self as identity—who you are in local space and time—and your Self as holonomy, your cosmic beingness bridging together so that they now have access to each other.

And when you are ready, when you feel this bridging and empowerment, wake up and open your eyes. And continue to wake up more and more, letting the knowledge you have gained and the experience you have known continue to deepen within you.

DISCUSSION

Allow this experience to become familiar, this capacity to orchestrate states of consciousness. Look at some of the situations and possibilities in your life from the perspective you have now and notice if they seem any different. For some people, the paradoxes and puzzles of their lives resolve themselves on a new level as the interconnectedness of all that we are is deeply experienced. In the "leaky margins" that are induced in this exercise, feelings and information flow together in new combinations and the creative possibility emerges. If this happens for you, celebrate it and enjoy.

Exercise 2

The Creative Intention

TIME: 30 to 60 minutes

For this exercise you will take the two orders—explicate and implicate—back and forth between here and the holoverse, creating a process in which every aspect of our being is in loving yearning and resonance, every cell and molecule in loving yearning for its unfoldment. Then you will bring the energy-momentum of that yearning and that unfoldment to the creative intention itself.

PREPARATION

I suggest that you read this exercise carefully to feel its movements, rhythms, and metaphors before doing it. The "mmmmm's" throughout serve to remind you to hum and move continuously; each "mmmmm" in the course of the text, unless otherwise noted, indicates a pause of three to five seconds. This is all flexible and arranged to be of service to your spontaneous creativity.

Before you begin, reflect on what you would like to accomplish, be, or have happen in your life before too long. Your intention should help, not harm, and its actualization should be a happy addition to the physical, mental, and spiritual growth of yourself and the planet.

First, take twenty minutes to wander around—outdoors if possible, engaging and conversing with the forms of nature. During this time—whimsically or seriously, however you like—think about your creative intention. Find in this meditative time something specifically important for you to be, to do, to have, to become in order to become a good co-creator, a good *explicate* of the larger reality.

The intention is looking for you, too. Be open to it. You will know when it's right, when it's appropriate. Ask yourself these questions and write the answers down:

What is trying to form itself through me?

What do I want from the holoverse?

What does the holoverse want from me?

What do we want together?

Return in twenty minutes with an interesting, juicy, living sense of what your creative intention is. This sense may be more kinesthetic than verbal. *Feel* your creative intention trying to become manifest.

THE EXERCISE

Begin with a kind of moving chant, a resonating hum, letting your whole body vibrate very subtly, your arms and hands lifted aloft like branches of a tree shimmering and creating a field of frequency. If you need to get up and move at any point during this experience, you can—keep the humming going, keep the vibrations going while you move.

Begin a humming and vibrating chant . . . *mmmmm* . . .

Now put forth your creative intention . . . *mmmmm* . . . literally into every cell . . . *mmmmm*. Let it flutter and pulsate . . . *mmmmm* . . . literally into every cell of your being. A very subtle "hmmmm" sound, just keep that up . . . *mmmmm* . . . very gentle . . . *mmmmm* . . . very subtle . . . *mmmmm*. This will go on for some time . . . *mmmmm*. (Fifteen seconds.)

Let a kind of delicious rippling wave of frequencies hum throughout your being . . . *mmmmm* . . . your body, your protein structures, your cells, your atoms, your mind, the force fields around you, the creative intention moving as waves, like a series of interference patterns . . . *mmmmm*. (Fifteen seconds.)

You and all the waves are one with your creative intention . . . *mmmmm*.

Try putting your fingers in your ears, creating a resonance chamber, and let that vibration pulsate through you . . . *mmmmm*. (Forty-five seconds.) This resonance moves through every part of you so that it is a microphase of desire and intention . . . *mmmmm*. (Sixty seconds.)

All right, now that is coded. Now we can go about building up the nonequilibrium system of yearning.

Knowing that your intention is now in every cell, continue the subtle vibrational movement and the humming, the very subtle listening . . . *mmmmm* . . . and feel the desire of the atom, its yearning for other atoms, its yearning to become molecule . . . *mmmmm* . . . the yearning of the form for the atom . . . *mmmmm* . . . and feel the momentum of the desire, of the creative intention of that atom . . . *mmmmm*. (Thirty seconds.) Let the yearning find its form, find what the atom needs . . . *mmmmm*. (Forty-five seconds.)

You are now becoming a molecule composed of these atoms. Continue to hum and vibrate through your body, you arms and hands . . . *mmmmm*. Feel the yearning, the desire, the exploration of the world of the molecule in its explicate order, and feel the yearning of God for the molecule . . . *mmmmm*. Feel these two and the tension of the two pulling and moving toward each other, into each other. Feel the consonance of the molecule's yearning, the full momentum of the molecule girded by the momentum of the atoms . . . *mmmmm*. (Sixty seconds.)

And the molecules, illuminated by the living force, are becoming *cells*—and *be* a cell, totally a cell, a cell in yearning. Feel the yearning of the implicate primary order for the cell, for its becomings, and *be* the momentum of that yearning and that desire for the cell buttressed by the yearning of its molecules and atoms . . . *mmmmm*. (Sixty seconds.)

And the cell evolves into greater and greater complexity, into interrelated systems, and these body systems are desirous and yearning and have passion for a kind of completion, fulfillment, and creative intention . . . *mmmmm* . . . the Being of the implicate order yearning for the body systems . . . *mmmmm* . . . and *be* that yearning . . . *be* its momentum and let it feel welcome to unfold its possibilities . . . *mmmmm*. (Forty-five seconds.)

And now you are a body, a complete human body, and *be* the yearning of that body . . . *mmmmm* . . . and *be* the yearning of the primary implicate order to bridge between body and Being and Being and body. *Be* the yearning and the exploration of its possibilities, powered and encouraged by the momentum of atom and molecule and cell and body system, and the systems of systems that orchestrate the body . . . *mmmmm*. (Sixty seconds.)

That body is a fetus seeking to be born, and *be* the yearning of that fetus . . . *mmmmm* . . . feeling the creative intention in the fetus . . . empassioned by the yearnings of atom, molecule, cell, system, and body . . . *mmmmm* . . . and feel God yearning for the fetus to be manifest . . . unfolded . . . to become what it can be . . . *mmmmm*. (Sixty seconds.)

And now you are the infant, the baby, and *be* the passion of the infant, the creative intention, the future-coded desire of the infant . . . *mmmmm* . . . supported by the yearning of atom and molecule and body system and fetus, the passion becoming greater, more complex, more realities added, more dimensions . . . *mmmmm* . . . *mmmmm*. Find the forms that are looking for you . . . *mmmmm*. (Thirty seconds.)

Now, in the becoming, the yearning, the passion and intention of the child, let the forms unfold as you find them, let the connections be made, nurtured by the yearning of the infant, the fetus, the body, the body systems, the cell, the molecule, the atom . . . *mmmmm* . . . the desire and *passion* becoming more and more coherent and complex . . . and the coherent complexity of spirit yearning for the embodied form of the child. (If it helps to close off your ears to make your sounds, do so . . . *mmmmm*. Change the sound if you like; move your tongue around against your teeth and the roof of your mouth, experiment with rhythms of frequency.) Let the passion unfold the child . . . *mmmmm*. (Sixty seconds.)

Now you are the yearning, the intention of the adolescent, reaching to forms, new complexities, the fervor of the adolescent encouraged by the passion of the child, the fetus, the whole body and the body systems, the cells and molecules and atoms and within the atoms the realm of pure frequency . . . *mmmmm* . . . all these systems becoming more and more complex, the yearnings of the adolescent becoming greater and deeper . . . *mmmmm*. (Sixty seconds.)

Going now into the passion of the mature years, the desires and yearnings, the creative intention . . . *mmmmm* . . . the lovings of the mature years, the reaching out for new creations, new forms . . . *mmmmm*. (Sixty seconds.)

Becoming now the passion of the elder yearning for Being, the matrix upon which the outer forms are woven . . . *mmmmm*. (Sixty seconds.)

Coming now, the coming of death, the yearning of death for the yielding of life into another form . . . *mmmmm*. (Thirty seconds.)

Becoming the passion of male and female, yang and yin yearning for union . . . *mmmmm*. (Thirty seconds.)

Letting all of these forces move now, mounting in a momentum of desire . . . *mmmmm* . . . the passion of the planet and of nature, yearning for form and expression: you are that—That Art Thou, filled with and buttressed by all the other yearnings, becoming more complex . . . *mmmmm*. (Thirty seconds.)

Feel and *be* the desire of the explicate order for union with the implicate order, of spirit with nature and nature with spirit . . . *mmmmm* . . . the passion of yourself for God and God for you . . . *mmmmm*. (Fifteen seconds.)

The passion of the implicate order for the explicate, feel and *be* the passion of God for you . . . *mmmmm*. (Fifteen seconds.)

Let it all rise in you, getting more and more complex. Deepen with it, and let the passion of implicate for explicate and explicate for implicate go back and forth in resonance . . . *mmmmm*.

And sing the song of total coherence. Let that hum become your hymn to the holoverse. Let the coherence move through every part of your being . . . *mmmmm*. (Continue singing.) Every part of your being is all Being, you are incarnate *bodhisattva*, God-manifest in self . . . *mmmmm*. (Continue singing.) Let yourself show it, the hologram knowing the Hologram, the union with the Source. Sing it forth and let it be expressed totally . . . *mmmmm*. (Ninety seconds. Continue singing.)

And with this as background going on all the time, put forth your creative intention—and *be it*!

Send it throughout the entire order of Being as waves traversing and interconnecting with the totality of Being.

Send out your creative intention and let the World begin to green with the manifestations of the Source. (Thirty seconds. Continue singing.)

All the momentum, energy, and passion that has accrued from the totality of all you have experienced—give this energy now to the creative intention and send it out through the holoverse.

Use your hands as vibrating tendrils and *be* your intention as you send it out. *Be* the sending force and the taking in. Be all these things and let your intention soar through you as you continue your song of yearning and union . . . *mmmmm*.

You have all the assistance you need from the abundance. Allow yourself to be found by God and gifted from this abundance. Feel and know the forms emerging . . . *mmmmm*. (Thirty seconds.)

Now be silent, and allow the deepening to take place. Absolute quiet. (Allow two full minutes for this.)

Now, live out your intention quietly but deeply, letting all your senses and images be engaged in the process. Let it become progressively more and more real to you and, as it unfolds, let it show you some of the pathways and possibilities which you might not have consciously imagined. (Allow one minute for this.)

Feel your creative intention taking root in yourself, sending down into your body-being deep roots of connection and grounding. Actually place your hands on your belly and with a little grunt feel the rooted grounding of the creative intention taking place within you.

Let your arms lift from your sides and feel them as branches and tendrils reaching out across space and time to make connection with circumstances and people who would be necessary to help bring your creative intention into manifest reality. Feel these branches of your being as luminous arteries, channels in which your creative will can reach out and make the appropriate connections in the mind field of reality that knows no distinctions in space and time. (Allow one minute for this.)

Feeling these connections being made, bring your arms back to the belly, giving an appropriate grunt and allowing this nexus of connections you have just made with the world out there to join the now rooted aspects of your creative intentions. Live out now, as in a waking dream, the changes that may have been wrought in your creative intention by virtue of your having sent that intention out into the world, finding that the intention has now deepened and broadened in scope, having gained much from its venture with other beings and events. (Allow one minute for this.)

Again, let your arms rise as branches and again send your creative intention out on the stream of your creative will. Let it find a further nexus of connections in the world out there, with thoughts becoming substance and aspiration moving into manifestation.

Feel your intention seek out and bond with the needed persons and events to bring it to creative fruition. If it helps, make high-pitched sounds in your throat as you seek out these connections.

Again, with an earth-grounding grunt, slap your hands back on your belly and hold them there as you live out richly the deepening course of your creative intention. (Allow one minute for this.)

For the third and final time let your will be the bearer of intention to the universe at large. Make connections and bring the newly yeasted intention back to its roots in your body, receiving it there to be lived out and known. (Allow one minute for this.)

Again, be silent, absolutely quiet. (Allow one minute for this.)

Know yourself to belong to two worlds. You are a citizen of two realms, you are identity and holonomy, you are of the order of the One and the Many, which are ultimately the same. The Source is in you and you in the Source. You are seeded, you are coded, and as you water the fields of your being with belief and delight and expressiveness while recognizing the other seeds and forms in which you quicken, then you will grow and green the world. Knowing this and having this—*this* is your potent birthright: citizen of two realms. (Allow one minute for this.)

Do not be afraid to re-enter the world and do what you must do, for you are more now than a little local being.

You are crew, you are harvest, you are *bodhisattva*, you are apotheosis.

You are the doer, the doing, and the done; the writer, the writing, and the written; the speaker, the speaking, and the speech; the friend, the befriending, and the befriended . . . That Art Thou.

And whenever you begin to forget, just recall these moments and what you've done and do likewise, entering into the desirings of the parts for the whole and of the whole for the parts, seeded with the forms of your creative intention, and receiving from the abundance of the Source.

The Creative Intention

Epilogue

I see a change. It is vested in the greatest rise in expectations the world has ever seen. It is so far-reaching in its implications that one might call it evolution consciously entering into time, the evolutionary potential asserting itself. It needed a certain critical mass, a certain merging of complexity, crisis, and consciousness to awaken. Now it is happening.

The change comes slowly. A sleeping giant, it wakes in the hearts and minds of millions. Four hundred thousand years of being humans-in-search-of-subsistence, seven thousand years of being humans-in-search-of-meaning, and two centuries of modern economic and social revolution have prepared the way for the deepest quickening in human and cultural evolution. The events of recent centuries were the social and political churnings of the change. They were the manifestations of the deep seismic seizures happening and rehappening in the depths of ourselves. And what is happening constellates around the ideas of human freedom and human possibilities. The idea of freedom is expanding because the idea of what it is to be a human being is expanding.

The traditional views of freedom and the possible human have served as moral beacons, drawing forth the highest aspirations and noblest actions of those who sighted them. The uncompromising light brought oppression into high relief and sparked the courage needed to confront the squalor of social evils. But now the beacons must be tuned to even greater brilliance. The old gleamings are no longer adequate to the time, and to follow them is to fall among the shadows that confound, leading us to shores both dangerous and archaic. Perhaps this is why so much of current social and political thought is lacking in confidence and why so many governmental and organizational decisions are ridden with perilous banality. Short-term solutions to complex problems blight both landscape and inscape with a crazy-quilt patchwork of Band-Aids. Each of our so-called "successes" generates ten new problems and becomes in the collapsed space/time of the global village a world-eroding failure. Our national and international policies are mostly the results of sophisticated cause-effect, stimulus-response patterns appropriate to much simpler societies, which themselves were grounded in the cultural trance of tribe or village. The societywide slavery seen in Orwell's *1984* or Huxley's *Brave New World* are but the logical projections of what could happen to complex societies that insist on maintaining atavistic psychologies. These atavisms persist because of the lack of a thrilling and appropriate notion of freedom, one that joins the new vistas of the nature of human possibilities to the consideration of social and educational programs that would nurture these possibilities. Better that we extend that notion now and hope that by extending the horizon of human possibilities other domains will similarly improve.

Never before has the responsibility of the human being for the planetary process been greater. Never before have we gained power of such magnitude over the primordial issues of life and death. The density and intimacy of the global village, along with the staggering consequences of our new knowledge and technologies, make us directors of a world that, up to now, has mostly directed us. This is a responsibility for which we have been ill prepared and for which the usual formulas and stop-gap solutions will not work.

We find ourselves in a time in which extremely limited consciousness has the powers once accorded to the gods. Extremely limited consciousness can launch a nuclear holocaust with the single push of a button. Extremely limited consciousness can and does intervene directly in the genetic code, interferes with the complex patterns of life in the sea, and pours its wastes into the protective ozone layers that encircle the earth. Extremely limited consciousness is about to create a whole new energy base linking together computers, electronics, new materials from outer space, biofacture, and genetic engineering, which in turn will release a flood of innovation and external power unlike anything seen before in human history. In short, extremely limited consciousness is accruing to itself the powers of Second Genesis. And this with an ethic that is more Faustian than godlike.

We must therefore begin to do what has never been done before. We must assume the *Imago Dei* and humbly but tenaciously educate ourselves for sacred stewardship, acquiring the inner capacities to match our outer powers. We must seek and find those physical, mental, and spiritual resources that will enable us to partner the planet.

But how can we bring on the *Change*? How can we possibly undertake so giant a task when failure of nerve is rife throughout the planet, when we are everywhere experiencing a breakdown of all the old ways of knowing, doing, being? We don't even know what to tell the children anymore; how can we dare so great a venture? For we are clearly at the end of one age and not quite at the beginning of the new one. We are the people who are treading air over the abyss, the people of the parentheses.

But as anyone who has ever worked on a farm or in a garden knows, breakdown is always the signal for breakthrough. After the harvest, during winter's parentheses of life, the sere and decaying stalks of the previous year's vegetation collapse to provide the nutrients for the spring breakthrough of the reseeded earth. So too with ourselves. I am reminded of a recent conversation had while running after a seventy-eight-year-old retired nurse in Helsinki as she bounded up the stairs to open a conference on human possibilities:

So many people are losing heart, but not me! I have
lived through four wars, have seen unbelievable suffering and misery, and you know what? I am full of hope for
the human race. We are tied to each other in ways not
possible before. We must now begin to live and grow
together to become what we can be. I have dedicated
the rest of my life to helping make this possible. I have
no money and few have ever heard of me outside of
Finland, but no matter. The time is ripe, ripe, ripe, and
I know that what I do will make a difference.

This remarkable woman is a member of a new breed of heroes, one
that we might call the *people of the breakthrough*, men and women who
find in the present parentheses an extraordinary opportunity for seeding
and nurturing both personal and social transformation. I find them
everywhere—in citizens' volunteer associations, in store-front self-help
agencies, in teachers who stay after school to help the child whom
society forgets, in physicians who are attempting to treat the whole person. Young and old and in between, and from all walks of life, they demonstrate some remarkable similarities in both commitment and belief.

For the most part, they feel that as of now the future is wide open,
and that what we do truly makes a difference as to whether humanity
fails or flourishes. They have little interest in protecting their own turf,
and therefore freely network and exchange ideas, information, and
resources. If meaning eludes them, they act *as if* it were there and keep
on working until it shows up. Nor are they afraid of the bouts of despair
that occasionally attend the quest for the Pattern that Connects, knowing full well that this suffering is integral to the coming of wisdom.

Most important of all, they do their homework, by which I mean
that they have a healthy and spirited appreciation of the complexity and
capacities of their own being, and regularly spend time in discovering,
refining, and applying the latent potentials of their own body-minds.
There is little of narcissism here, as daily they rid themselves of un-
needed rancor and deliberately pursue ways both mental and physical of
deepening into the Depths of which they are a part. In this they become
in some sense citizens of a larger universe, who take time to prepare
themselves so that they can listen to the rhythms of awakening that may
be pulsing from a deeper, more coherent Order of Reality.

They rarely make the papers or show up on the media, *because*
they do not care for the credit, *because* most of their activities are ones
of quiet and creative persistence and not of the order of catastrophe or
the grandstand play, *because* their news is good news. They are the
most important people in the world today, these *people of the breakthrough*, and it is for them that I write this book.

I see a change. And you are part of it.

NOTES

Chapter 1

1. Ralph Waldo Emerson, "Conduct of Life: Beauty," in *The Complete Works of Ralph Waldo Emerson* (Boston: Houghton Mifflin, 1903), Vol. 6, pp. 298–299.

2. R. A. Schwaller de Lubicz, *The Temple in Man*, translated by Robert and Deborah Lawlor (Brookline, Mass.: Autumn Press, 1977).

3. See, for example, F. M. Alexander, *The Use of the Self* (London: Re-Educational Publications, 1955) and *Man's Supreme Inheritance* (London: Chaterson, 1946); Moshe Feldenkrais, *Awareness Through Movement* (New York: Harper & Row, 1972), *Body and Mature Behavior* (New York: International Universities Press, 1975), and *The Case of Nora* (New York: Harper & Row, 1977); *Elsa Gindler Bulletin of the Charlotte Selver Foundation*, Winter 1981, pp. 1–44. For a study of the work of Charlotte Selver, see Charles Brooks, *Sensory Awareness* (New York: Viking, 1974).

4. For an excellent study of biofeedback, see Barbara Brown, *New Body, New Mind* (New York: Harper & Row, 1973).

Chapter 2

1. Paul Friedlander, *Plato*, Vol. 1, translated by Hans Meyerhoff (New York: Pantheon, Bollingen Series LIX, 1958), p. 49.

2. *The Bhagavad-Gita*, translated by Swami Shripurohit (New York: Vintage Books, 1977), p. 36.

3. Antoine de St. Exupéry, *The Little Prince* (New York: Reynaud & Hitchcock, 1943), pp. 18–19.

4. René Dubos, *The Dreams of Reason* (New York: Columbia University Press, 1961), p. 164.

5. Lore Segal, *The Juniper Tree and Other Tales from Grimm*, Vol. 2 (New York: Farrar, Straus & Giroux, 1973), p. 256.

6. Eli Spitz, *The First Year of Life* (New York: International Universities Press, 1965), p. 136.

7. Randall McClellan, "Music and Altered States of Consciousness," in *Dromenon*, Winter 1979, pp. 3–8.

Chapter 3

1. J. E. Bogen, "Some Educational Aspects of Hemispheric Specialization," in *Dromenon*, February 1979, pp. 16–20. Also in *UCLA Educator*, Spring 1975; Barbara Brown, *New Body, New Mind* (New York: Harper & Row, 1973); Jeanne Chall and A. Mirsh, eds., *Education and the Brain* (Chicago: University of Chicago Press, 1978);

Marilyn Ferguson, *The Brain Revolution* (New York: Taplinger, 1973); Michael Gazzaniga et al., *The Integrated Mind* (New York: Plenum, 1978); Karl Popper and John Eccles, *The Self and Its Brain* (New York: Springer International, 1978); William Powers, *Behavior and the Control of Perception* (Chicago: Aldine, 1973); Karl Pribram, *Languages of the Brain* (Englewood Cliffs, N.J.: Prentice-Hall, 1971); Richard M. Restak, *The Brain: The Last Frontier* (New York: Doubleday, 1979); Stephen Rose, *The Conscious Brain* (New York: Knopf, 1973).

2. A. R. Orage, *Psychological Exercises and Essays* (New York: Samuel Weiser, 1974), p. 8.

Chapter 4

1. Cicero, *De Oratore*, translated by E. W. Sutton and H. Rackham (Cambridge, Mass.: Harvard University Press, Loeb Classical Library, 1926), Vol. 2, p. 358.

2. Frances A. Yates, *The Art of Memory* (Chicago: University of Chicago Press, 1966), p. 16.

3. Quoted in Yates, p. 10.

4. I observed this process while studying and testing Dr. Mead's methods of memory recall, which I described in my article, "The Mind of Margaret Mead," *Quest/77*, June 1977.

5. Milton H. Erickson, "A Special Inquiry with Aldous Huxley into the Nature and Character of Various States of Consciousness," in *Advanced Techniques of Hypnosis and Therapy: Selected Papers of Milton H. Erickson*, Jay Haley, ed. (New York: Grune & Stratton, 1967), pp. 277–298.

6. Erickson, p. 294.

Chapter 5

1. Arthur Koestler, *The Act of Creation* (New York: Macmillan, 1964), p. 63.

2. Paul D. MacLean, "A Meeting of Minds," in *Dromenon*, Fall-Winter 1980, pp. 12–20. See also Paul D. MacLean, "On the Evolution of Three Mentalities," in *New Dimensions in Psychiatry: A World View*, Vol. 2, ed. by Silvano Arieti and Gerard Chryanowski (New York: Wiley, 1977).

3. MacLean discusses this in the articles cited above.

Chapter 6

1. Koestler, op cit., p. 95.

2. The philosophy of "as if" is described particularly in William James, *The Will to Believe* (New York: Dover, 1956) and William James, *Pragmatism and Other Essays* (New York: Washington Square Press, 1963).

Chapter 7

1. Jacques Hadamard, *The Psychology of Invention in the Mathematical Field* (New York: Dover, 1954), pp. 142–144.

2. Reported in E. R. Jaensch, *Eidetic Imagery* (London: Routledge & Kegan Paul, 1930).

3. To explore under laboratory conditions the altered states and imagery-producing potentials of audiovisual programs, we created our own "environment" with the invaluable assistance of New York artist Don Snyder. Slides were projected over the surface of an 8-by-8-foot semicircular rear-projection screen. The subject sits behind the screen, close enough so that the images occupy his or her entire field of vision and thus has the feeling of almost being "in" the slide projection. Music and sound come to the subject either through headphones or from speakers situated at his or her sides. The visual program consists of dissolving 2-by-2-inch slides (many of them polarized, giving a constantly moving and flowing design) projected by two projectors and motion adapters over the entire surface of the screen. The program is exactly repeatable since the sound tape controls at preprogrammed intervals both the changing of the slides and the duration (one to twenty seconds) of the slide dissolves. Most of the programs contain from 120 to 160 slides and last from thirty to forty-five minutes. The slides, wholly original, are abstract and intended either to elicit specific emotional and projective responses or to facilitate and encourage free projection—a "seeing into" of the abstraction, which itself is as free of suggestive material as possible.

Ordinarily, the audiovisual environment induces a mildly altered state of consciousness or trance, and, in a minority of cases, more profoundly altered states or deep trances. Characteristic responses include such phenomena as time disorientation, empathy, anxiety, euphoria, body-image changes, religious and erotic feelings, projected imagery, pronounced relaxation, feelings of mild intoxication, a strong sense of wanting to go into, or being drawn into, the image.

4. The problems of abstract time are given a fine elucidation in Jacques Ellul, *The Technological Society* (New York: Vintage Books, 1964).

5. A remarkable long-term experiment describing changes over a fifteen-year period in delinquent teenagers' attitudes toward time and gratification is found in Anthony Davids and Bradley Falkoff, "Juvenile Delinquency Then and Now: Comparison of Findings from 1959 and 1974," *Journal of Abnormal Psychology*, Vol. 84, No. 2, 1975, pp. 161–164.

6. For a profound discussion of the effects of technology on the sense of duration, see Enrico Castelli's study *Il Tempo Esaurito* (Rome: Bussola, 1947). I discuss the phenomenon of the decline of language and grammar and the pathology of time in my article "Prometheus Rebound: An Inquiry into Technological Growth and Psychological Change," in *Technological Forecasting and Social Change*, Vol. 9, 1976, pp. 241–258.

7. Linn Cooper and Milton Erickson, *Time Distortion in Hypnosis*, 2nd edition (Baltimore: Williams and Wilkins, 1959).

8. Perhaps the most useful and intensive analysis of this phenomenon that has come to us from the ancient world is found in Plato's discussion of the nature of "inspired mania" in the *Phaedrus*. There, Plato discussed the analogies and similar roots that exist between mediumship, poetic creation, and certain pathological manifestations of the religious consciousness, all three of which have the appearance of being "given" from somewhere else. μανίας θείᾳ δόσει διδομένης (*Phaedrus* 244A). In the same passage, Plato speaks of "possession (κατοχαχή) by the Muses" and declares this to be indispensable to the production of the best poetry. However, as E. R. Dodds observes, whereas Plato on the one hand accepted the poet, the prophet, and the Corybantic as "being in some sense channels of divine or daemonic grace, he nevertheless rated their activities far below those of the rational self, and held that they must be subject to the control and criticism of reason, since reason was for him no passive plaything of hidden forces but an active manifestation of deity in man, a daemon in its own right." (*The Greeks and the Irrational* [Boston: Beacon Press, 1957], p. 218.)

9. Friedrich Nietzsche, "Composition of Thus Spake Zarathustra," from *Ecce Homo*, translated by Clifton Fadiman. In Brewster Ghiselin, ed., *The Creative Process* (Berkeley: University of California Press, 1952), pp. 201–203.

10. Quoted in Peter McKeller, *Imagination and Thinking: A Psychological Analysis* (New York: Basic Books, 1957), pp. 136–137.

11. J. R. R. Tolkien, *The Letters of J. R. R. Tolkien*, selected and edited by Humphrey Carpenter (Boston: Houghton Mifflin, 1981), p. 145.

12. Jean Cocteau, "The Process of Inspiration," in Ghiselin, *op cit*, pp. 81–82.

13. Amy Lowell, "The Process of Making Poetry," in Ghiselin, *op cit*, pp. 109–112.

14. Wolfgang Amadeus Mozart, "A Letter," quoted in Ghiselin, *op cit*, pp. 44–45.

15. Dreams have long been associated with creativity, and it is amusing to review some of the better-known examples of creative people tapping into their dreams for inspiration. Here is a brief assemblage of such stuff as dreams and creative breakthroughs are made of. In the fifth century A.D. Synesius described problem-solving dreams. Voltaire was said to have dreamed the entire canto of *La Henriade*. Giuseppe Tartini composed *The Devil's Trill* with auditory materials from a dream. Charlotte Brontë used induced dreams to have experiences she could not have in waking life and then used these experiences in her writings. Robert Louis Stevenson created stories in his sleep—that is, he dreamed them and then recorded the dreams. Poe, Hazlitt, and Charles Lamb regularly used dream materials in their writings. Newton and Jerome Cardan found solutions for mathematical problems in dreams. The French philosopher Condorcet solved, in a dream, a mathematical problem that he had long been unable to solve in a waking state. William Blake dreamed of a new, and workable, method of engraving, and he drew upon both dreams and waking visual imagery for much of what we find in his painting, poetry, and other works. H. V. Hilprecht made an archaeological discovery in 1893 after the facts were revealed to him in a dream. Descartes appears to have encountered the basic notions of analytic geometry in a dream. And, of course, F. A. Kekule discovered in a dream the ring structure of benzene, which led the poet Robert Graves to intone in *Marmosite's Miscellany* (London, 1925):

> The maunderings of a maniac signi-
>   fying nothing
> I hold in respect; I hear his tale out.
> Thought comes often clad in the
>   strangest clothing:
> So Kekule the chemist watched the
>   weird rout
> Of eager atom-serpents writhing in
>   and out
> And waltzing tail to mouth. In that
>   absurd guise
> Appeared benzine and anilin, their
>   drugs and their dyes.

Such dreams and fancies are part of the folklore of creativity studies and are abundantly documented in many sources. Among the best, however, are Peter McKeller, *op cit*, pp. 113–147; and Norman MacKenzie, *Dreams and Dreaming* (New York: Vanguard, 1965), pp. 126–141.

16. As examples of some curiosa in the service of creativity, Balzac would drink a hundred or more cups of coffee a day as a stimulus to creativity; Dr. Johnson did much the same with tea; Zola needed strange refractions of artificial light; Kipling required a very heavy black ink to express himself; Descartes wrapped his head in towels and buried himself in bed to do his best work; Proust did likewise, and also sealed off his room from any wandering air currents; Kant also worked in bed with a curious arrangement of the blankets and used a tower as a mental focus while working on the *Critique of Pure Reason*; Leibnitz thought lying down; Rousseau exposed his head to the glare of the sun; Milton composed with his head leaning over his easy chair; and Shelley lay with his head close to a fire.

17. The need to become inspired, to unlock the unconscious and set the creative process free, has destroyed many artists of stature, especially when alcoholic drunkenness has become the key. What begins as a mechanism of disinhibition of the creative process all too often takes its toll in brain damage and the permanent disordering of cognitive functions. The list of writers and artists who regularly worked when under alcoholic intoxication is too long to present here; a very brief enumeration would have to include Catullus, Horace, Ovid, Tasso, Cervantes, Marlowe, Bacon, Jonson, Franz Hals, Carew, Hobbes, Herrick, Jan Steen, Addison, Parnell, Handel, Pope, Savage, Swift, Gluck, Goldsmith, Sheridan, Schiller, Coleridge, Lamb, Kleist, Balzac, De Quincey, Byron, Gerard de Nerval, Poe, Musset, Baudelaire, Swinburne, Verlaine, Maupassant, Joyce, Hart Crane, Faulkner, Mailer, Dylan Thomas, and Brendan Behan. Some symbolists such as Rimbaud used alcohol and drugs to achieve a systematic derangement of the senses. In the twentieth century we have the heirs to this tradition in the surrealists and their exploration of the dream, drugs, trance, and other altered states. A thoughtful appraisal of this phenomenon is to be had in Arthur Jacobson, *Genius: Some Revaluations* (New York: Greenberg, 1926).

18. A medical curiosity associated with the creative process has to do with the often observed phenomenon that some brilliant and promising people appear to become creative only after the onset of the symptoms of tuberculosis. The toxins of tuberculosis have facilitated the release of creative personalities in many notable instances, including Molière, Watteau, Rousseau, Mme. de Staël, Jane Austen, Paganini, Weber, Shelley, Keats, Elizabeth Barrett Browning, Chopin, Beardsley, Charlotte Brontë, Kingsley, J. A. Symonds, Stephen Crane, and Katherine Mansfield. (See the discussion in Jacobson, *op cit*, pp. 5–7, where it is noted that "the toxins of tuberculosis are keys wherewith some individuals can unlock the unconscious . . . so the tuberculous Emerson walking in a trance-like state, during which he 'receives' and records short but complete messages.") With the decline of tuberculosis we rarely hear of it in relation to creativity, but there is no doubting its former importance and association with creative states.

19. Attention has occasionally been called to a brilliant phase of creative outburst in highly talented people whose nervous systems have been invaded by syphilis just preceding the final debacle. Examples of this type of releasing toxemia are Maupassant, Nietzsche, Heine, Baudelaire, and Verlaine.

20. Prior to its disintegrative phase, the beginning symptoms of schizophrenia are often manifested in many altered states of consciousness, some of them commonly associated with the creative process or the nurturing of that process. Most students of this phenomenon, including Kubie (*Neurotic Distortions of the Creative Process*), Koestler (*The Act of Creation*), and Kretschmer (*The Psychology of Men of Genius*), tend to regard the initial creative phase as a mere flash in the pan that is never sustained for long enough periods to be truly creative. There are, however, too many cases of long-term schizophrenia coupled with long-term and productive "acts of creation" in persons like Gerard de Nerval to call that thesis into question. Some of the recent discussions and investigations of researchers such as Wilson Van Dusen in *The Natural Depth of Man* (New York: Harper & Row, 1972) and R. D. Laing suggest the value of "treating" some kinds of schizophrenia cases as creative interludes rather than as pathologies. The long-term work in this methodology remains to be done, but its premises are hopeful for their inherent humaneness if not for their romanticization of schizophrenia. It should also be noted that many geniuses and highly creative people tend to have hypersensitive nervous systems that may be abnormal but are also superior, more finely tuned, and more responsive, not *just* pathological—that is, conducive to altered states of consciousness characterized by novel perceptions, imagery, hypnoid states, and a richer, more intense dream life. They may also have a different—not just pathological—brain chemistry that is conducive to the emergence or maintenance of mental faculties that are inhibited or for some reason less fully developed in "ordinary persons." We will go on equating genius with derangement as long as we tend to see differences from the normal kinds of mental functioning, especially on nonverbal levels, as examples of psychopathological phenomena. Why not say of Blake's visions that they are evidence that the visionary faculty latent in all men was developed to a superior state in Blake? That makes much more sense than to speak of Blake's hallucinations.

Whether a mental function should be called pathological depends upon both the use to which it is put and the end result—the product. Mentally ill people sometimes have hallucinations, and so do artists (if we call vivid imagery a hallucination). Schizophrenics hear voices and so do philosophers, composers, and some other creative sane people. Beethoven "heard" music, as have other composers. John Doe might be held to be psychotic on that basis, but he is not psychotic just because he is not Beethoven. Small wonder that people are reluctant to speak of their altered states of consciousness, experiences that, as we are learning, virtually all people have, and with considerable richness. These experiences are not usually as rich as those experienced by geniuses or highly creative people, or by highly disturbed schizophrenics. Both are extremes—one of mental illness, the other of superior human functioning of a certain type (and sometimes bought at the expense of other functions, but still often a far cry from psychosis).

Freud sought to explain the work of Leonardo in terms of a penis-in-the-mouth fantasy. Perhaps we should not expect genius to be understood by average people, or average psychiatrists, when even men of genius are so far from understanding one another.

21. F. W. H. Myers, *Human Personality and Its Survival of Bodily Death* (New York: Longmans, Green, 1954), Vol. 1, p. 72.

22. See, for example, Robert Masters' and my discussion of this phenomenon in our books *The Varieties of Psychedelic Experience* (New York: Holt, Rinehart, and Winston, 1966) and *Psychedelic Art* (New York: Grove Press-Balance House, 1968). See also my study, "Phenomenology of the Psychedelic Experience," in Richard Hicks and Paul Fink, *Psychedelic Drugs* (Philadelphia: Grune and Stratton, 1969).

Chapter 8

1. This is my translation, based upon the text described by Charles Eliot in his work, *Japanese Buddhism* (New York: Barnes and Noble, 1969), pp. 109–110.

2. Jorge Luis Borges, "The Aleph," *The Aleph and Other Stories, 1933–1969* (New York: Bantam Books, 1971).

3. Karl Pribram, *Languages of the Brain* (Englewood Cliffs, N.J.: Prentice-Hall, 1971), pp. 140–166. See also Karl Pribram, *Holonomy and Structure in the Organization of Perception*, reprint from the Department of Psychology, Stanford University (Stanford, California: Stanford University Press, 1974).

4. David Bohn, "Quantum Theory as an Indication of a New Order in Physics, Part B," *Implicate and Explicate Order in Physical Law, Foundations of Physics*, 3:139, 1973.

5. Quoted in John Curtis Gowan, *Operations of Increasing Order* (privately published by the author, 1426 Southwind Circle, Westlake Village, CA 91361, 1980), p. 309.

6. Lawrence Domash, "The TM Technique in Quantum Physics," in D. W. Orme-Johnson and J. T. Farrow, eds., *Scientific Research on the TM Program,* Vol. 1 (Maharishi European Research University, 1977), pp. 652–670.

7. *Brain/Mind Bulletin*, May 21, 1979. A full discussion of Prigogine's theory is found in his book *From Being to Becoming* (San Francisco: Freeman, 1980).

8. Rammurti S. Mishra, *The Textbook of Yoga Psychology: A New Translation and Interpretation of Patanjali's Yoga Sutras* (New York: Julian Press, 1963).

9. For the Vedic concept of *Purusha*, see *Hindu Scriptures*, translated by R. C. Zaehner (New York: Dutton, Everyman's Library, 1966), The Rig-Veda, X, xc, pp. 8–10; The Atharva-Veda, X, ii, pp. 15–18.

BIBLIOGRAPHY

Alexander, F. M. *Man's Supreme Inheritance*. London: Chaterson, 1946.

———. *The Use of the Self*. London: Re-Educational Publications, 1955.

Bogen, J. E. "Some Educational Aspects of Hemispheric Socialization." *Dromenon*, February 1979. Also in *UCLA Educator*, Spring 1975.

Bohn, David. "Quantum Theory as an Indication of a New Order in Physics, Part B." *Implicate and Explicate Order in Physical Law, Foundations of Physics* 3:139, 1973.

Borges, Jorge Luis. *The Aleph and Other Stories, 1933–1969*. New York: Bantam, 1971.

Brain/Mind Bulletin, May 21, 1979.

Brooks, Charles. *Sensory Awareness*. New York: Viking, 1974.

Brown, Barbara. *New Body, New Mind*. New York: Harper & Row, 1973.

Castelli, Enrico. *Il Tempo Esaurito*. Rome: Bussola, 1947.

Chall, Jeanne, and Mirsh, A., eds. *Education and the Brain*. Chicago: University of Chicago Press, 1978.

Cicero. *De Oratore*. Translated by E. W. Sutton and H. Rackham. Cambridge, Mass.: Harvard University Press, 1926.

Cooper, Linn, and Erickson, Milton. *Time Distortion in Hypnosis*. Baltimore: Williams and Wilkins, 1959.

Davids, Anthony, and Falkoff, Bradley. "Juvenile Deliquency Then and Now: Comparison of Findings from 1959 and 1974," *Journal of Abnormal Psychology*, Vol. 84, No. 2, 1975.

Dillard, Annie. "Teaching a Stove to Talk" in *Atlantic Monthly*, February 1981.

Dodds, E. R. *The Greeks and the Irrational*. Boston: Beacon Press, 1957.

Dubos, René. *The Dreams of Reason*. New York: Columbia University Press, 1961.

Eliot, Charles. *Japanese Buddhism*. New York: Barnes and Noble, 1969.

Eliot, T. S. "Burnt Norton." *The Four Quartets*. New York: Harcourt, Brace, Jovanovich, 1971.

Ellul, Jacques. *The Technological Society*. New York: Vintage Books, 1964.

Elsa Gindler Bulletin of the Charlotte Selver Foundation. Winter 1981.

Emerson, Ralph Waldo. "Conduct of Life: Beauty." *The Complete Works of Ralph Waldo Emerson*. Boston: Houghton Mifflin, 1903.

Erickson, Milton H. "A Special Inquiry with Aldous Huxley into the Nature and Character of Various States of Consciousness." *Advanced Techniques of Hyp-*

nosis and Therapy: Selected Papers of Milton H. Erickson, Jay Haley, ed. New York: Grune & Stratton, 1967.

Feldenkrais, Moshe. *Awareness Through Movement*. New York: Harper & Row, 1972.

———. *Body and Mature Behavior*. New York: International Universities Press, 1975.

———. *The Case of Nora*. New York: Harper & Row, 1977.

Ferguson, Marilyn. *The Brain Revolution*. New York: Taplinger, 1973.

Friedlander, Paul. *Plato*, Vol. 1. Translated by Hans Meyerhoff. New York: Pantheon, 1958.

Gazzaniga, Michael, et al. *The Integrated Mind*. New York: Plenum, 1978.

Ghiselin, Brewster, ed. *The Creative Process*. Berkeley: University of California Press, 1952.

Gowan, John Curtis. *Operations of Increasing Order*. Privately published by author, 1426 Southwind Circle, Westlake Village, CA 91361, 1980.

Hadamard, Jacques. *The Psychology of Invention in the Mathematical Field*. New York: Dover, 1954.

Hicks, Richard, and Fink, Paul. *Psychedelic Drugs*. Philadelphia: Grune & Stratton, 1969.

Houston, Jean. *Lifeforce: The Psycho-Historical Recovery of the Self*. New York: Delacorte, 1980.

———. "The Mind of Margaret Mead." *Quest/77*, June 1977.

———. "Prometheus Rebound: An Inquiry into Technological Growth and Psychological Change." *Technological Forecasting and Social Change*. Vol. 9, 1976.

Jacobson, Arthur. *Genius: Some Revaluations*. New York: Greenberg, 1926.

Jaensch, E. R. *Eidetic Imagery*. London: Routledge and Kegan Paul, 1930.

Koestler, Arthur. *The Act of Creation*. New York: Macmillan, 1964.

Kretschmer, Ernst. *The Psychology of Men of Genius*. London: Kegan Paul, Trench, Trubner, 1931.

Kubie, Lawrence. *Neurotic Distortions of the Creative Process*. New York: Farrar, Straus & Giroux, 1961.

MacKenzie, Norman. *Dreams and Dreaming*. New York: Vanguard, 1965.

MacLean, Paul D. "A Meeting of Minds." *Dromenon*, Fall-Winter 1980.

———. "On the Evolution of Three Mentalities." *New Dimensions in Psychiatry: A World View*, Vol. 2, Silvano Arieti and Gerald Chryanowski, eds. New York: Wiley, 1977.

Masters, Robert, and Houston, Jean. *The Varieties of Psychedelic Experience*. New York: Holt, Rinehart and Winston, 1966.

———. *Psychedelic Art*. New York: Grove Press/Balance House, 1968.

———. *Mind Games*. New York: Viking, 1972.

———. *Listening to the Body*. New York: Delacorte, 1978.

McClellan, Randall. "Music and Altered States of Consciousness." *Dromenon*, Winter 1979.

McKeller, Peter. *Imagination and Thinking: A Psychological Analysis*. New York: Basic Books, 1957.

Mishra, Rammurti S. *The Textbook of Yoga Psychology: A New Translation and Interpretation of Patanjali's Yoga Sutras*. New York: Julian Press, 1963.

Myers, F. W. H. *Human Personality and Its Survival of Bodily Death*. New York: Longmans, Green, 1954.

Orage, A. R. *Psychology Exercises and Essays*. New York: Samuel Weiser, 1974.

Orme-Johnson, D. W., and Farrow, J. T., eds. *Scientific Research on the TM Program*, Vol. 1. Maharishi European Research University, 1977.

Popper, Karl, and Eccles, John. *The Self and Its Brain*. New York: Springer International, 1978.

Powers, William. *Behavior and the Control of Perception*. Chicago: Aldine, 1973.

Pribram, Karl. *Holonomy and Structure in the Organization of Perception*. Reprint from the Department of Psychology, Stanford University, Stanford, Calif.: Stanford University Press, 1974.

————. *Languages of the Brain*. Englewood Cliffs, N.J.: Prentice-Hall, 1971.

Prigogine, Ilya. *From Being to Becoming*. San Francisco: Freeman, 1980.

Restak, Richard M. *The Brain: The Last Frontier*. New York: Doubleday, 1979.

Rose, Stephen. *The Conscious Brain*. New York: Knopf, 1973.

St. Exupéry, Antoine de. *The Little Prince*. New York: Reynaud and Hitchcock, 1943.

Schwaller de Lubicz, R. A. *The Temple in Man*. Translated by Robert and Deborah Lawlor. Brookline, Mass.: Autumn Press, 1977.

Segal, Lore. *The Juniper Tree and Other Tales from Grimm*, Vol. 2. New York: Farrar, Straus & Giroux, 1973.

Spitz, Eli. *The First Year of Life*. New York: International Universities Press, 1965.

The Bhagavad-Gita. Translated by Swami Shripurohit. New York: Vintage Books, 1977.

Van Dusen, Wilson. *The Natural Depth of Man*. New York: Harper & Row, 1972.

Yates, Frances A. *The Art of Memory*. Chicago: University of Chicago Press, 1966.

Zaehner, R. C., translator. *Hindu Scriptures*. New York: Dutton, 1966.

Persons interested in subscribing to or acquiring particular issues of *Dromenon* journal should write to G.P.O. Box 2244, New York, NY 10001.

Audio tapes of related lectures and seminars given by Jean Houston are available, as are psychophysical exercises developed at The Foundation for Mind Research. Interested persons should contact Human Capacities Corporation, Box 600, Pomona, NY 10970.

INDEX

The Possible Human was composed in the typefaces
Caledonia and Helvetica by Achorn Graphics, Worcester, Massachusetts.

Printed and bound by The Haddon Craftsmen.